IMAGES
of America

EARLY SAN ANGELO

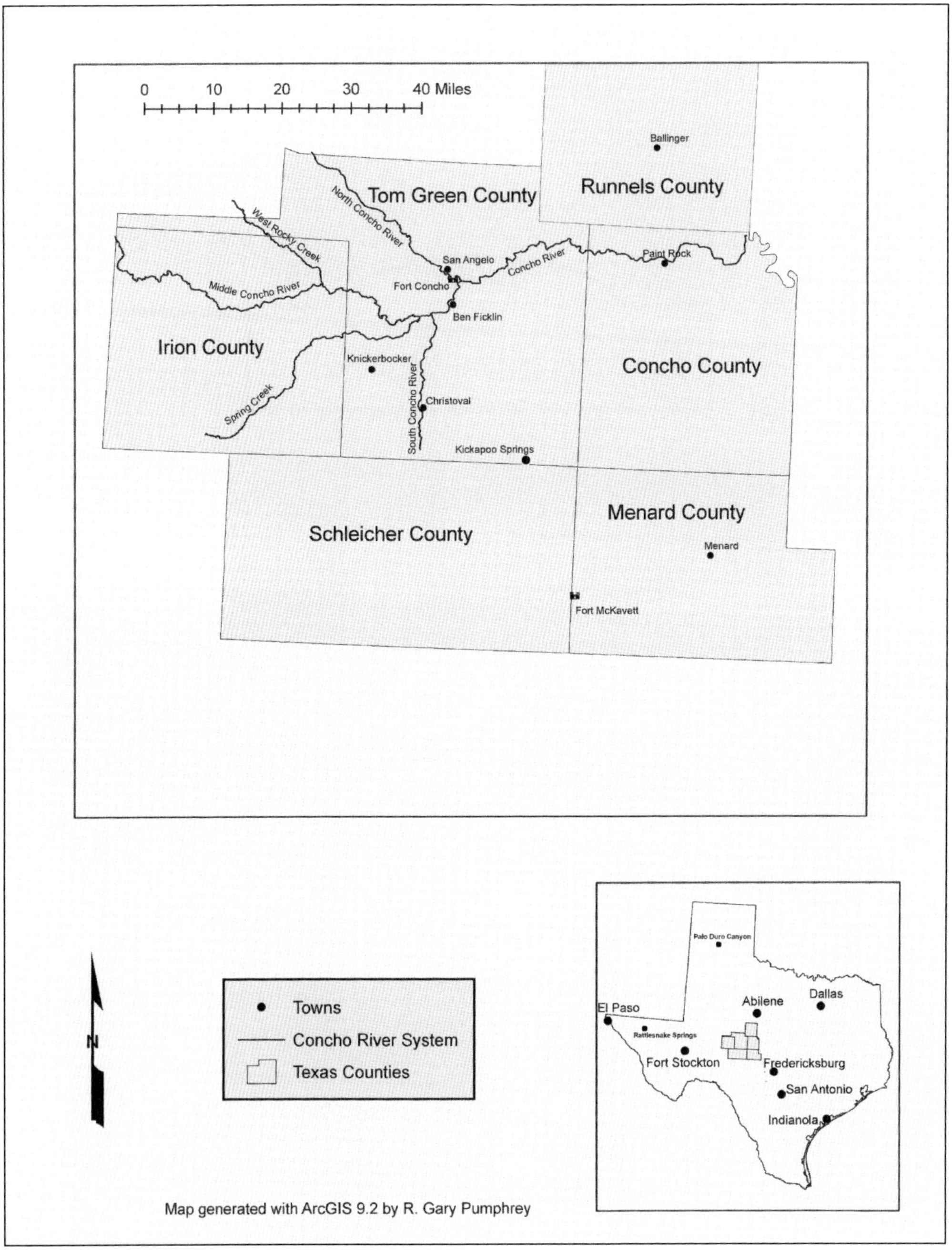

This map shows San Angelo, the Concho Valley, and their location in Texas.

On the Cover: This photograph shows the corner of Beauregard and Chadbourne Streets, looking south, in 1907. The impressive structure on the left is the First National Bank Building. (Courtesy of Fort Concho National Historic Site.)

IMAGES
of America

EARLY SAN ANGELO

Virginia Noelke

ARCADIA
PUBLISHING

ISBN 978-0-7385-8476-8

Published by Arcadia Publishing
Charleston, South Carolina

Printed in the United States of America

Library of Congress Control Number: 2011922445

For all general information, please contact Arcadia Publishing:
Telephone 843-853-2070
Fax 843-853-0044
E-mail sales@arcadiapublishing.com
For customer service and orders:
Toll-Free 1-888-313-2665

Visit us on the Internet at www.arcadiapublishing.com

To all who have preserved our legacy: the buildings, records, stories, and photographs of the Concho Valley

Contents

Acknowledgments

This pictorial history of early San Angelo begins with the fort period and ends in the 1920s, before an oil boom would add yet another dimension to the life of the city. The goal is to tell the story of urban development in one western community. We are fortunate that a rich photographic record is available to help relate the tale.

Two important archives of early San Angelo photographs exist today, and most of the images in this volume appear courtesy of the West Texas Collection of the Angelo State University Library (WTC) and the archives at the Fort Concho National Historic Site (FC). Susanne Campbell and Shannon Sturm at the university and Evelyn Lemons at Fort Concho have been invaluable guides to the photographs and experts in their reproduction. These women have also contributed much useful information to the narrative that follows. I could not have done this work without them. I also want to thank a group of people who agreed to read the manuscript and check for inaccuracies: Bob Bluthardt, director of the Fort Concho National Historic Site; Susanne Campbell; Shannon Sturm; Evelyn Lemons; Barbara Hesse; Prof. Walter Noelke; and Prof. Arnoldo DeLeon. All remaining mistakes are mine alone.

Prof. Gary Pumphrey spent many hours preparing the map on page 2. His work is much appreciated because it allows the reader to locate most of the places mentioned in the book.

I also want to thank Lauren Hummer and the staff at Arcadia Publishing for their professional guidance in the book-making process. They make it almost easy!

INTRODUCTION

San Angelo is located in the western part of Texas, where three tributaries combine to form the Concho River. This river is not the longest or widest river in the state, but it has tremendous appeal because it is a considerable distance from other rivers and because of the resources nearby. The Concho River is surrounded by excellent grasslands, and travel is easy in the area. Pecan and fruit trees grow along the riverbanks, game is abundant, and the weather is generally mild.

For centuries, the Concho Valley has attracted visitors. Ancient campsites are a common feature in the area, and old stone tools can be found everywhere. For at least 1,000 years, Native American visitors recorded their presence with striking pictographs at nearby Paint Rock. Today, we understand that people with names such as Apache, Jumano, and Kickapoo foraged and traveled throughout this area in prehistoric times. The eastern branch of the Comanche War Trail crossed the branches of the Concho River just west of where San Angelo is located today. Surely there were many other native visitors as well.

After 1500, Spanish explorers showed interest in the Concho Valley. A shipwreck on the Texas coast brought Cabeza de Vaca and Esteban to the area when they fled their Indian captors and sought a route to Spanish settlements in Mexico. Francisco Coronado came from Mexico looking for mythical kingdoms to conquer. Numerous Spanish priests visited the Concho River hoping to baptize Indian converts and perhaps set up a permanent settlement where San Angelo now sits. They found beautiful lavender Concho pearls in addition to a number of nomadic Indians. These discoveries were not inducement enough to cause Spain to settle in remote western Texas rather than in New Mexico or San Antonio.

In the 19th century, people from the United States developed a strong interest in the region. Searching for trading opportunities, gold mines, rivers, and whatever wonders might exist, government and private expeditions explored western Texas. Explorers such as Zebulon Pike and George Kendall risked attack or imprisonment when they ventured into the area when it was Spanish or Mexican territory. After 1849, the United States owned the Concho Valley, and the exploration increased. The federal government scouted the area for resources and potential railroad routes. Private businessmen would soon follow.

In the 1850s, the Butterfield Overland Stage carried travelers through the Concho Valley on the way from Illinois to the California goldfields. Freighters carried goods on this southern route, and wagon trains of pioneers also chose this long trail, hoping for a warm trip to the West Coast without so many mountains to climb. A few brave souls relocated to the area to manage stage stands or grow livestock. Soon after the Civil War, drovers moved vast herds of cattle through the area on the Goodnight-Loving Trail. All of these enterprising frontiersmen had a common problem—attacks and raids by the native population. As more and more people came to the Concho River area, the Indian population felt increasingly under pressure. Native Americans had their lifestyles and their livelihoods to protect, and violence would escalate. Settlers and travelers both demanded US government protection from attacks, raids, and theft.

In 1867, the US Army authorized a new line of forts to be built in western Texas to deal with these problems. Fort Concho was located at an ideal spot on the Concho River, and it would be active in pacifying the frontier for the next 22 years. Military protection emboldened settlers to flock to the region and take advantage of the economic opportunities created by the fort and the Concho Valley. The military post naturally spawned a city, which would be called San Angelo. In the beginning, the small town located across the river from the fort was a somewhat disreputable collection of saloons, stores, and brothels designed to separate the soldiers from their paychecks. Quickly, however, the boom was on, and the town grew and diversified.

Agricultural enterprises were the primary businesses in the area. The last decades of the 19th century saw sheep and cattle booms in both Texas and the United States. Ranching seemed a dramatic, surefire way to make a fortune, and the Concho Valley proved to be excellent for livestock production. A variety of people came from many parts of the world to take advantage of these opportunities. Cotton was another important crop. People in town provided capital, sold supplies, and helped market the agricultural products.

Early San Angelo had many talented individuals who helped it grow. In 1875, M.C. Ragsdale moved to town with his family. He was a professional photographer from South Carolina who looked for a spot in Texas where an enterprising man could support his family. San Angelo was his choice. Ragsdale maintained his studio here for more than 40 years, capturing the development of the area in photographs. In 1884, Oscar Ruffini came to San Angelo to superintend the building of the Tom Green County Courthouse. He also liked the possibilities he saw in the Concho Valley and decided to stay, making his living as an architect. The work of these professionals, along with the efforts of many civic leaders, boosters, builders, and hard workers, somehow lifted San Angelo from the ranks of a struggling frontier town to a thriving western city. Enthusiastic residents thought of the town as a haven of opportunity; they even called it "The End of the Rainbow."

One

Fort Concho

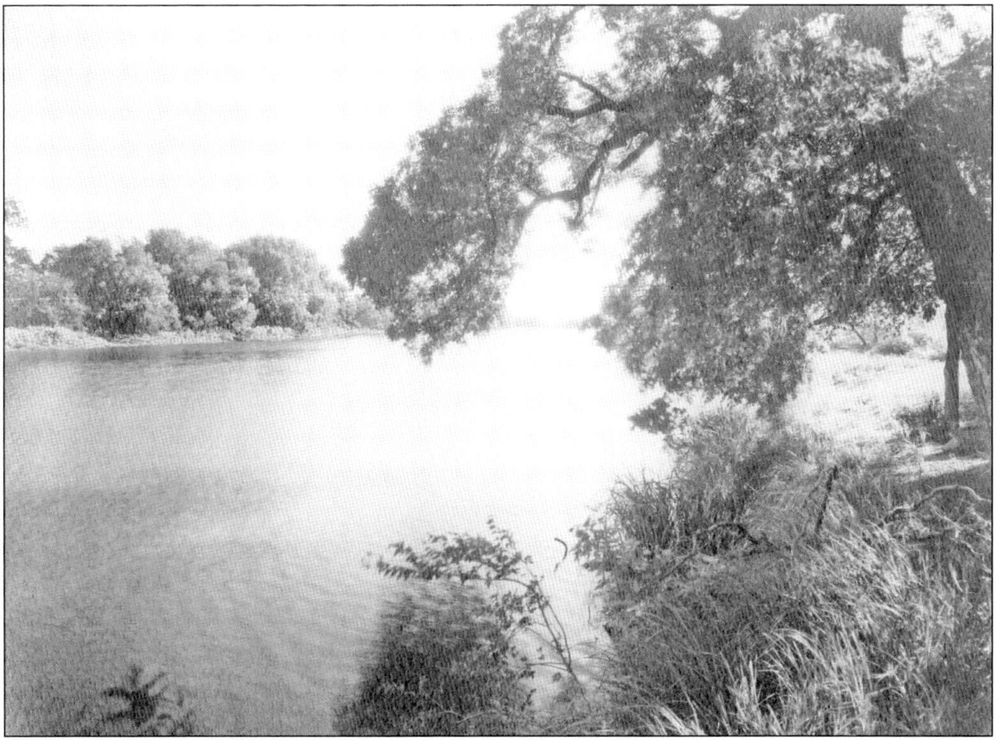

It started with the river. The federal government established many forts in Texas to protect settlers and transportation routes from attacks by Native Americans. As the line of settlement moved westward, more forts were established. In arid West Texas, water was critical. In November 1867, a site was chosen on the Concho River to build a military facility, which would be called Fort Concho. The river had been an oasis for travelers for centuries. In the last third of the 19th century, it would provide precious water for the fort and the town of San Angelo, which would develop along its banks. (FC.)

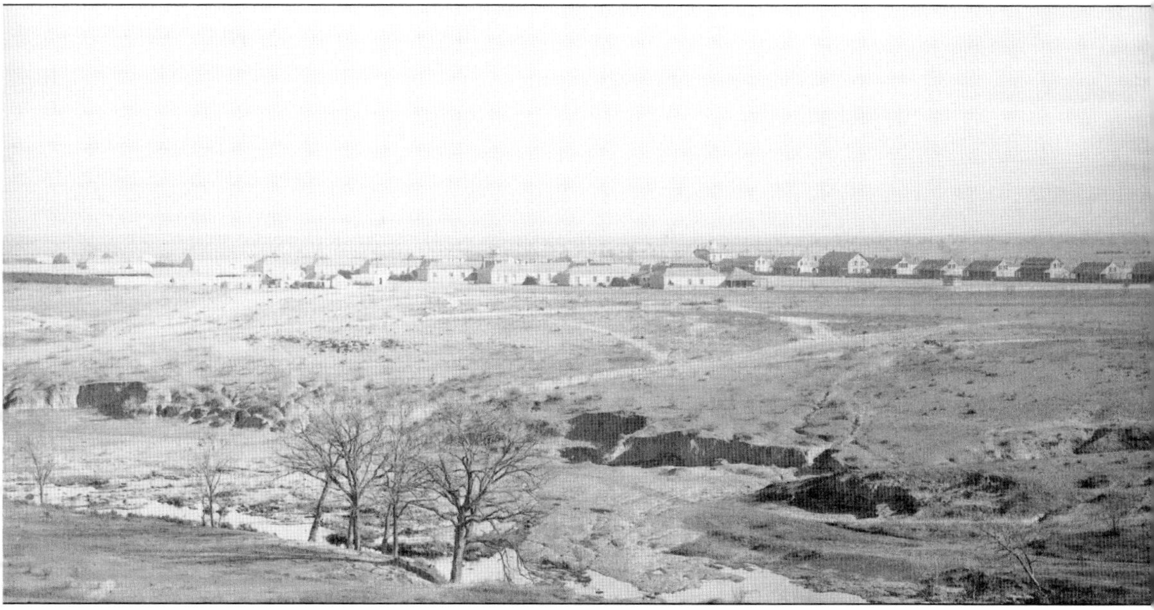

This view of Fort Concho shows an orderly collection of barracks, officers' quarters, and other military structures. As reported in *The Handbook of Texas Online* in an article labeled "Fort Concho," Capt. Robert G. Carter remembered Fort Concho in the 1870s as "one of the most beautiful and best ordered posts on the Texas border." He called the barracks "commodious and handsome" and the houses of the officers "tasty, elegant, [and] imposing." When troops began to arrive in 1868, this is not the picture they saw. It would take many years to build the fort. (FC.)

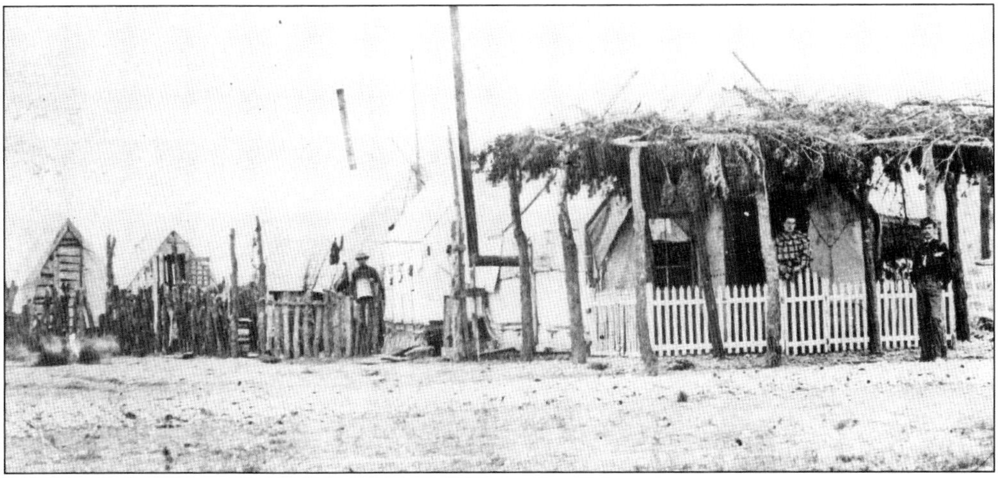

The first buildings completed at the fort were the commissary and the quartermaster's storehouse. By the end of 1868, the hospital was being built, but all personnel lived in tents. This photograph shows an early officer's house. Residents made a valiant effort to add a porch and a picket fence to improve their tent. The stone wall on the right of the photograph shows what was to come. German stonemasons came from Fredericksburg, Texas, to construct substantial buildings in an area where timber was scarce. When stone artisans were not available, soldiers would do their best to build in that tradition. Tent living would then be limited to scouts and campaigns. (WTC.)

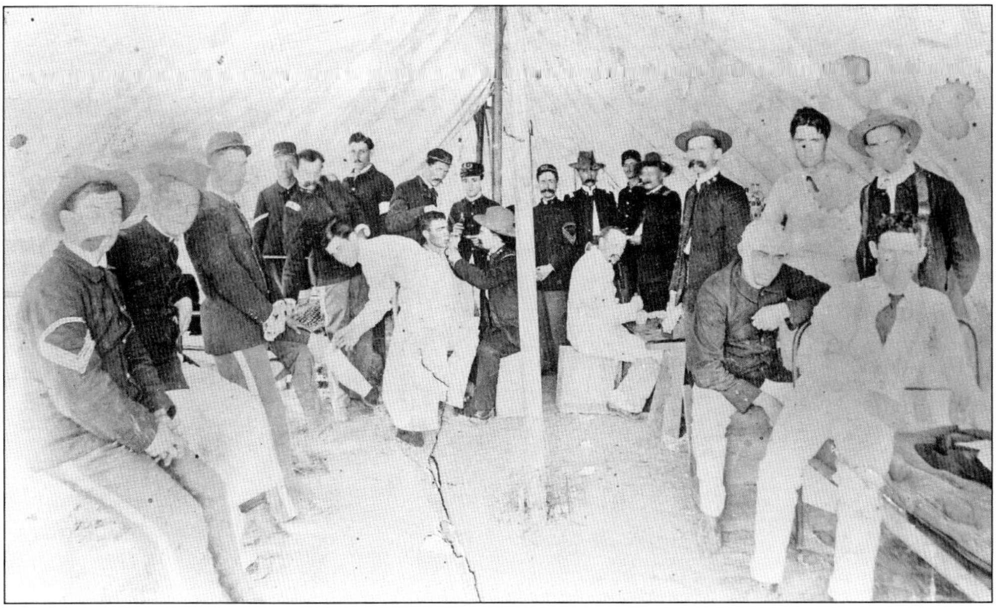

In the beginning, even medical care was delivered in a tent. This photograph shows soldiers at sick call. The post surgeon at Fort Concho oversaw four such tents—with no heat and no privacy. Throughout the life of the fort, the surgeons and their assistants also treated civilians. There was often no other medical care available in the area. (WTC.)

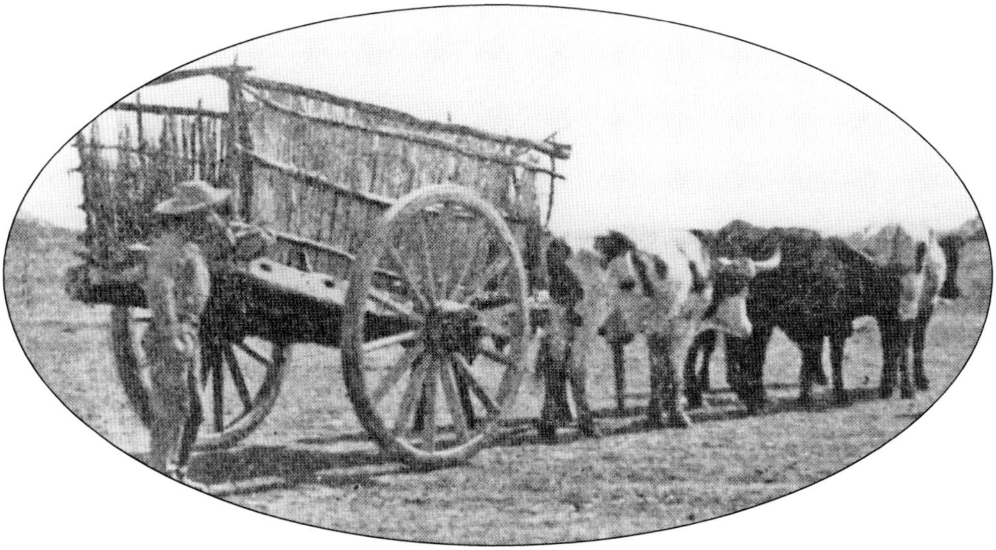

The building process was definitely hampered by a long and difficult supply line. Local building materials such as adobe and pecan wood were not considered satisfactory, and the railroad did not reach San Angelo until 1888, just one year before the fort was abandoned. Supplies came by ox wagons or mule trains operated by Mexican, German, or American teamsters. This picture shows a very simple conveyance. But even larger and more sophisticated freight operations could not supply Fort Concho adequately. Anything that could not be produced locally typically came from Indianola on the Texas coast via San Antonio and then to the fort, a trip of about 400 miles. The road between San Antonio and San Angelo was rough and hilly. Drought might stop the freight wagons because the animals had nothing to eat. Wet weather created mud and sometimes flood conditions, which could stop a wagon for days at the time. Supplies were in critical demand at times. In one instance, the post surgeon had to ride more than 50 miles to Fort McKavett to borrow medical supplies. (WTC.)

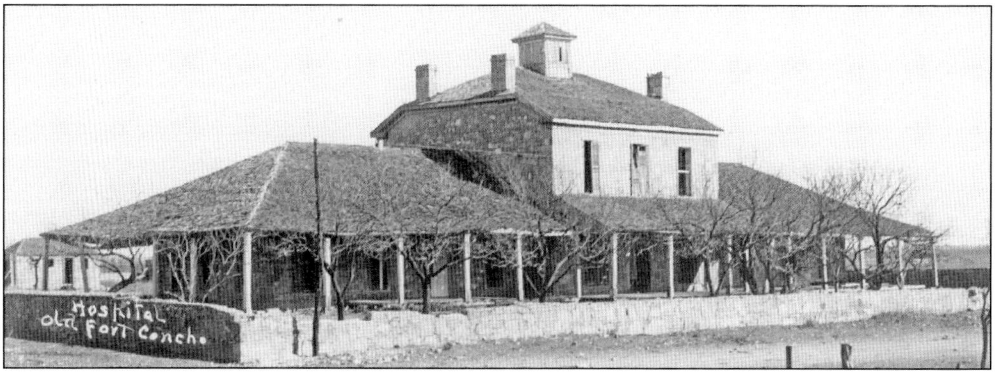

The most imposing structure at the fort was the hospital. Gen. William T. Sherman came for an inspection in 1871 and said it was elegant but too large and a waste of money. This building, however, had multiple uses. The belvedere on top the hospital was a good place to watch for prairie fires or approaching enemies. At night, a light in the belvedere would guide troops back home; at least, that is, until someone realized it provided a target for the enemy, or indeed anyone who wanted to practice their marksmanship. The upper floor had multiple uses once it was discovered that it was very difficult to get patients and corpses up and down the narrow stairs. Newcomers sometimes lived at the hospital until proper housing became available. The large space was rarely wasted. (FC.)

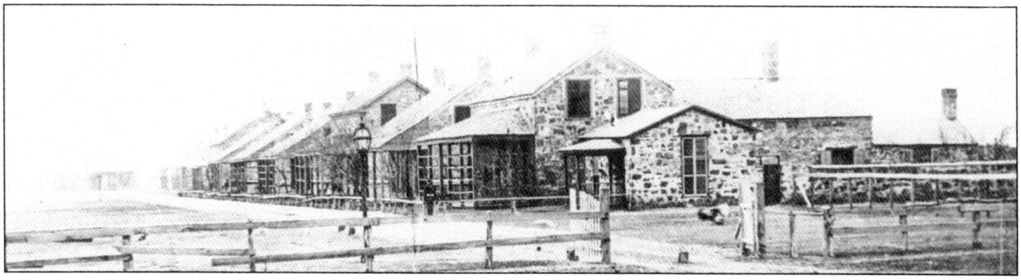

This is a view of the officers' quarters on the south side of the parade ground. Col. Benjamin Grierson was the commander of Fort Concho from 1875 to 1882. He had been a music teacher before the Civil War created a military career for him. Grierson did an excellent job of completing the building program at the fort and making the facility beautiful. He lived in the first building in this row, to which he added an office, a kitchen, and a carriage house, making the building in the foreground the most imposing home on the post. He had decided to add the office at his home so that he could avoid walking to the headquarters building several times a day in front of the other officers' quarters. The wives of other officers were always anxious to visit, seek favors, and generally further the careers of their husbands. Grierson preferred to avoid those time-consuming meetings as much as possible. (FC.)

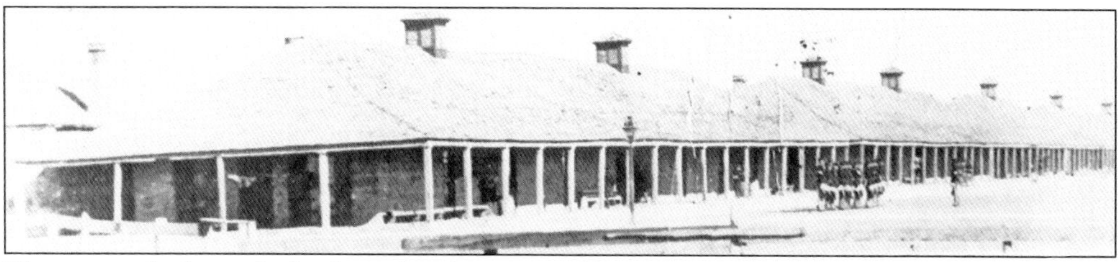

These were the barracks for the enlisted men. A soldier's life at Fort Concho was highly organized. Bugles sounded reveille and taps each day. The flag on the parade ground was raised and lowered, there were inspections, and guards were posted. Here, one can see soldiers involved in their regular work. They might be assigned building or repair duties, work in the garden, or haul water and supplies. The worst assignments went to the occupants of the guardhouse. (FC.)

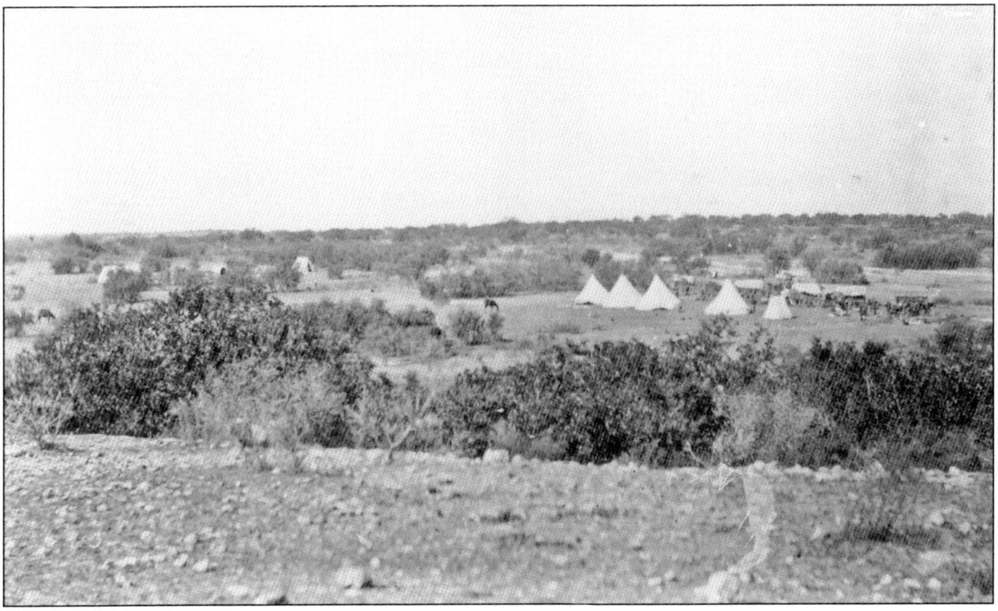

Capt. George Wedemeyer took this picture of soldiers camping at Kickapoo Springs, Texas, in 1887. Soldiers had many assignments away from Fort Concho. They might be called upon to guard a wagon train or a herd of cattle. They might be scouting for Indian renegades after receiving reports of attacks on ranch houses or thefts of horses. Other assignments might include mapping, stringing telegraph line, or building roads in the area. (FC.)

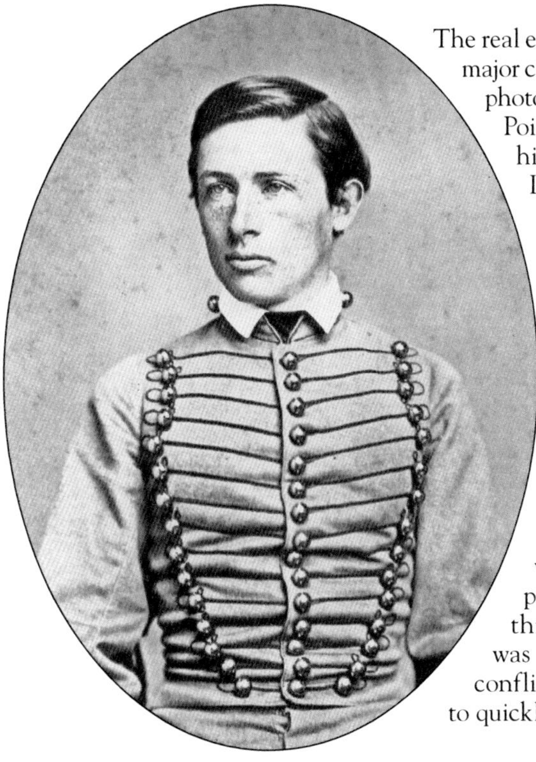

The real excitement for a soldier was battle, and several major campaigns originated at Fort Concho. This is a photograph of Col. Ranald S. Mackenzie as a West Point cadet. Gen. Phillip Sheridan said he was his best field commander in the Indian Wars. In command of the 4th Cavalry, Mackenzie carried out a brilliant campaign against the Comanche, Kiowa, Cheyenne, and Arapaho who were raiding on the northern Texas frontier. In September 1874, he led several companies along with Indian scouts against the enemy in Tule Canyon and Palo Duro Canyon in the Texas Panhandle. The soldiers destroyed the Indians' camp, burned food and supplies, and killed hundreds of horses, and the Indians were forced to return to the reservation. Mackenzie brought 124 women and children back to Fort Concho, where they were held hostage for a brief period. This campaign ended Indian raids in this northern area of Texas. Many felt that he was an innovator of the concept of total war: a conflict fought against both civilians and soldiers to quickly end a military threat. (WTC.)

The major remaining obstacle to the Euro-American settlement of West Texas was the Apache leader Victorio. In 1877, he left the San Carlos Reservation in Arizona with around 300 Mescalero, Chiricahua, and Apache and began attacking ranches, stagecoaches, and other profitable targets in New Mexico, Texas, and Mexico. Benjamin Grierson led the 10th Cavalry to stop these incursions. In the summer of 1880, Grierson used his knowledge of the limited water sources in far western Texas to set up a decisive battle with the Apache band at Rattlesnake Springs. Much weakened, Victorio retreated to the New Mexico mountains and was later killed in Mexico. The 10th Cavalry and Grierson himself fought valiantly in this last extended campaign that originated at Fort Concho. (FC.)

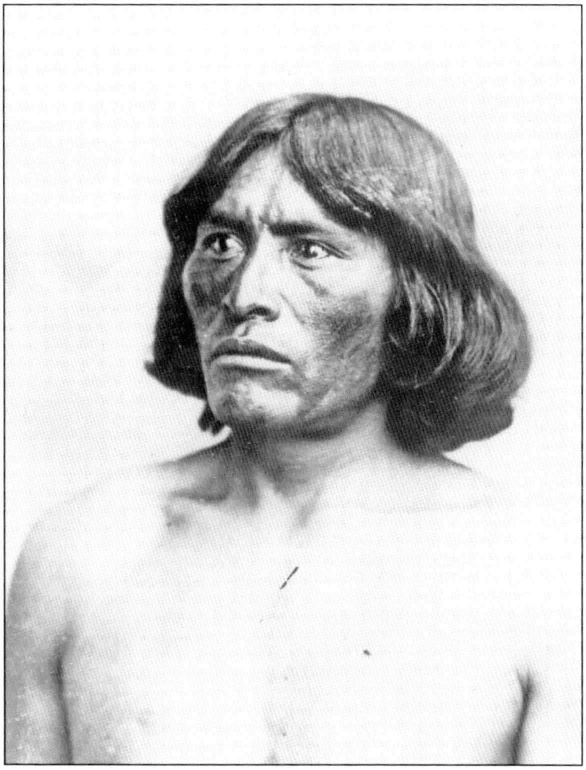

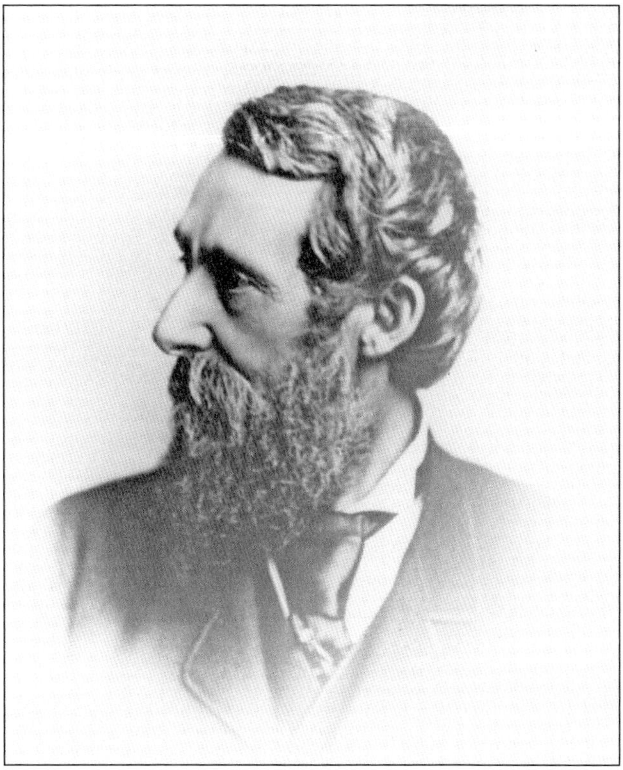

This portrait shows Benjamin Grierson in civilian clothes and highlights his humanitarian side. The 10th Cavalry was the most famous regiment of Buffalo Soldiers in the Indian Wars. Fort Concho was home to four black regiments—9th Cavalry, 10th Cavalry, 24th Infantry, and 25th Infantry. Grierson was a great defender of the black troopers. He also supported President Grant's peace policy and Indian rights in general. These views sometimes led to conflict with his contemporaries, including Ranald Mackenzie, who favored a more forceful solution to the "Indian problem." The 10th Cavalry and Grierson stayed at Fort Concho for seven years, from 1875 to 1882, and made an indelible mark on the mission there. (FC.)

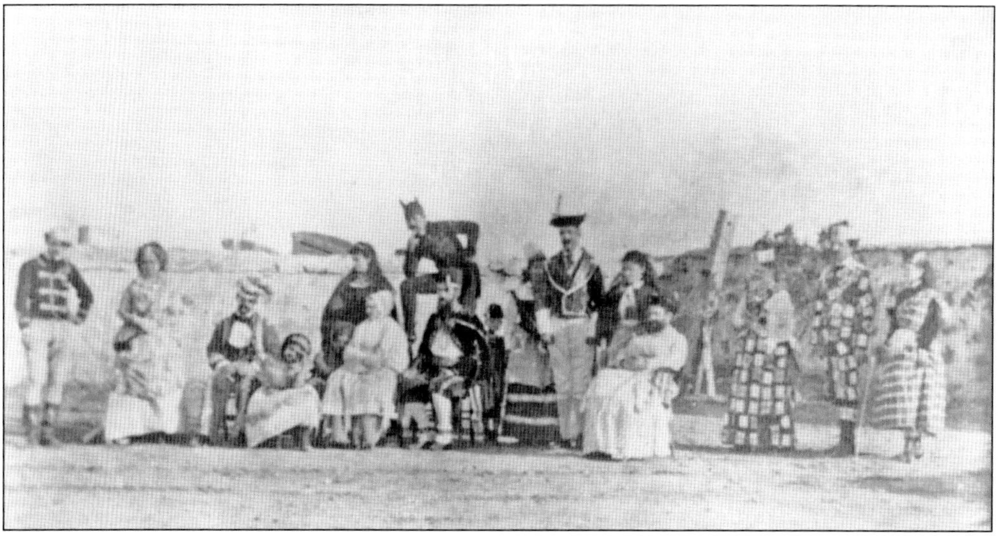

Benjamin and Alice Grierson were leaders of the social life at the fort. Colonel Grierson had a musical background, played several instruments, and took pride in the regimental band. He and the band frequently entertained soldiers, officers, and their families. Alice, Benjamin's wife, organized many celebrations in their home, taking pride in setting a fine table and providing lively dancing. Here, the Griersons and others are dressed in costume for a play. (FC.)

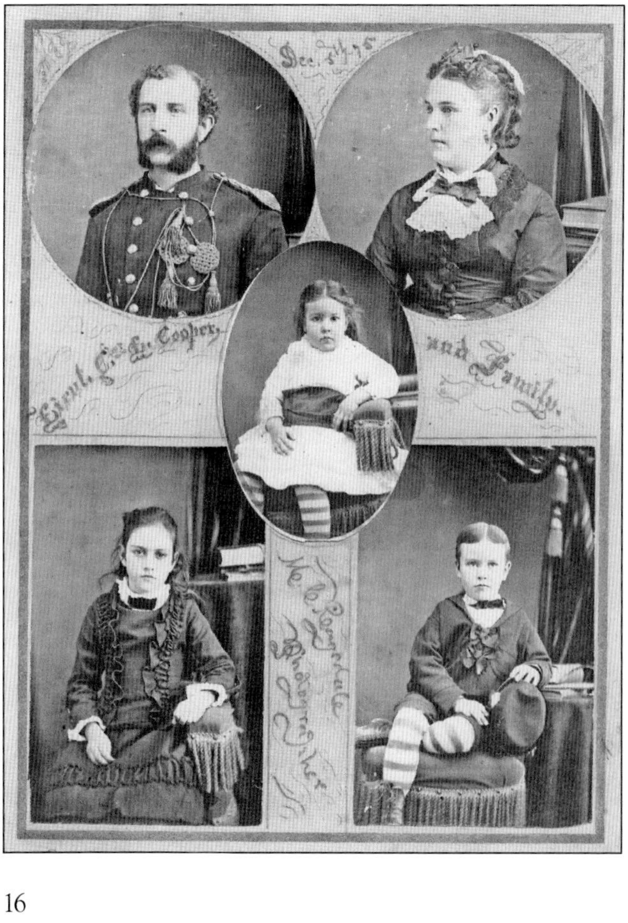

Officers often brought their wives and children to live at the fort. This is the family of Lt. Charles Lawrence Cooper, an officer of the 10th Cavalry. His daughter Forrestine, or Birdie, is on the lower left in this picture. She wrote several novels about the West as well as her memoirs. One of the chapters in her memoirs is entitled "Life was Never Dull at Fort Concho." Her father was the post commissary officer, and he provided her with baby mice for pets and a military burial ceremony for them when they died. There were pranks, practical jokes, weddings, and Christmas to amuse her. She also speaks of the very tight bond that existed between her and the other children of the regiment. (FC.)

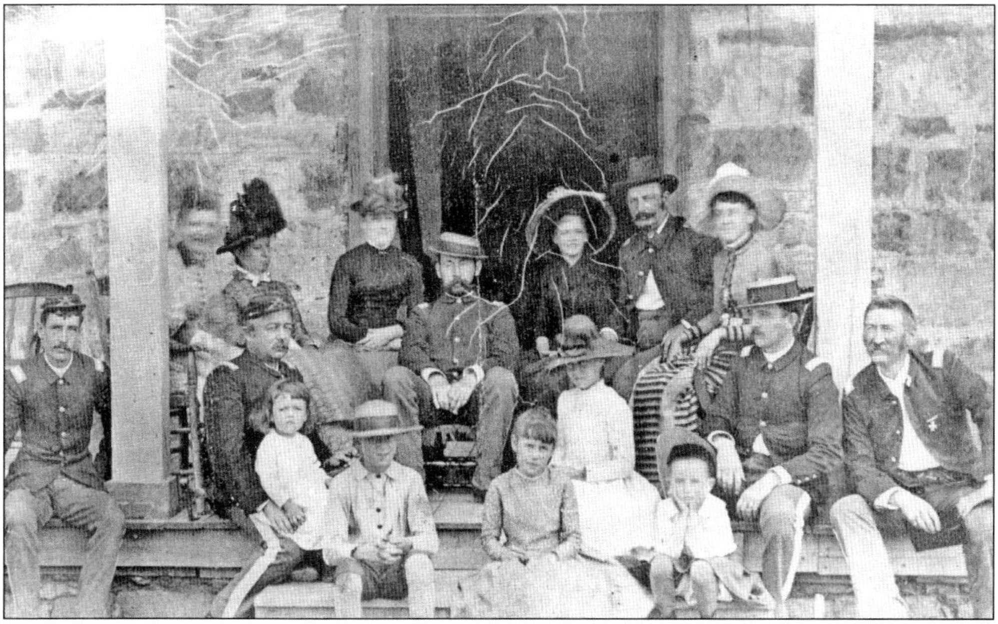

This photograph shows a gathering of officers, wives, and children on the porch of Capt. George Wedemeyer's home. Diaries speak of parties to celebrate many occasions. The Fourth of July might mean horse races, picnics, and band music. Arrivals and departures might call for a party. In an isolated setting, one could complain about the conditions or make the best of it. Captain Wedemeyer is at bottom right in the picture. (WTC.)

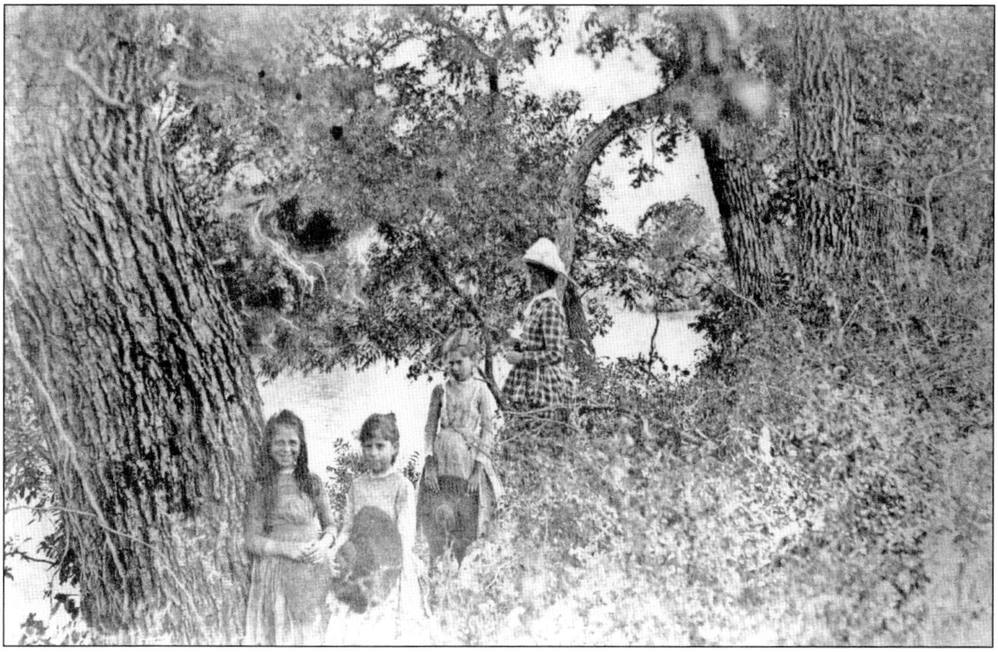

Here, a daughter of Captain Wedemeyer takes some children on an outing by the river. Birdy Cooper wrote glowingly about the freedom she had as a child at Fort Concho. Men, women, and children went on fishing expeditions, had swimming parties, or even hunted buffalo nearby at Twin Mountains. (WTC.)

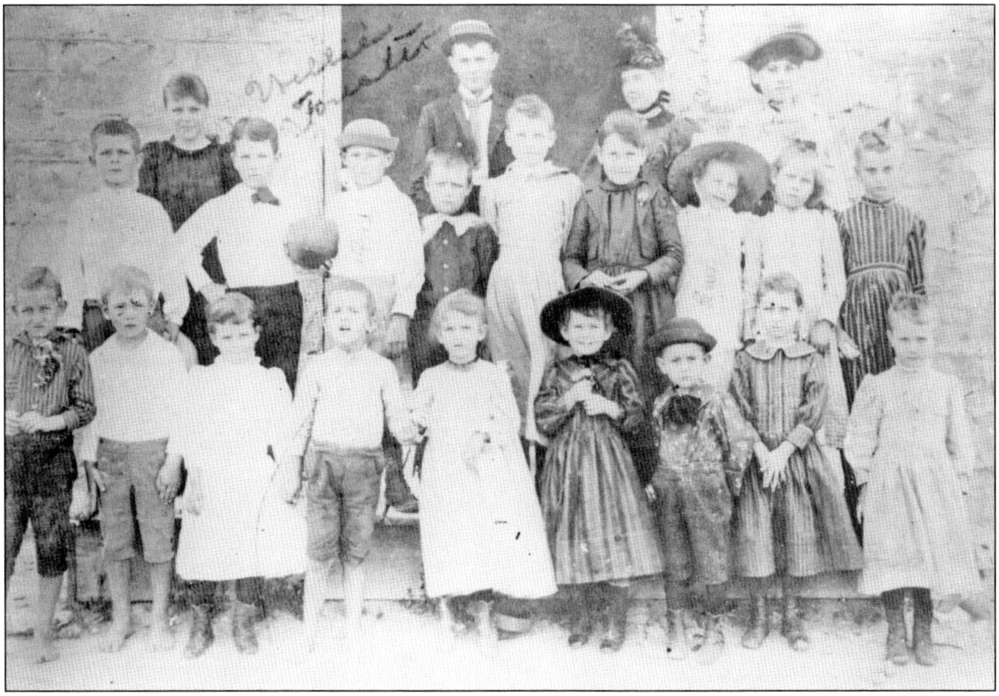

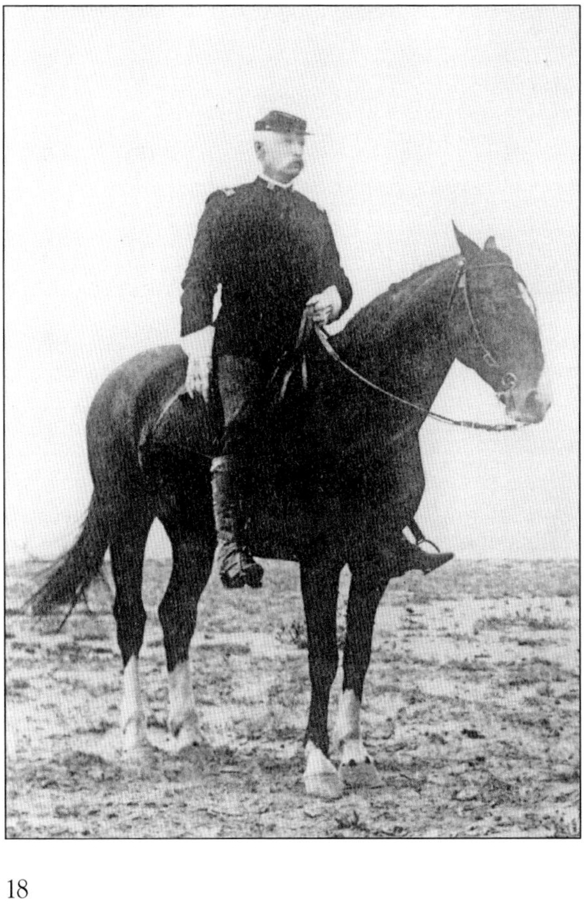

But the children at the fort were not always free to do as they wished. They attended school at the fort after the construction of this building during the Grierson years. The structure, located at the end of officer's row, was both the schoolhouse and the chapel. (FC.)

Capt. William Davis Jr., of the 10th Cavalry, married Colonel Grierson's niece in December 1878. He was one of four officers who married at the fort. According to the wedding guests, the festivities were especially stylish, and the newly married couple left in a stagecoach for their wedding trip. (WTC.)

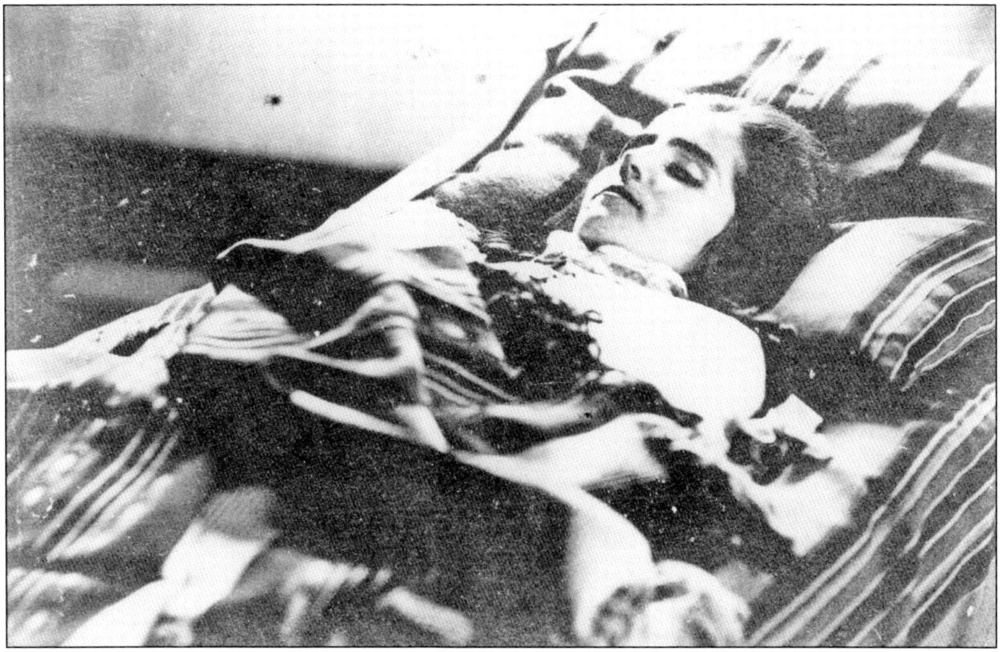

The story of Fort Concho is not entirely one of games and parties. This sad picture shows Edith Grierson, age 13, in her casket. She died of typhoid in 1878. The commander and Alice mourned this very popular young lady, as did everyone at the fort. Tragedy and hardship were common, but most fort inhabitants expected that and still made the most of their stays. (FC.)

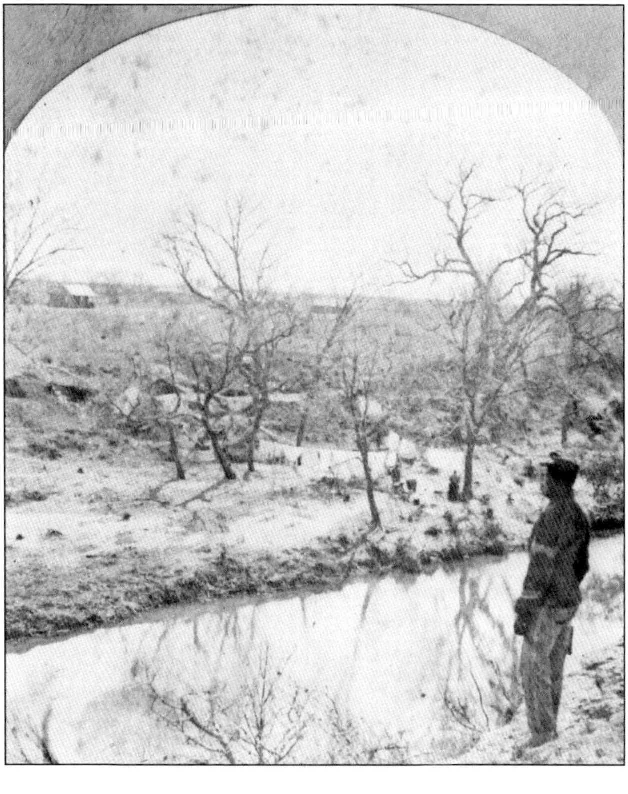

Enlisted men at the fort lived a simpler life. If they had families, the wives and children could not live on post. This poignant photograph shows a lonely trooper looking across the river at a rough settlement occupied by wives, laundresses, and other camp followers. Grierson did have a sturdy building constructed for their use during his tenure at Fort Concho. Laundresses received rations and were paid a small sum by the military. Census data reveals that many men and women worked as servants at the post, and most of them were black. (FC.)

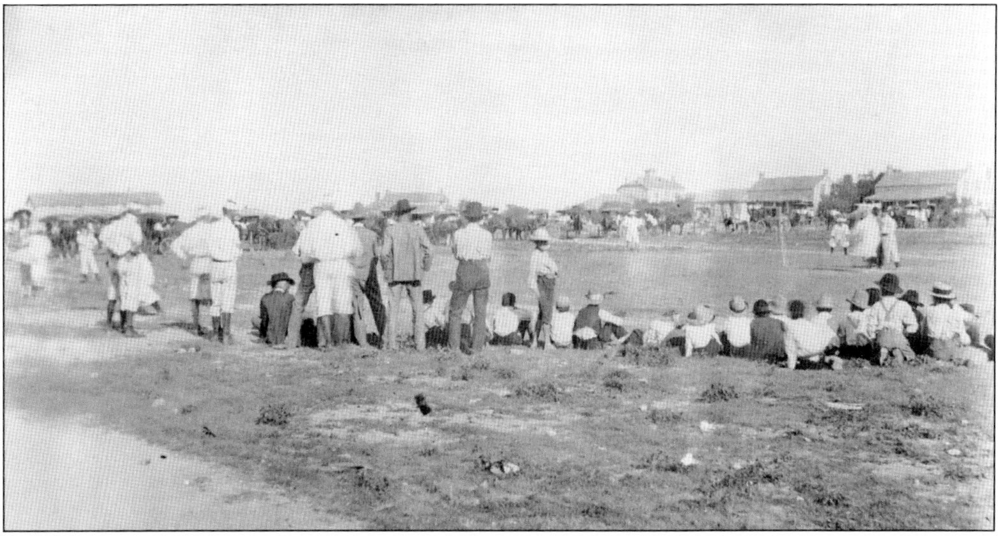

Baseball was a popular entertainment at the fort. Enlisted men also enjoyed parties and holiday celebrations. Companies would take turns hosting dances and dinners. The Fourth of July celebration might feature a parade with the regimental band playing, horse races, and special food. This picture of a baseball game on the parade ground may or may not have been taken while the fort was active; playing baseball on the parade ground remained popular for many years. (FC.)

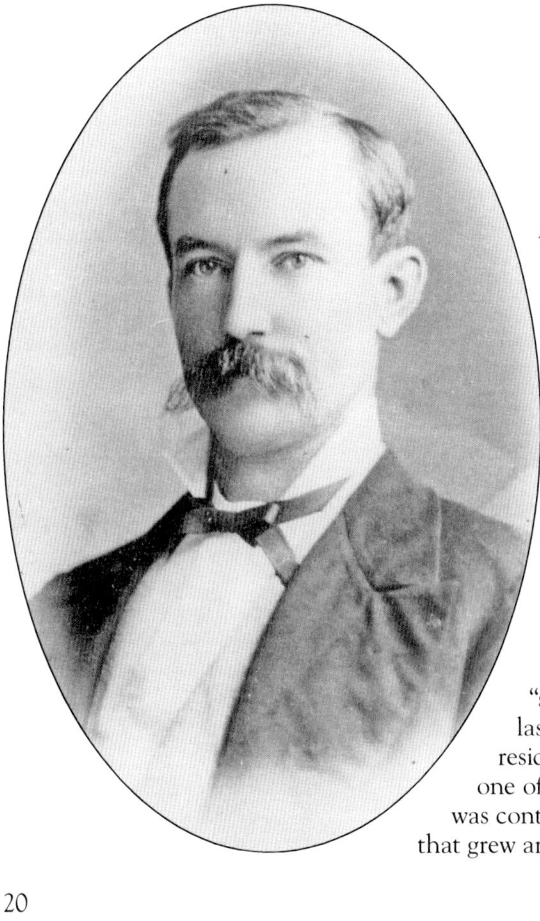

A soldier might seek entertainment at the post sutler's store. There he could get a drink, buy something special, play a game of billiards, or perhaps do a little gambling. This is a portrait of James Louis Millspaugh, who served as post sutler from 1876 to 1881. It was very lucrative to hold this position, but it could be trying. A man had to please a post council, consisting of three officers, who might require a new building, better merchandise, or tighter control of drinking and gambling. Still, a trader could make money from a guaranteed volume of business at the store plus the opportunity to contract supplies for other western forts. Millspaugh, described by a contemporary as a "small, dynamic, swashbuckling New Yorker," lasted for six years. He became a permanent resident and civic leader in San Angelo. Indeed, one of the greatest achievements of Fort Concho was contributing talented people to the community that grew around the outpost. (WTC.)

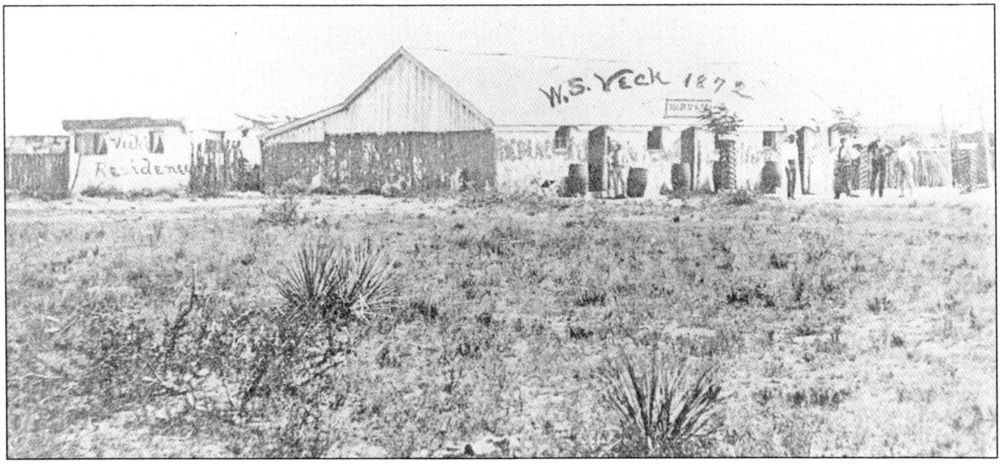

Soldiers could also leave the post to spend their money. This establishment, called by some the first store in San Angelo, was started by former post sutler W.S. Veck. It is interesting to note the size of his residence compared to the size of his store. San Angelo began with the mission to see that soldiers did not save any money. They were paid every two months, and most were under 30. In addition to stores, there were saloons, restaurants, barbershops, and brothels to entice a lonely soldier to quickly spend his paycheck. (FC.)

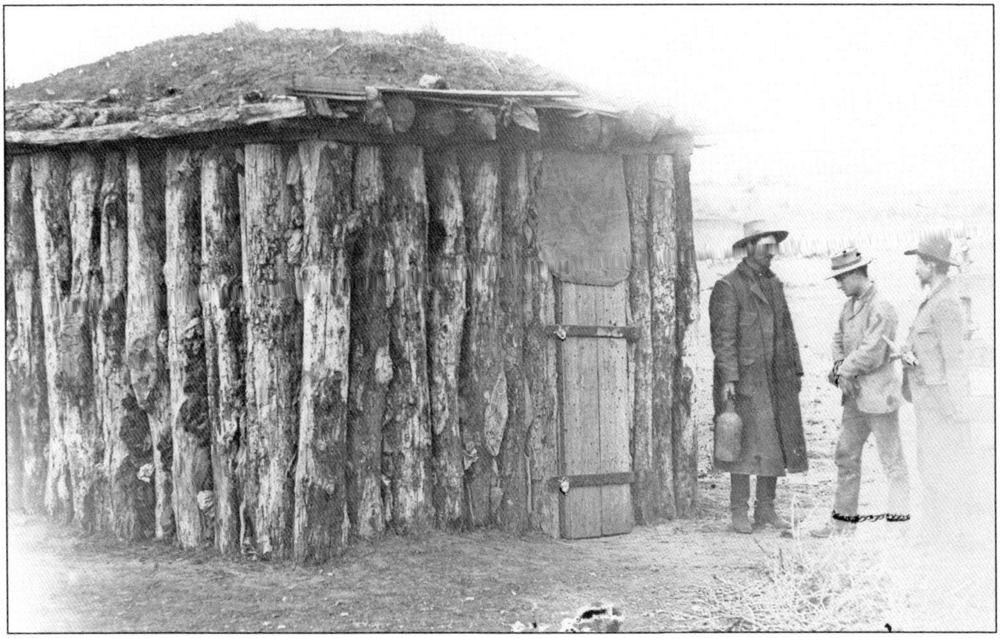

In the first years of its existence, San Angelo could be a dangerous place. The post surgeon reported that by 1871, one hundred murders had occurred within 10 miles of the fort. This picture shows the first jail in the community and perhaps indicates that law enforcement was somewhat primitive in the early days. Everyone in town was armed, and heavy drinking was a common pastime. To make things even more volatile, the Buffalo Soldiers at Fort Concho were stationed in a Southern state. Frequently, people in town showed their racial prejudices by yelling insults, picking fights, or even shooting at black soldiers. Another post surgeon said that as late as 1878 no officer left the garrison after dark because it was never safe in San Angelo at night. Enlisted men, however, frequently went to town. (WTC.)

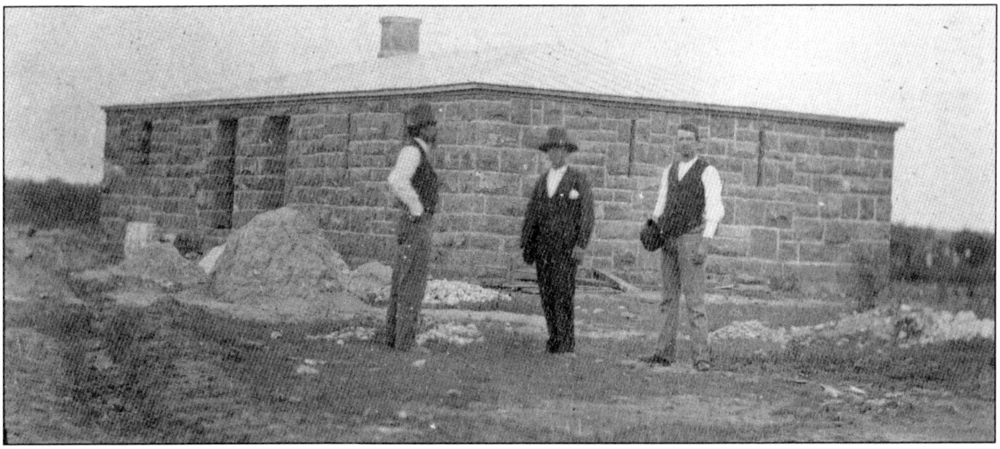

The most famous racial incident in San Angelo started in January 1881, when a Buffalo Soldier was killed in a local saloon. Soon thereafter, William Watkins of the 10th Cavalry was killed by a local rancher named Tom McCarthy. Watkins had been hired by McCarthy to play the banjo and sing and dance at a party where heavy drinking took place. Watkins was shot. Tension among all of the troops at the fort was extremely high. The gun that killed Watkins was proven to belong to Tom McCarthy, and he was handed over to the local sheriff, James Spears. Many soldiers feared McCarthy would escape justice. On February 2, Watkins was buried and about 100 soldiers marched to town, seized the sheriff, and demanded that McCarthy be released to them. Spears had "hidden" him in the Ben Ficklin Jail, shown in this early photograph. Ben Ficklin was a quiet community about four miles from San Angelo. By 1881, of course, the jail was completed. (WTC.)

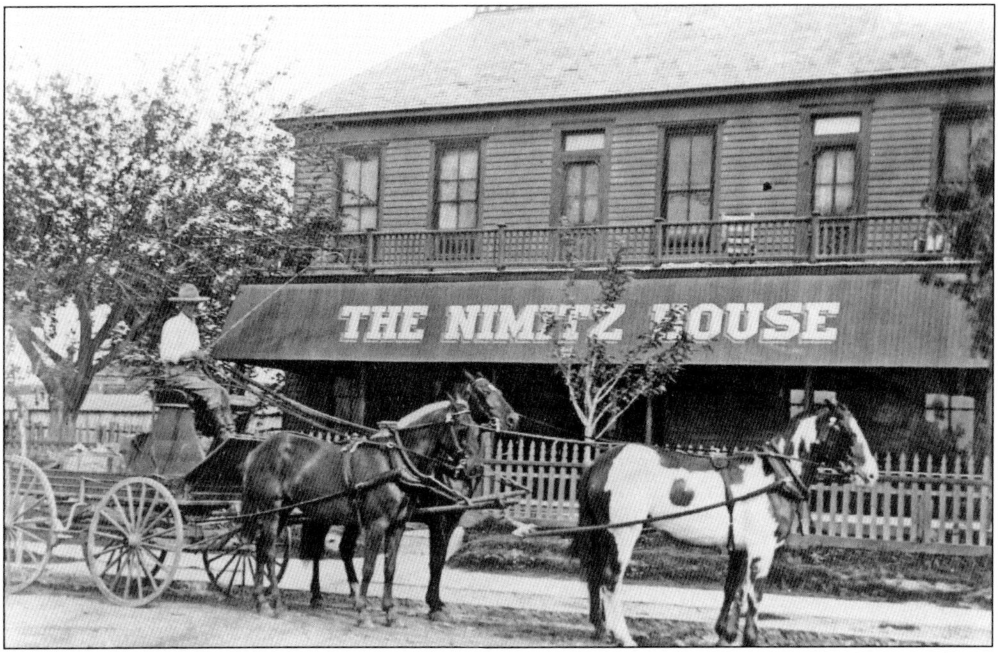

The Nimitz Hotel, shown here in more peaceful times, was the scene of a second incident involving black Fort Concho troopers. A rumor circulated that McCarthy was free and staying at the Nimitz, and this gossip prompted 30 to 40 armed soldiers to return to town. They fired about 200 shots at the hotel before they became convinced that he was not there. (WTC.)

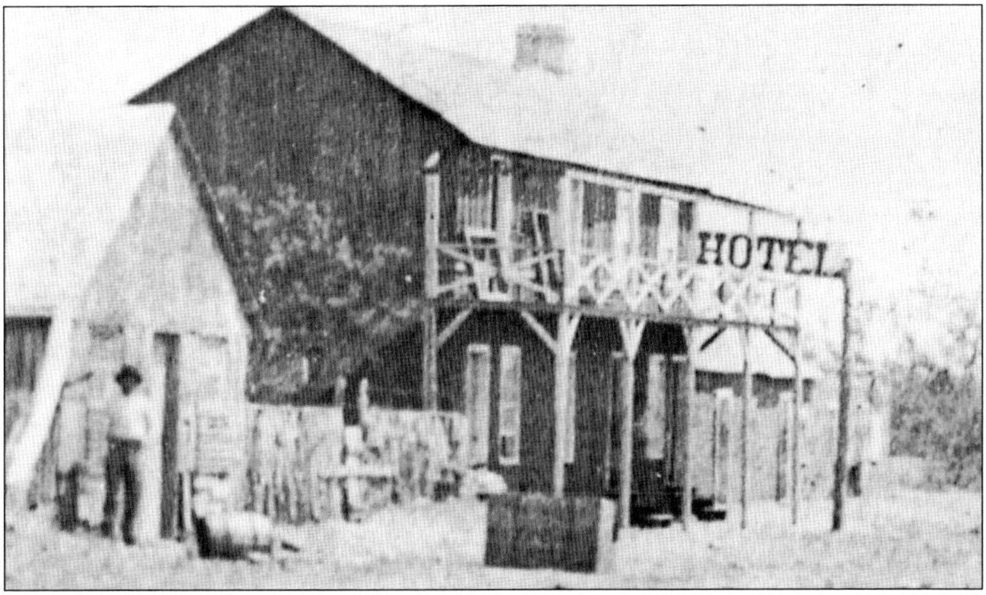

The soldiers next decided that McCarthy was being hidden at the Concho House Hotel, pictured here. The hotel owner, the intrepid Annie Ellen Tankersley, faced the soldiers and demanded that they leave her property. They returned to the fort. The next day, Texas Rangers, who were state lawmen, arrived in San Angelo and restored order. Commander Grierson was severely reprimanded for allowing his soldiers to shoot at local citizens in this undisciplined manner. McCarthy was tried for murder in November and released. The shooting was ruled accidental. (WTC.)

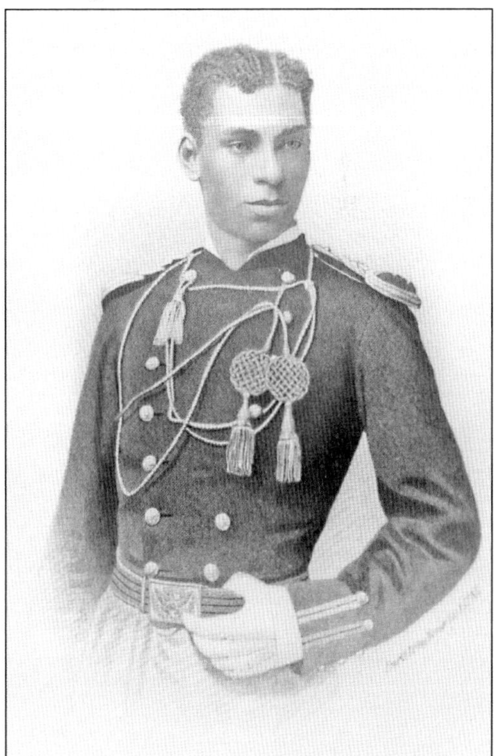

One of the most interesting people to serve at Fort Concho was 2nd Lt. Henry O. Flipper. He was the first African American to graduate from West Point, and when he joined the 10th Cavalry in 1880, he was the first black officer of the black regiment. This placed him in an awkward position. At one point, the commanding officer said he was not to eat in the quarters of the white officers. At the same time, he could not interact socially with the enlisted men. When he was later transferred to Fort Davis, he became quartermaster and was charged with financial irregularities. A court-martial convicted him of conduct unbecoming an officer. There were some minor irregularities involving funds, but Flipper always claimed that he was dismissed from the military because he had been too friendly with a white woman at Fort Concho. Flipper would fare better in civilian life as a successful engineer and businessman. The military was very ambiguous about integration in the 19th century. (WTC.)

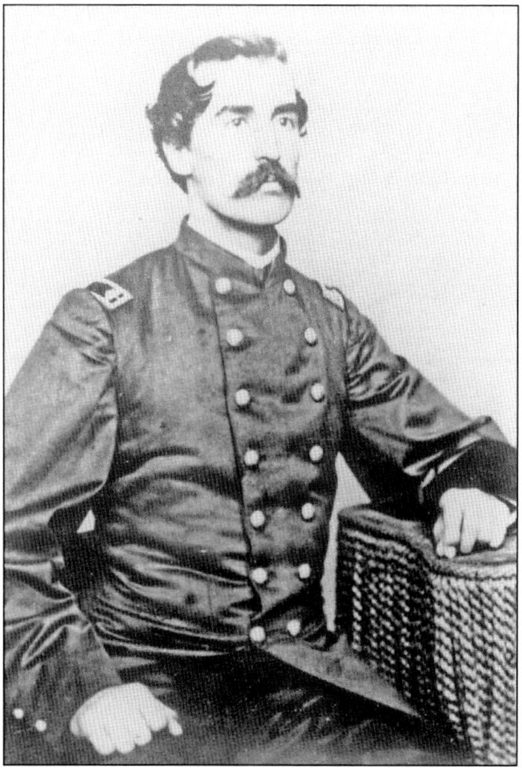

Dr. William M. Notson was post surgeon from 1869 to 1872. The men who held this position were crucial to the orderly operation of the fort. Notson was responsible for medical care, of course, but his duties extended in many other directions. He was in charge of sanitation and therefore the building program. He kept weather data, explored the natural history of the region, and even collected skulls, which he sent to the Army Medical Museum in Washington, DC. Notson's daily record of events was exacting, and his constant pressure for supplies at the isolated fort made life better for all who were stationed there. (FC.)

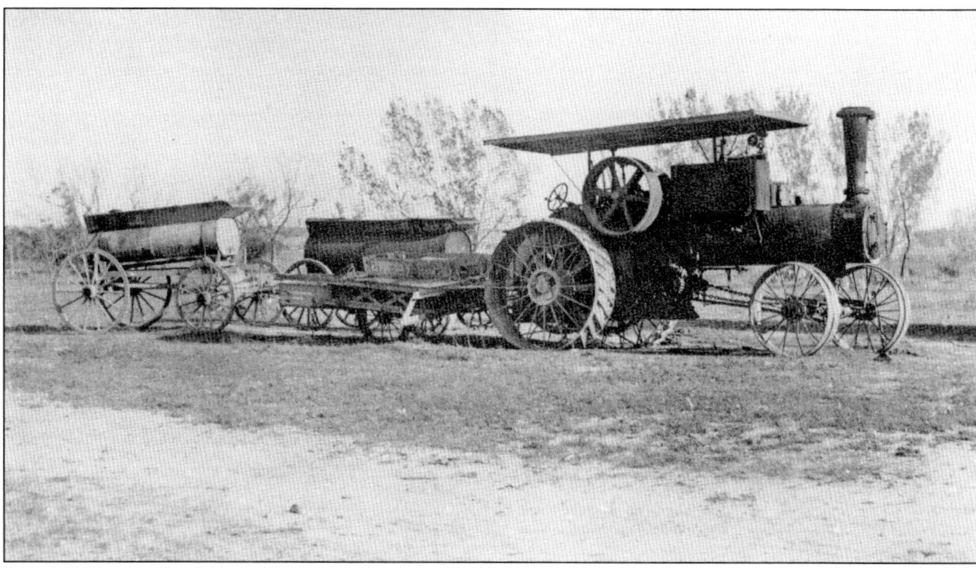

This photograph shows a steam tractor used at the nearby Bismarck Farm. Soldiers received a daily ration of beef, bread, and coffee. Fresh vegetables were a critical need at the fort; surgeon S.L.S. Smith reported rampant indigestion and gastrointestinal disorders among the troops. Fresh produce could not be brought from San Antonio, so the garrison had to buy from local farmers or grow its own. At times, the fort rented part of the Bismarck Farm to grow what it needed, and sometimes produce was grown at the fort itself. The surgeon oversaw this work until the job was taken over by the chaplain. (WTC.)

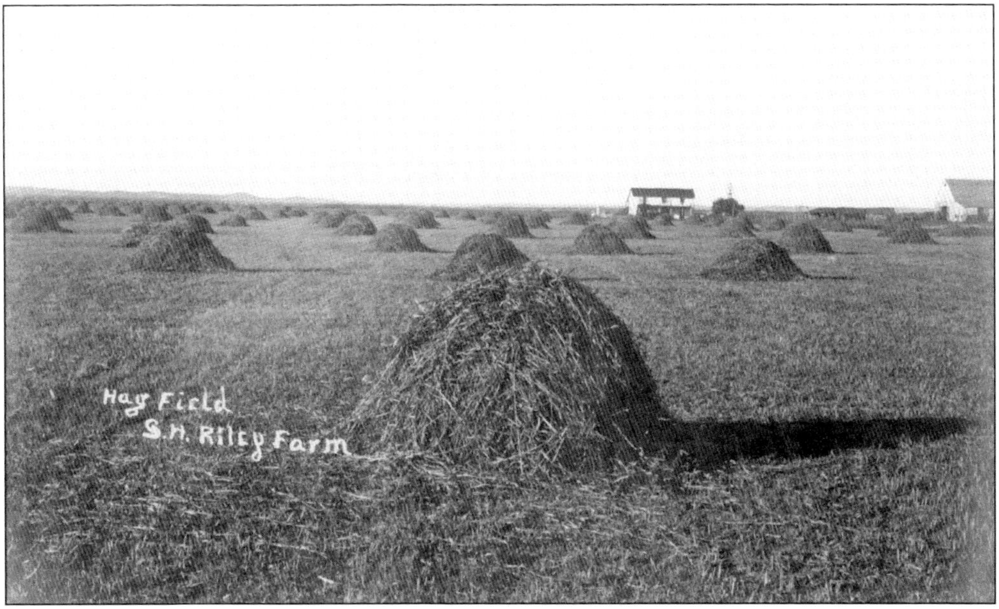

Many supplies were bought locally. A pen of cattle purchased from local ranchers was kept near the fort so that beef could be freshly slaughtered each day. Hay farms, such as the one in this picture, provided food for the horses and the cows. The local economy benefited from these purchases and many others. (FC.)

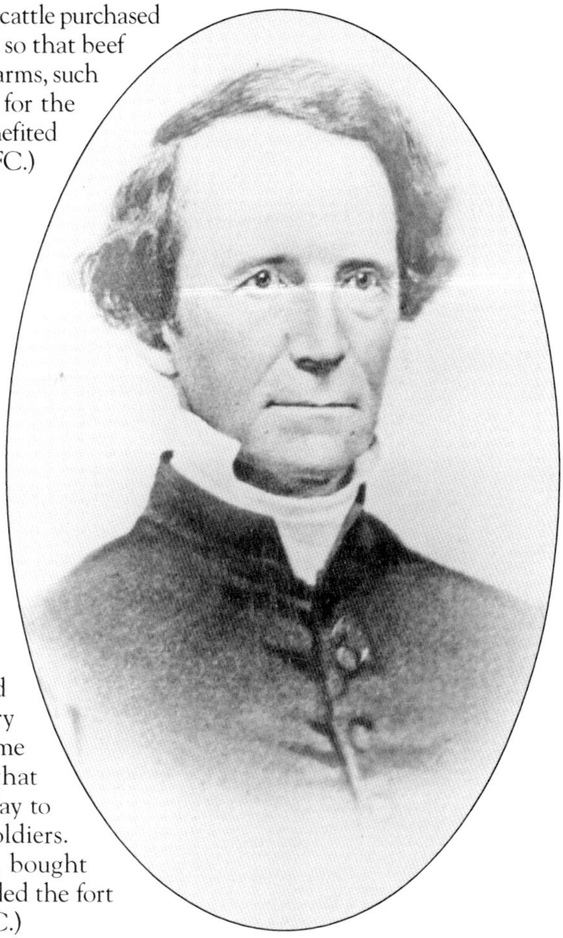

The Reverend Norman Badger was post chaplain from 1871 until 1876. He was a dedicated, hardworking Episcopal priest who would hold services for anyone—black or white, soldier or citizen, sinner or saint. When he first preached in nearby San Angelo, one contemporary observed that it was probably the first time God's name was spoken reverently in that place. Badger taught school during the day to white children and at night to black soldiers. In addition, he created a post library, bought periodicals and books for all to read, tended the fort garden, and supervised the bakery. (WTC.)

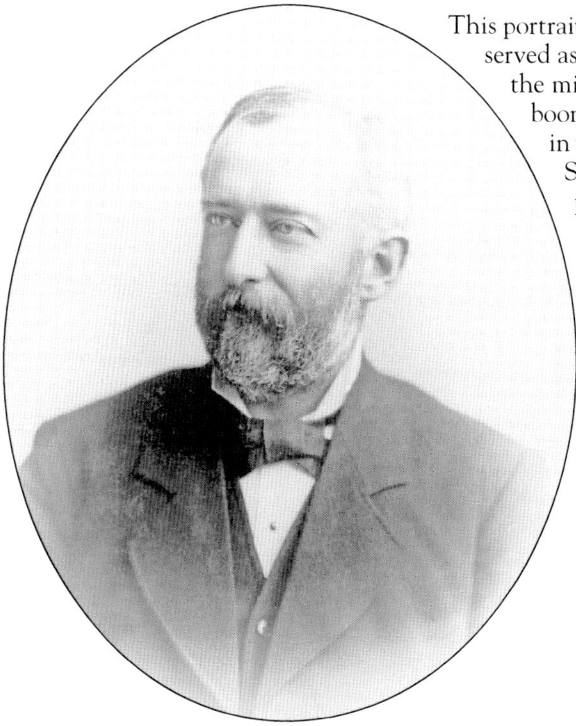

This portrait of Dr. S.L.S. Smith was taken when he served as post surgeon from 1878 to 1881. He left the military and stayed in San Angelo, a huge boon to the health of the growing population in town. Smith established the Pioneer Drug Store, where people could gather and visit, pick up their mail, and get medical advice or treatment. Later, he helped create the first hospital in San Angelo. (FC.)

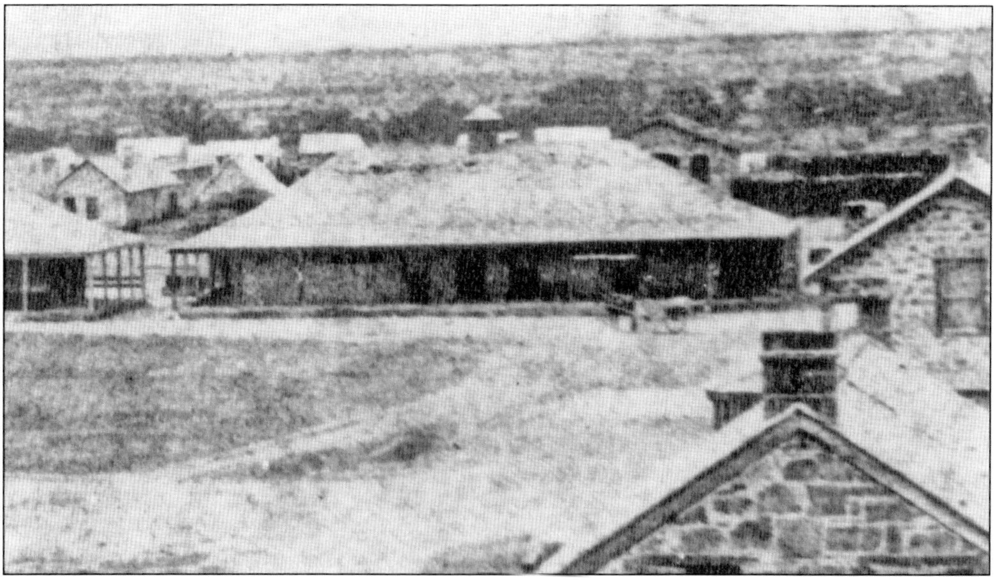

This is a view of the guardhouse, with barracks on the left. It was completed in 1871 with eight cells, which were frequently occupied. Pvt. Thomas Reger spent 326 of his 401 days at Fort Concho confined to this building for drinking. Desertion was amazingly common at the fort, since it was punishable by dishonorable discharge and imprisonment. Dr. Notson reported in July 1871 that there were 23 cases involving desertion. Black soldiers were not as likely to leave the post illegally. In the late 19th century, employment opportunities for African Americans were limited. The army offered a good and honorable job, which most black soldiers wanted to keep. They also had higher reenlistment rates than white soldiers. (FC.)

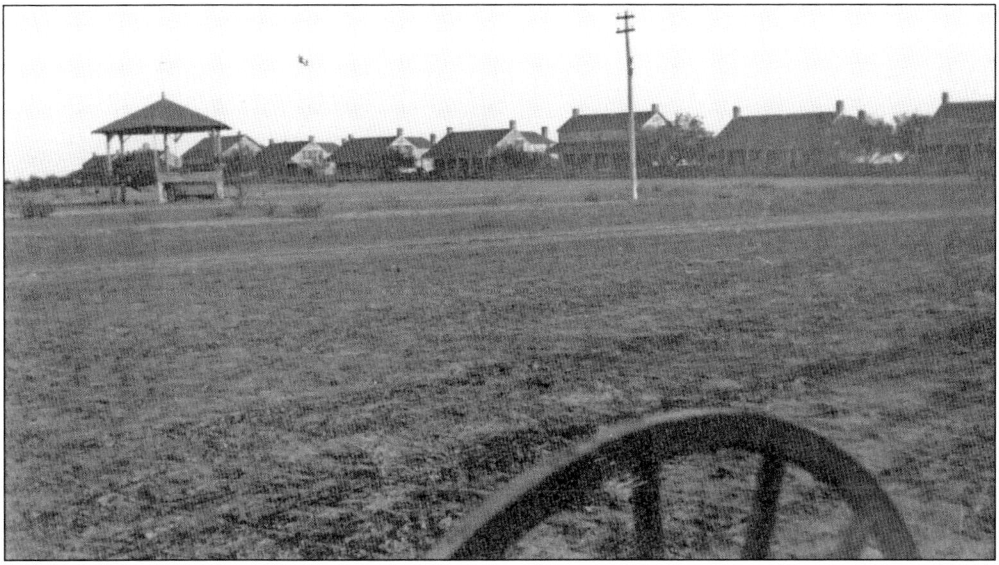

After the defeat of Victorio in 1881, the area around Fort Concho had little need for military protection. Captain Wedemeyer commented that it was ridiculous to go on scouts and have to follow well-traveled roads. Most of the countryside consisted of fenced pastures. On June 20, 1889, the last federal troops left San Angelo after one last salute was fired and the flag was lowered. Only the quartermaster was left to settle accounts. This is a view of the parade ground with a vacant band stand and officers' quarters. (WTC.)

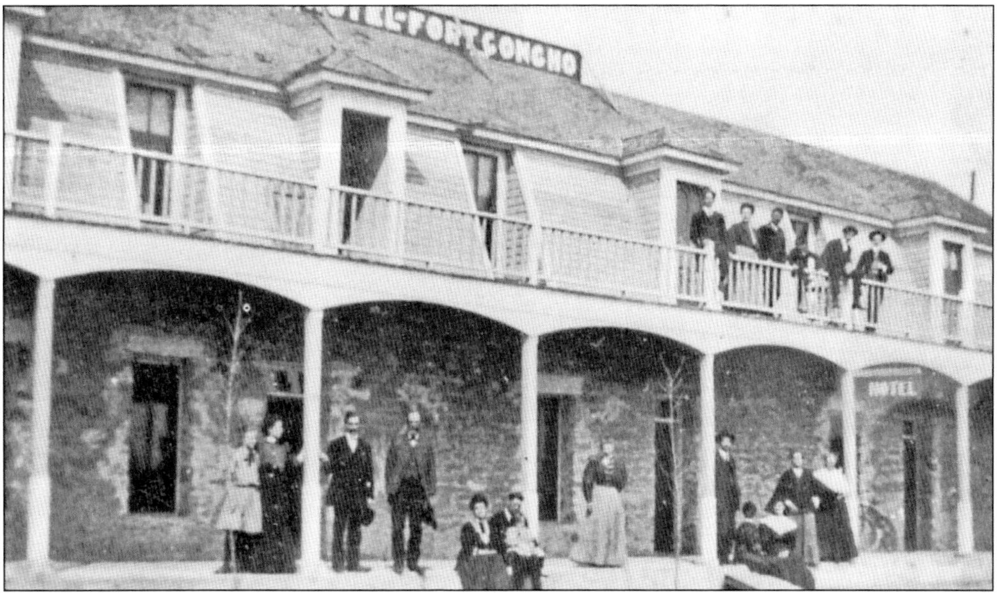

The fort was built on leased land, so ownership of all buildings went into private hands when the soldiers left. Local citizens had appealed to the federal government to fund some alternative use for these facilities, but that did not happen. In many ways, San Angelo was lucky that private citizens used the fort's buildings for homes, or storage, or, in this case, a hotel. The Fort Concho Hotel did not last long, but most of the structures at the fort benefitted from adaptive use. Today, the Fort Concho National Historic Site has many original buildings, making it the best preserved frontier fort west of the Mississippi. (WTC.)

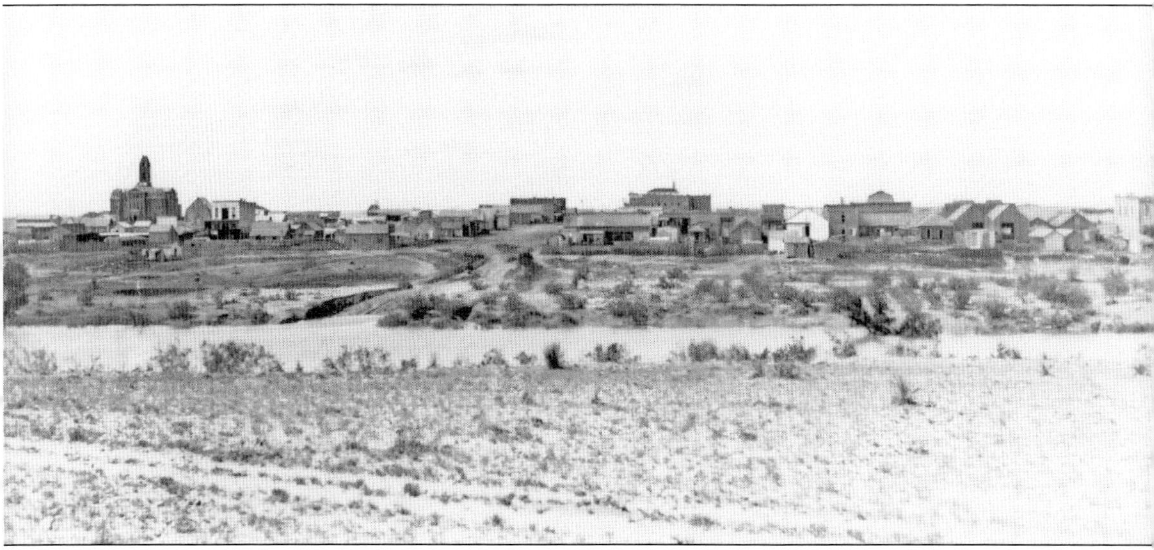

This 1886 photograph of San Angelo was taken by Captain Wedemeyer and shows what the city across the river was like as the fort was nearing closure. For 22 years, this military base did so much. It was home to companies from 15 regiments who worked hard and fought bravely to fulfill their mission. The US government in the late 19th century pursued a policy of facilitating western settlement at the expense of Native American rights and traditional lifestyles. In the 21st century, this policy seems callous and unfair, but the soldiers at Fort Concho did the job they were given in an admirable manner. While doing that job, roads were built, maps of the area were drawn, and resources were located. Personnel at the fort patronized local businesses and contributed to the development of a strong economy in San Angelo. Finally, the fort contributed people who decided to stay in San Angelo and help it grow. There is no way to measure how many people came to the area because there was a military post on the Concho River. When Fort Concho finally closed, there were many talented people in San Angelo to make certain that the community would continue and prosper. (FC.)

Two

Agricultural Enterprises

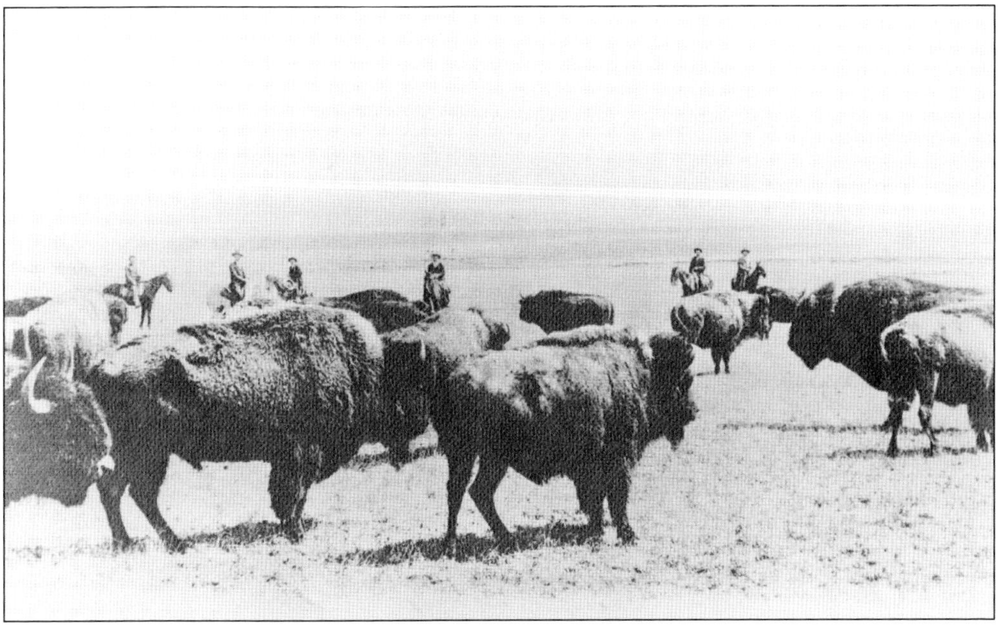

San Angelo grew and prospered while Fort Concho remained active, and the town would continue to develop after the soldiers left. Agriculture in its many forms would be the basis of the local economy for decades. The Concho Valley was at the southern end of the buffalo range on the western Great Plains, and San Angelo was an important center for buffalo hunters. These tough characters came to town to enjoy some city pleasures and sell the hides they had accumulated. In the 1870s, hundreds of thousands of hides were shipped from San Angelo by freight wagon. The killing of so many of these animals meant there would be less food for the Plains Indians and more grass for the cattle that would soon occupy the plains. (WTC.)

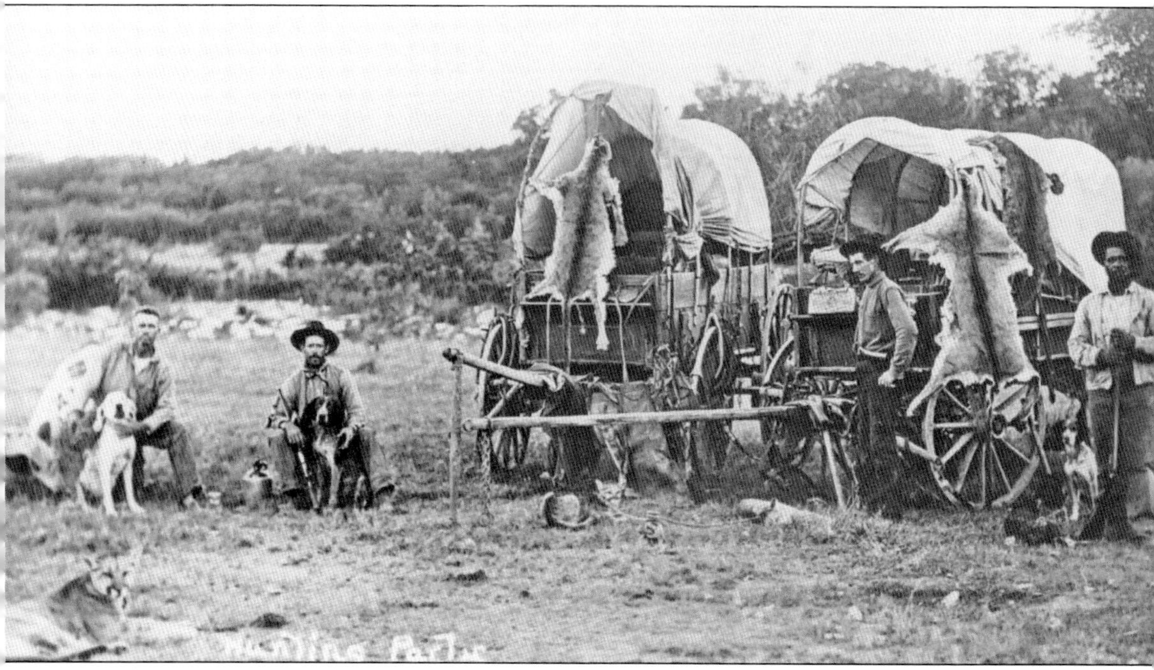

There were many valuable pelts in the Concho Valley. Trappers enjoyed hunting bear, bobcat, and fox, and a person could prosper from the enterprise. Businesses in San Angelo would market pelts for trappers just as they would sell wool for ranchers. (FC.)

The first cattle rancher in the Concho Valley was Richard Franklin (R.F.) Tankersley. He fought with the Texas Rangers in western Texas during the early 1860s. While he was there, he selected a place to later establish a cattle ranch. In 1864, he moved his family and his livestock to the headwaters of Spring Creek in Irion County. Before there was federal protection and before there were any neighbors except the Kickapoo and the Comanche, Tankersley raised livestock on the open-range principle—control some water, brand the cows, and let them grow and multiply with no fences and minimum supervision. His range at this point may have been as large as two million acres. He lost livestock to the Indians, and his wife, Annie, never sat on the porch without a gun on her knees, but he made money and ultimately acquired 20 sections of land to leave to his heirs. Marketing was an issue in this isolated place. In 1869, he drove 2,500 head of cattle to California to find buyers. By 1871, he had a local market, furnishing all of the meat to Forts Concho, Stockton, and McKavett. (WTC.)

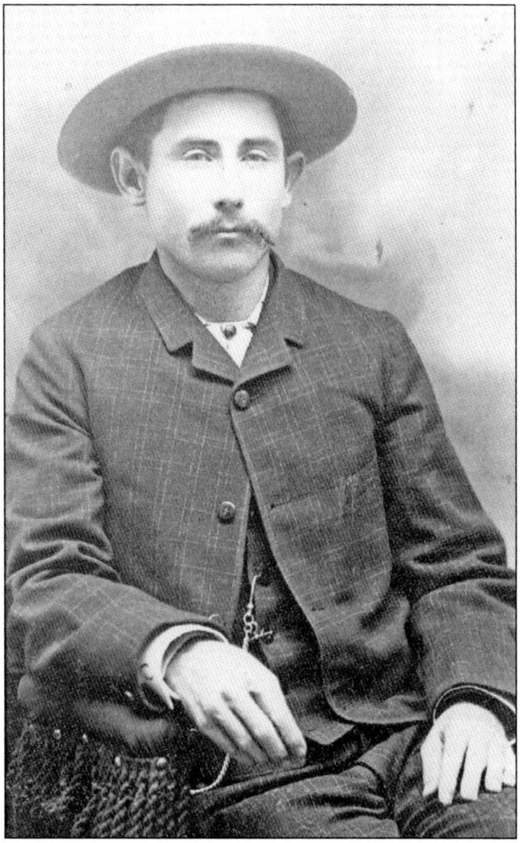

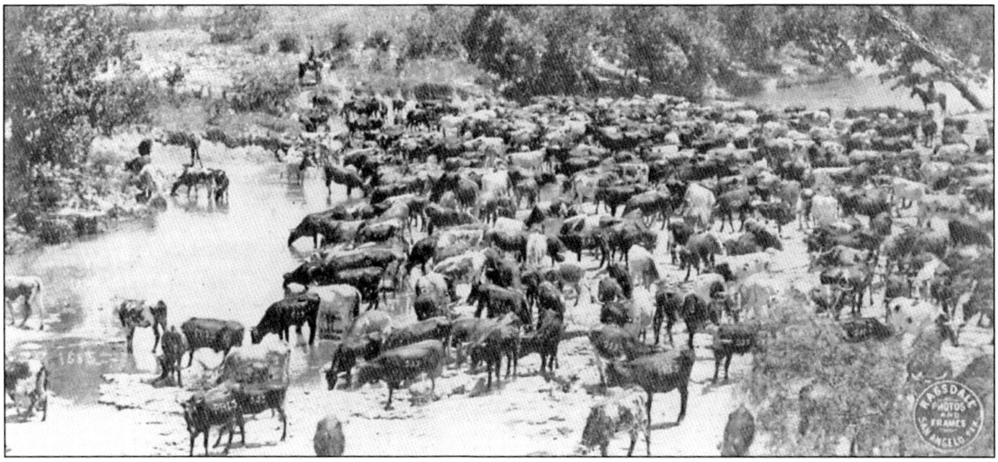

Raising cattle soon became widespread in the Concho Valley. A western cattle boom was in full swing in the 1870s and 1880s. Promotional pamphlets touted the existence of a "beef bonanza" on the Plains, a surefire way to get rich. Startup costs were minimal: cows and bulls and enough labor to round them up every year or so. The animals took care of multiplying on their own. Ambitious young men came from many places in the United States and Europe to cash in on this new frontier possibility. Santa Fe Railway reached San Angelo in 1888; an estimated 3,500 to 5,000 railcars of cattle were shipped annually, making San Angelo one of the largest range-cattle shipping points in the country. (WTC.)

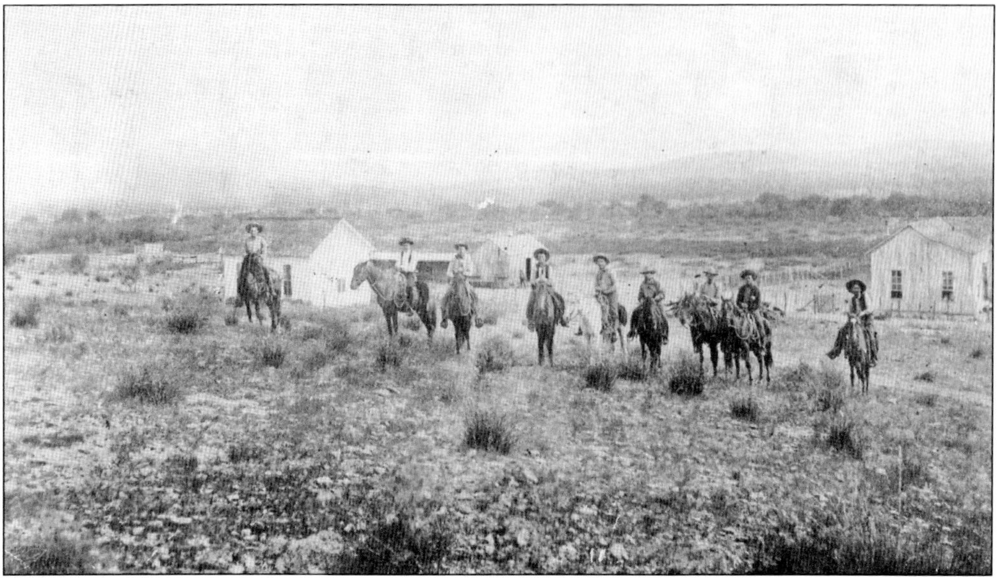

Cowboys soon had many places to work. This photograph, taken in 1887, shows the nine men who "rode the line" day and night on horseback at the Bar S Ranch. When landowners did not fence their ranches, they hired a few cowboys to keep the cattle from straying too far or getting in trouble. Later, ranchers would hire additional help for a roundup. The ranch boss on the far left in this picture is Lee Minor. The cowboy riding next to him is G.W. Tankersley, a son of R.F. and Annie. (WTC.)

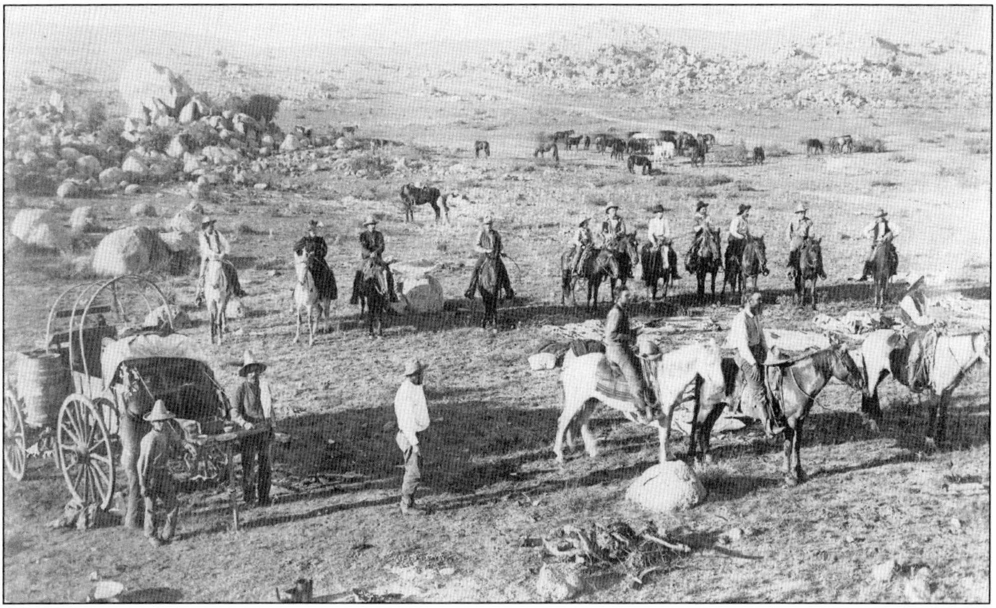

A label on this image reads, "The Spring Round-Up." A large crew was assembled to gather the cows and work them. The cattle were sorted by brand, and calves were branded with the brand of the mother. If a cow needed special attention, it was provided. Stock was chosen for market, and the rest were sent back for another year on the range. The roundup might include cowboys from several ranches; cooperation was essential when fences did not separate the herds. Even after fences were built, roundups were common on large ranches. (WTC.)

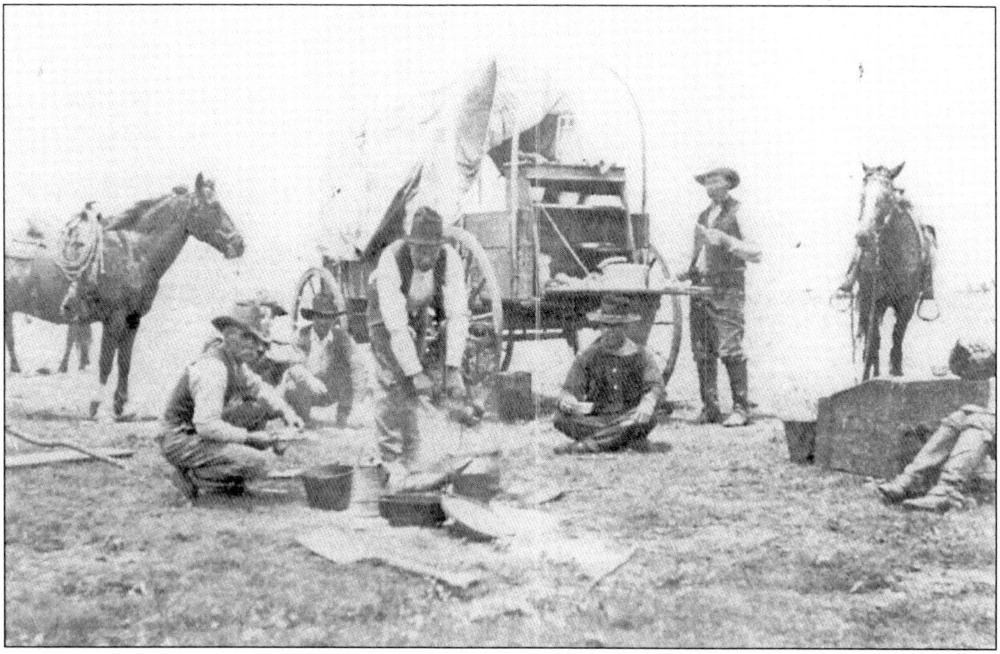

Breakfast, lunch, and dinner came from the chuck wagon when the work lasted for several days. When cowboys write about the "good old days," they often mention how good the food was on a cattle drive, especially because it was eaten outdoors with a great group of guys as companions. (WTC.)

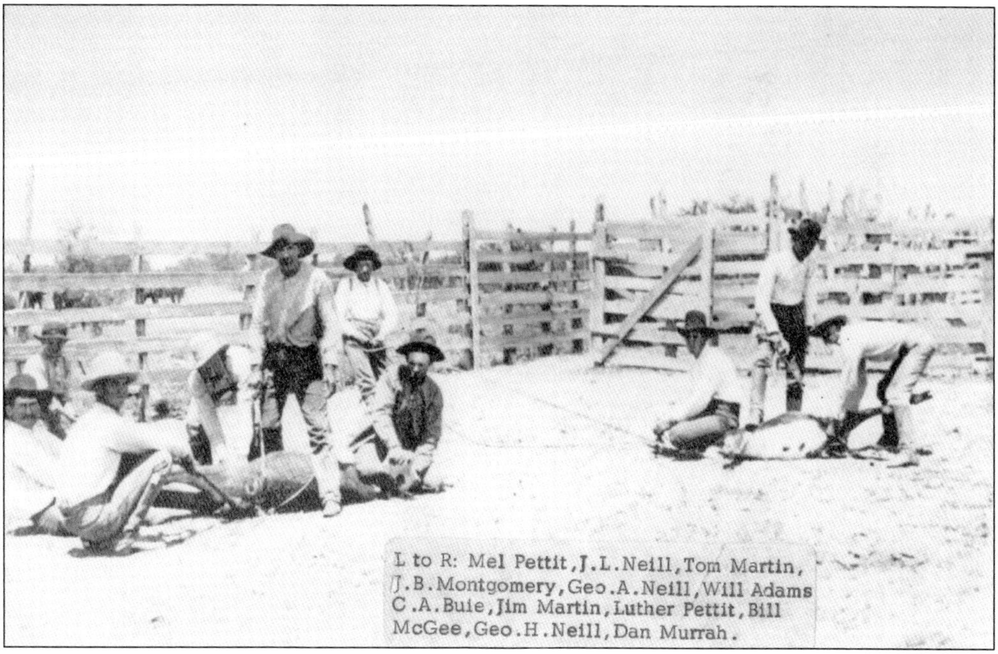

This is a c. 1903 branding scene on the Bird and Mertz Ranch in Schleicher County. Branding was crucial when cattle mixed freely on the open range. It remained necessary after fences were built in order to identify stolen property and to prove ownership. Brands were registered, and it made cattle theft difficult. (FC.)

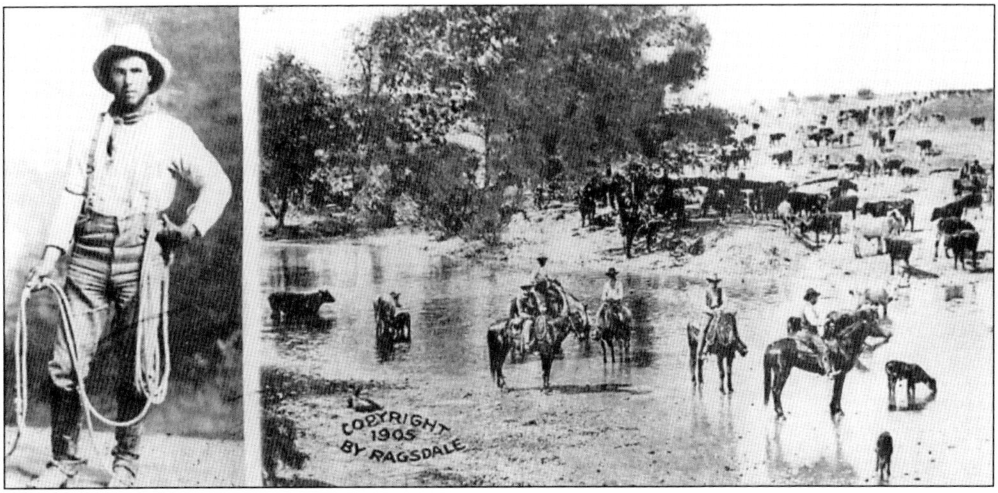

Cattle drives were a common way to get stock to market. The Goodnight-Loving Trail, for example, left the Cross Timbers in central Texas, followed the Concho River for a considerable distance, and then headed north after crossing the Pecos River. Even when rail transport was available, it was sometimes more economical to drive cows than to ship them. North-south cattle trails were especially common because the railroads generally ran in an east-west direction. The cowboy pictured here probably considered himself to be very lucky to have a job on a trail drive. This was the exciting work that made cowboy life attractive. (WTC.)

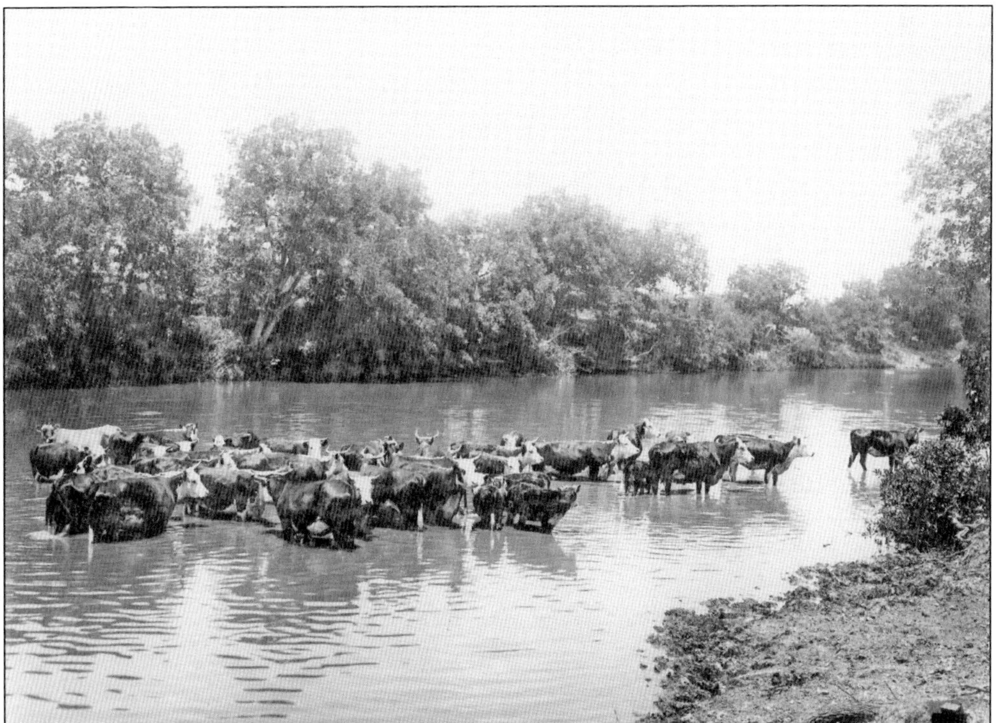

This photograph was taken in 1905 at the Lee Ranch, just west of San Angelo. The cattle seem to be enjoying their bath in the Spring Creek tributary to the Concho River. Having a large body of water that flowed though the ranch was an ideal condition. (FC.)

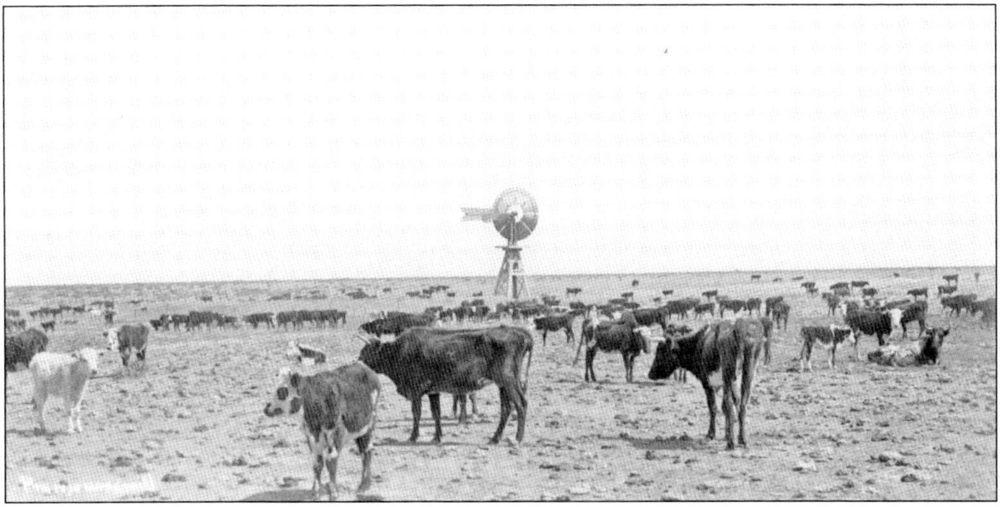

Windmills gradually became common in areas without natural springs or running water. The one in this picture is unusual because it is so short. The landowner was lucky enough to find water close to the surface, and the flat terrain meant low-moving winds. Digging a well and maintaining a windmill were expensive undertakings. (FC.)

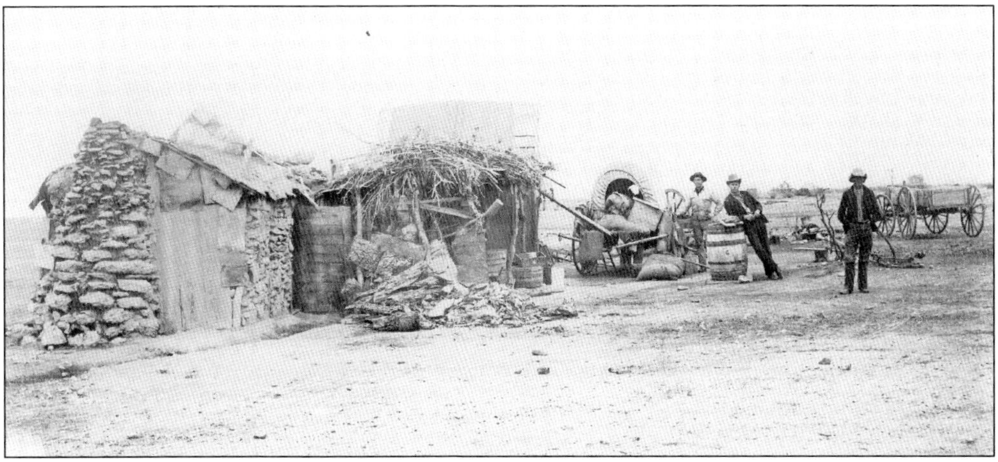

Ranch houses were often rough and primitive. The photographer calls this dwelling "a house on the prairie." It is likely that single men were the only inhabitants. (WTC.)

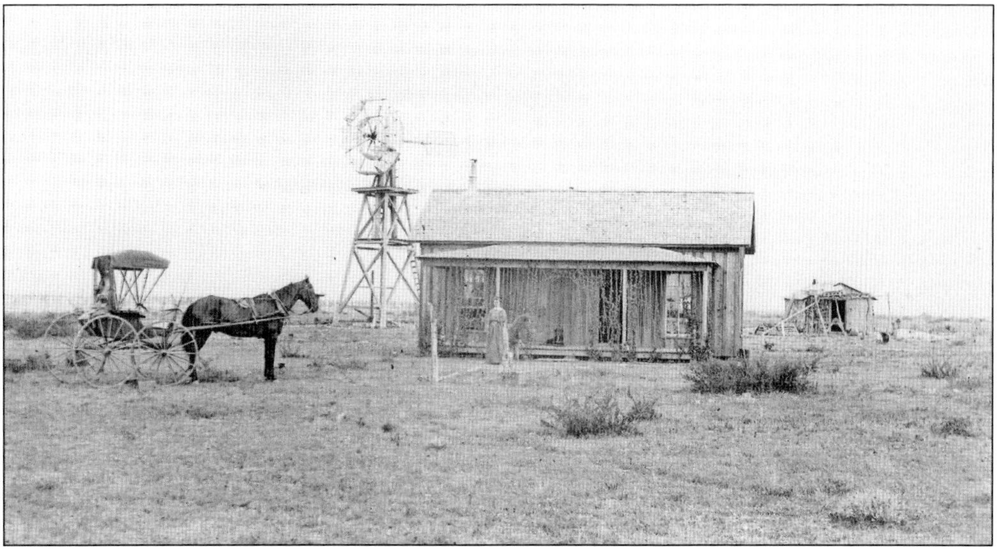

This ranch dwelling on the Kiowa Stock Farm was certainly orderly and livable. The windmill indicates running water, and the horse and buggy reveal that the lady in the picture could go to town when it became too lonely out in the country. The large size of cattle ranches in this arid part of western Texas meant there was often a considerable distance between a rancher and his or her closest neighbor. Visitors came infrequently and tended to stay for days rather than hours. (WTC.)

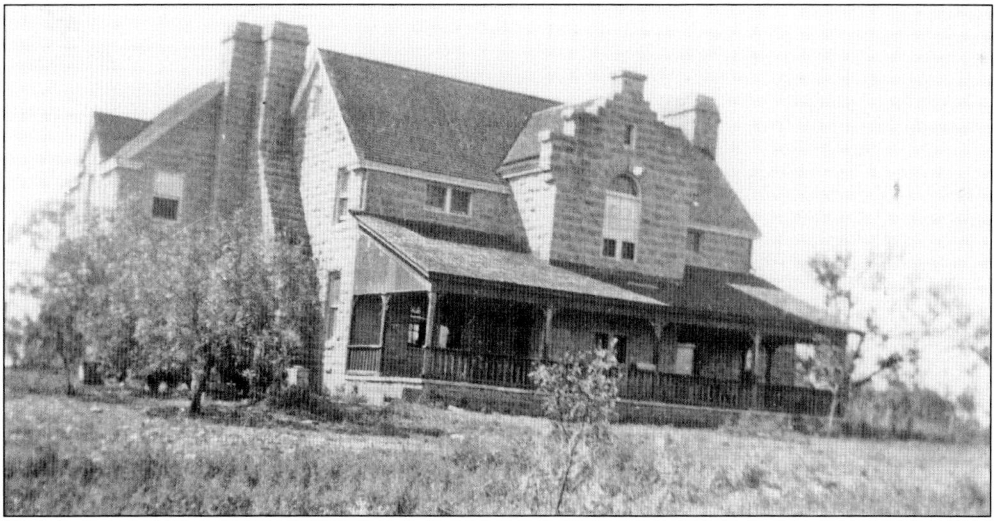

Some ranchers had grandiose ideas about how a person should live in the country. Welton Ostrander came from New York to Concho County to join his half brother John A Loomis in a ranching partnership. He brought carpenters and stonemasons from Syracuse, New York, to build this handsome nine-room house with basement and attic. He named the residence Thornfield and moved his wife, two daughters, and a maid to the home in 1885. The New York women stayed only a few months before Sarah, his wife, demanded that the family relocate to New York. There was also a problem with the cattle market. In the mid-1880s, there was a long-lasting, nationwide drop in prices due to bad weather, overstocking, and shrinking markets. This market break, which ended a dramatic cattle boom, was certainly another factor in the Ostranders' decision to move back east. (WTC.)

Cowboys enjoyed going to a photographer's studio to have their portrait made, whether they were in Abilene, Dodge City, or San Angelo. Many men and boys considered the life of a cowboy to be romantic and exciting. Untold numbers of boys and young men ran away from home in the east to go out west and become cowboys. Bob Percival poses with his gear at the M.C. Ragsdale studio in San Angelo. (WTC.)

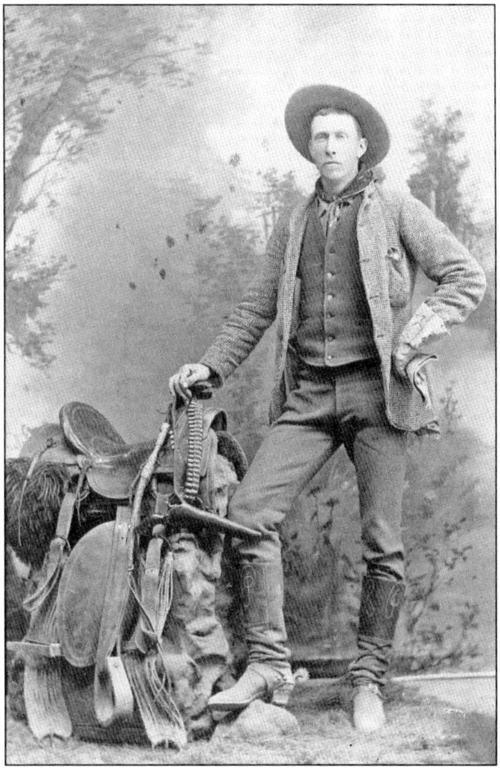

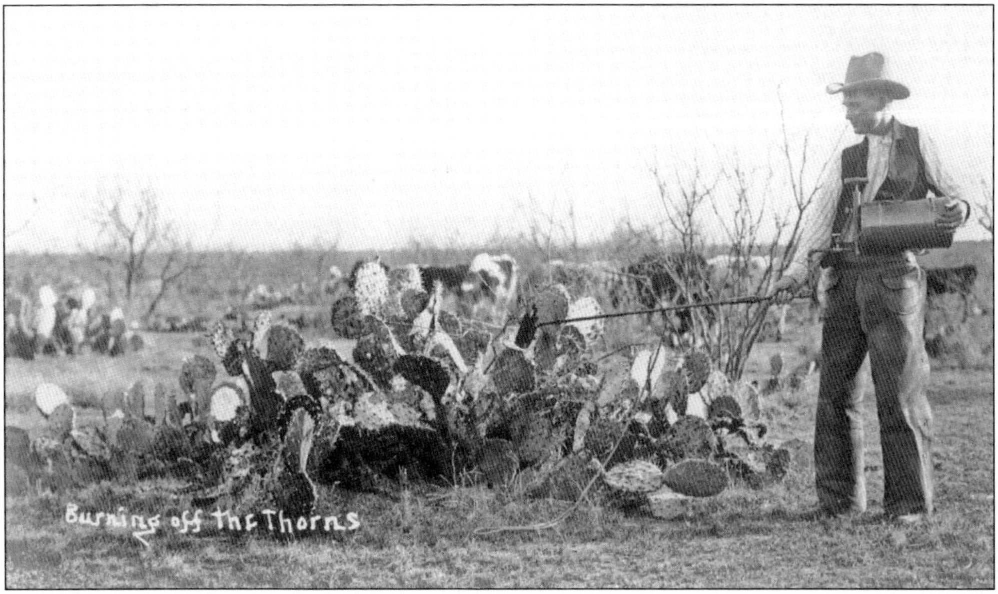

When cattle drives became less frequent, and horseback work was completed, a cowboy's life could quickly become less than glamorous. Here, a worker burns the thorns off cacti so the cows would eat the plants. This was a tried-and-true method of feeding cows in a drought. The activity could get exhilarating when rattlesnakes living under the cactus plant emerged to protest the torching of their dens. Repairing fences and painting the bunkhouse did not have as much potential for excitement. (FC.)

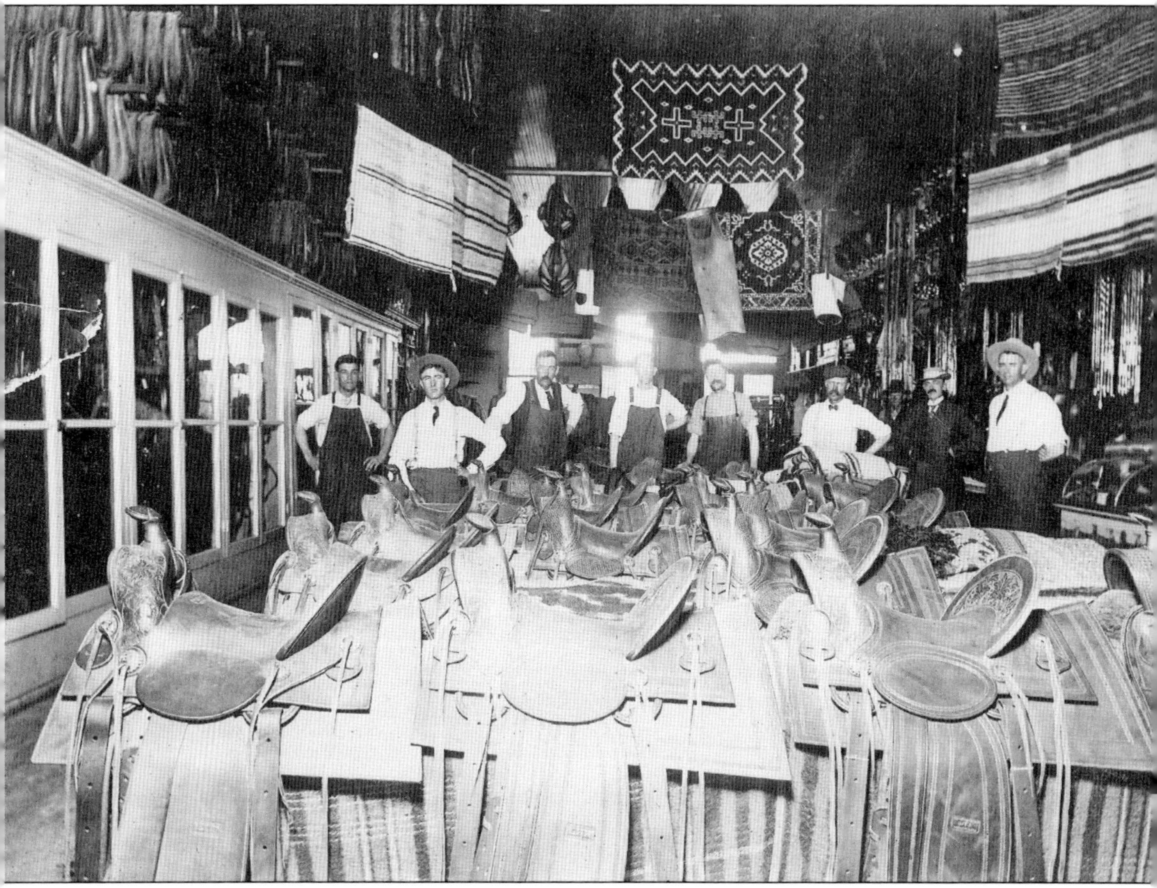

The cattle business was a huge boon for San Angelo merchants. This photograph shows the R.J. Andrew Saddle Shop in 1910, with Andrew standing on the right. Cowboys came to town for recreation and supplies just like the soldiers had in their day. Cowmen also needed banking services, food, clothes, help with shipping, and many other things. Ranchers and their employees were crucial to the economic health of the community. (WTC.)

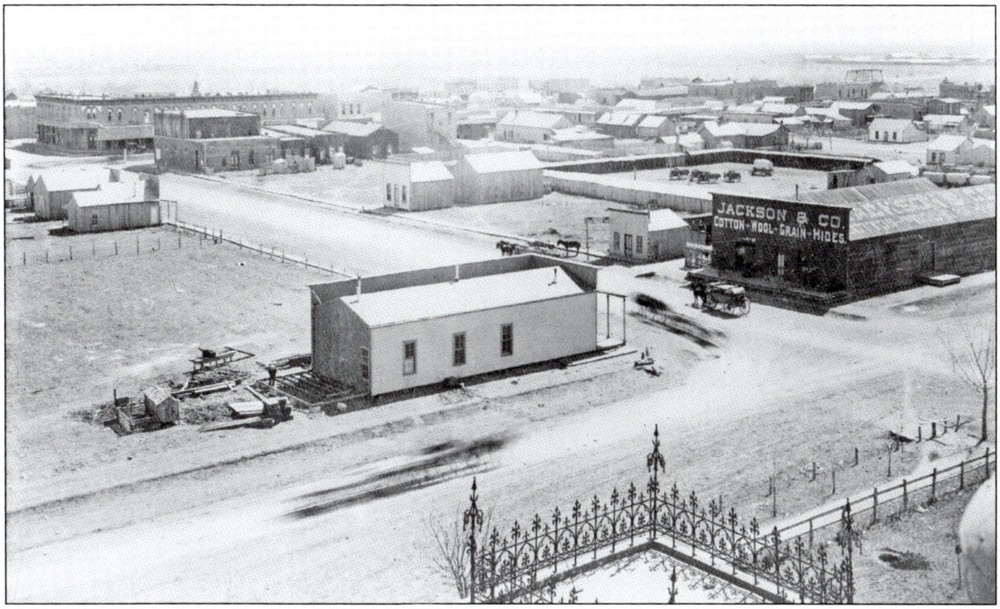

This photograph of the Jackson and Company building reveals an interesting city facility—the wagon yard, which was used by ranchers, farmers, and travelers. The large space to the left of the building was set aside for people traveling to town in wagons. These visitors could park their wagons and teams, buy feed, or even sleep in their wagons if hotel costs were too steep. In 1910, there were eight wagon yards operating in San Angelo, making the city and its stores much more accessible to rural people.

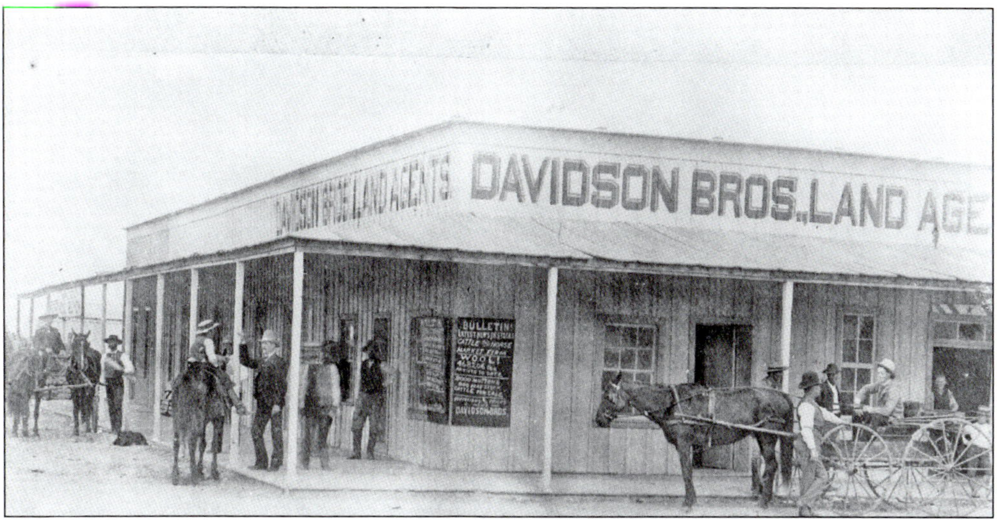

Yet another business established for the benefit of farmers and ranchers was the land agency. Here is a picture of the Davidson Brothers establishment. Charley Davidson is the gentleman on the porch talking to an unidentified young man on a horse. (WTC.)

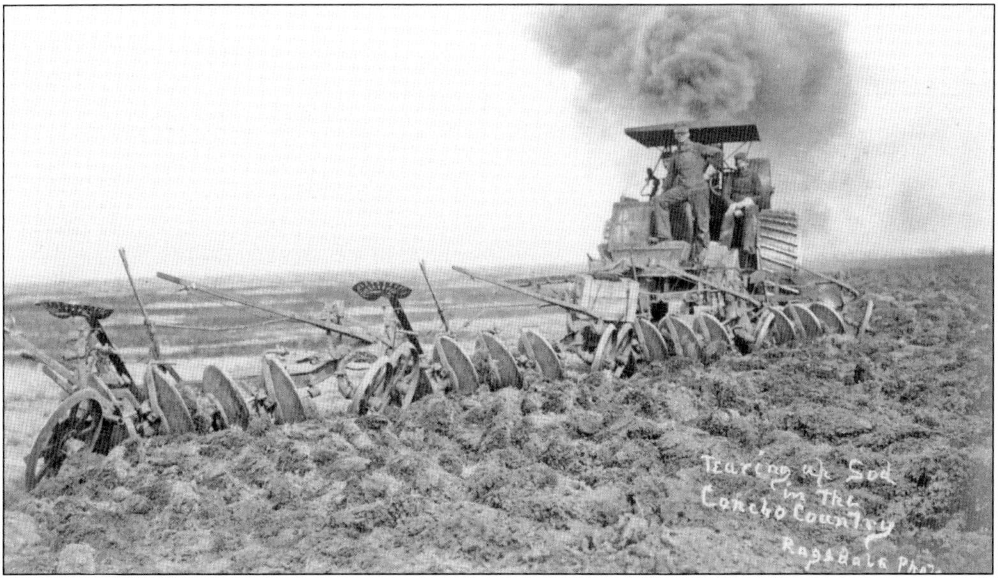

This interesting photograph shows a very large steam tractor and an even larger cutting blade tearing up the sod in the Concho country. One of the obstacles to planting crops in the western plains was the thick sod that ordinary plows could not cut through. Twenty-first-century scholars are critical of what these 19th-century farmers did to the land. The argument is that farming marginal land was harmful to the West, causing dust-bowl conditions and producing poor returns for the farmer. The Concho Valley, however, turned out to be an excellent place to grow cotton and many other crops. (FC.)

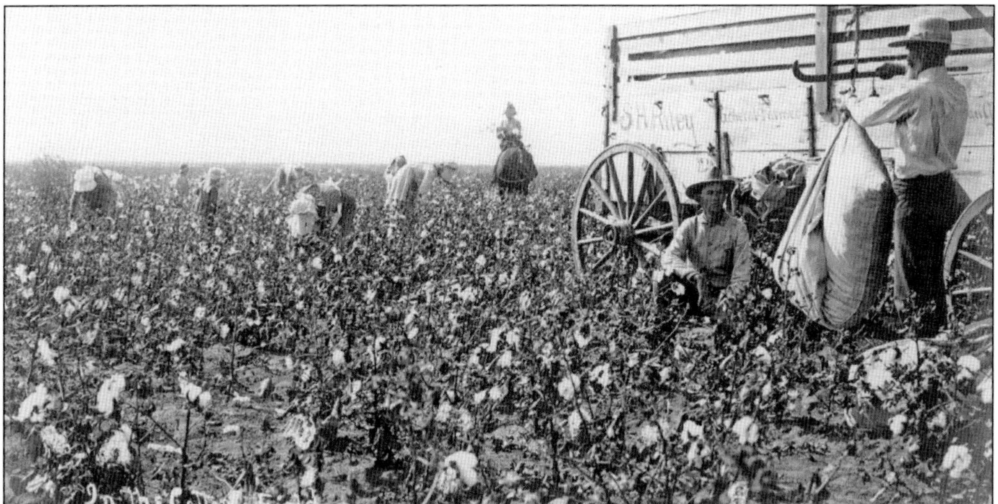

In a scene more reminiscent of Alabama than Texas, this photograph shows cotton pickers at work on the S.H. Riley farm. Dry land farming was the rule on early Concho Valley farms. Using a combination of techniques, such as frequent cultivation and mulching, most cotton farmers had to hope and pray that the rain came and that it arrived at the appropriate time. John Loomis, a sheep and cattle rancher, decided in the late 1880s that cotton farming was the way to make money. After investing in a steam tractor and building tenant houses and a cotton gin, he was ruined by dry weather, hail, and bollworms. He lost hundreds of thousands of dollars and exchanged his farm for a hotel in Oklahoma. There was no guarantee of success in agriculture. (FC.)

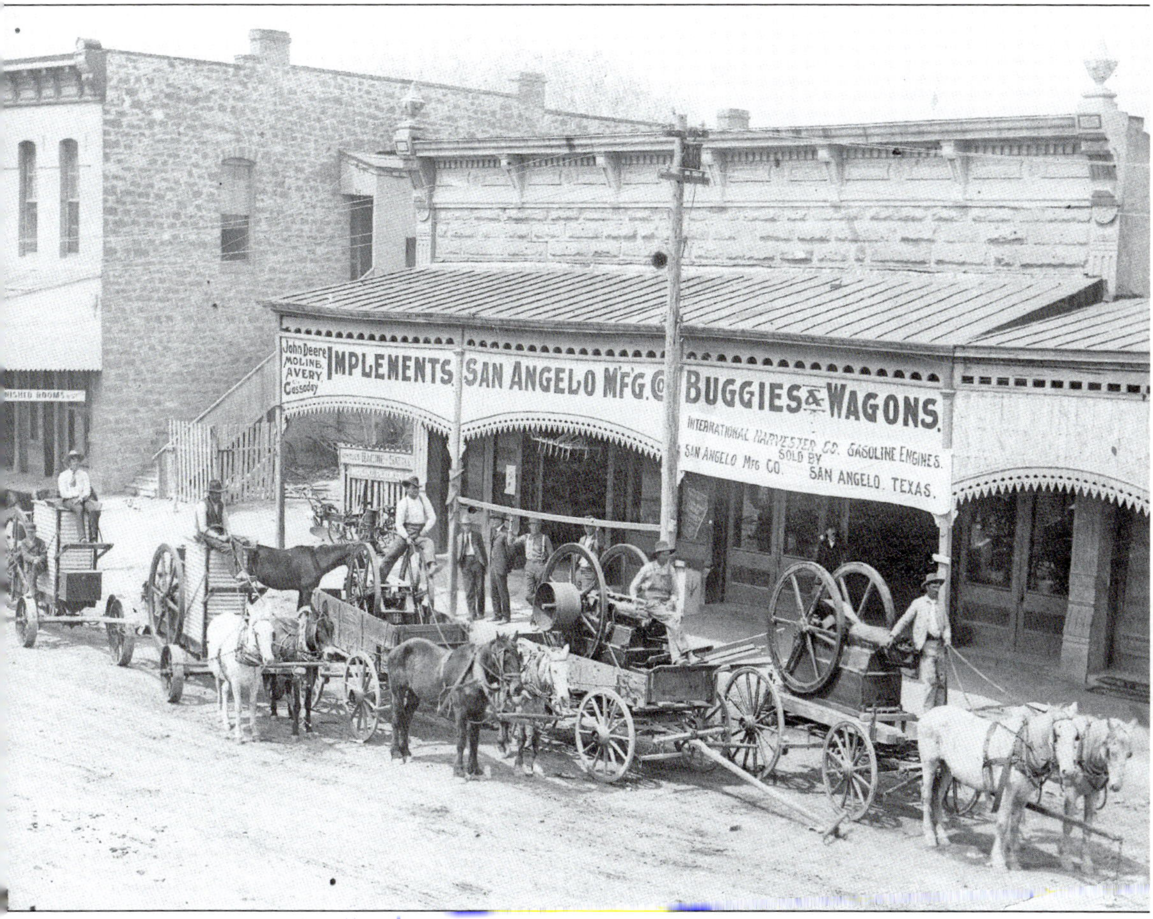

The San Angelo Mfg. Co. offered quite an array of farm equipment, buggies, and wagons. This photograph appears to be an advertisement for the firm, but it also shows how extensively farming developed in the Concho Valley. There were enough farmers in the area to support a company that both sold and manufactured farm implements. (WTC.)

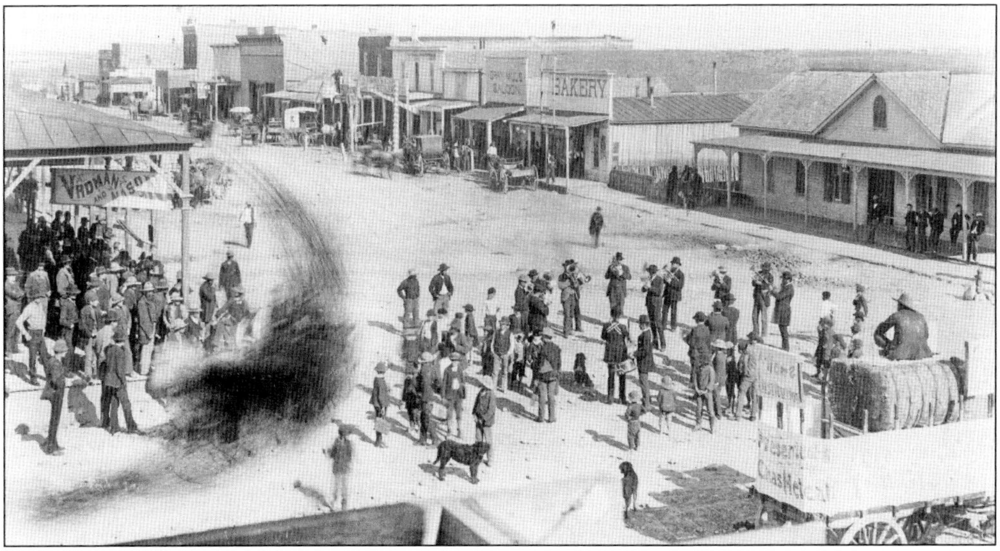

This picture, taken about 1889, shows San Angelo celebrating the first bale of cotton grown, picked, and ginned in Tom Green County. The city loved to have public celebrations to be sure, but the citizens of San Angelo clearly recognized the economic importance of farming to the community. The blur in the photograph was caused by a racing buggy that unexpectedly appeared after the photographer had set up a timed exposure. The band might be a bit impromptu, but it was there to make the occasion even more notable. (Private collection.)

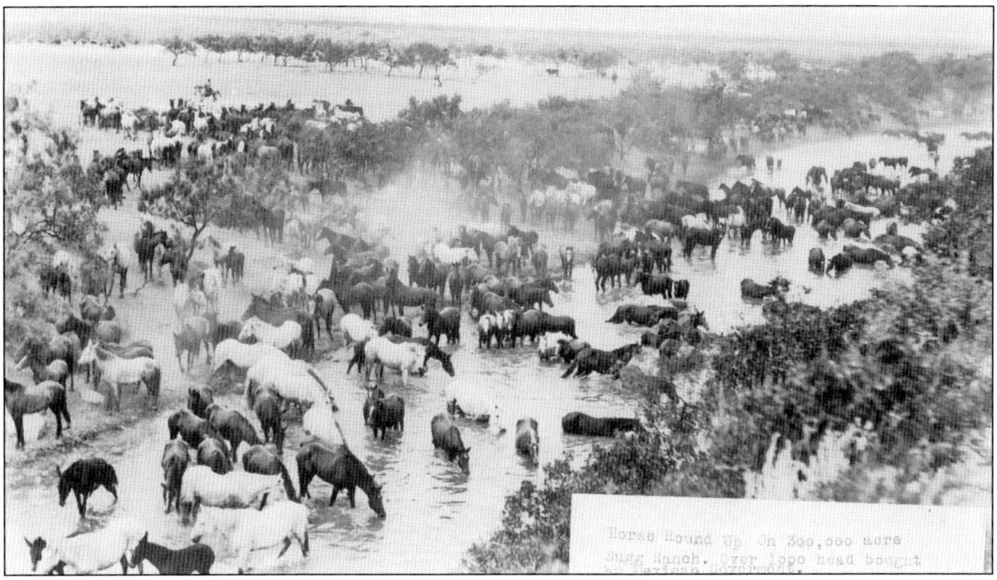

Horses were not only crucial to transportation and work in the region, but they were also a cash crop. This photograph shows a horse roundup on the J.D. Sugg ranch in Irion County. The purpose of this roundup was to provide the Mexican government with 1,000 horses. (FC.)

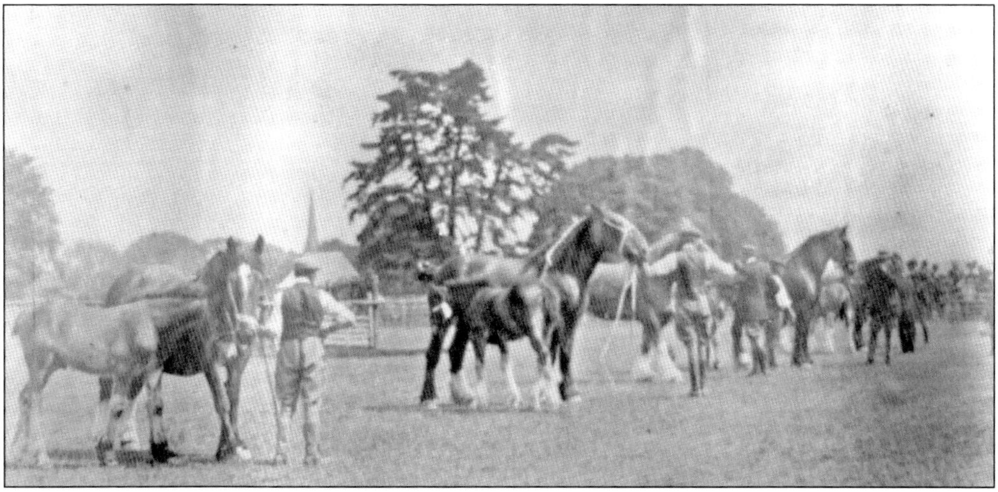

William Anson, often called "Billy," came to West Texas from England to raise horses. Since he was not the eldest son of a noble family, he would not inherit the family property. He came with two of his brothers to seek their fortune in the United States. This picture shows a lineup of fine stock at his Head of the River Ranch near Christoval, just south of San Angelo. (FC.)

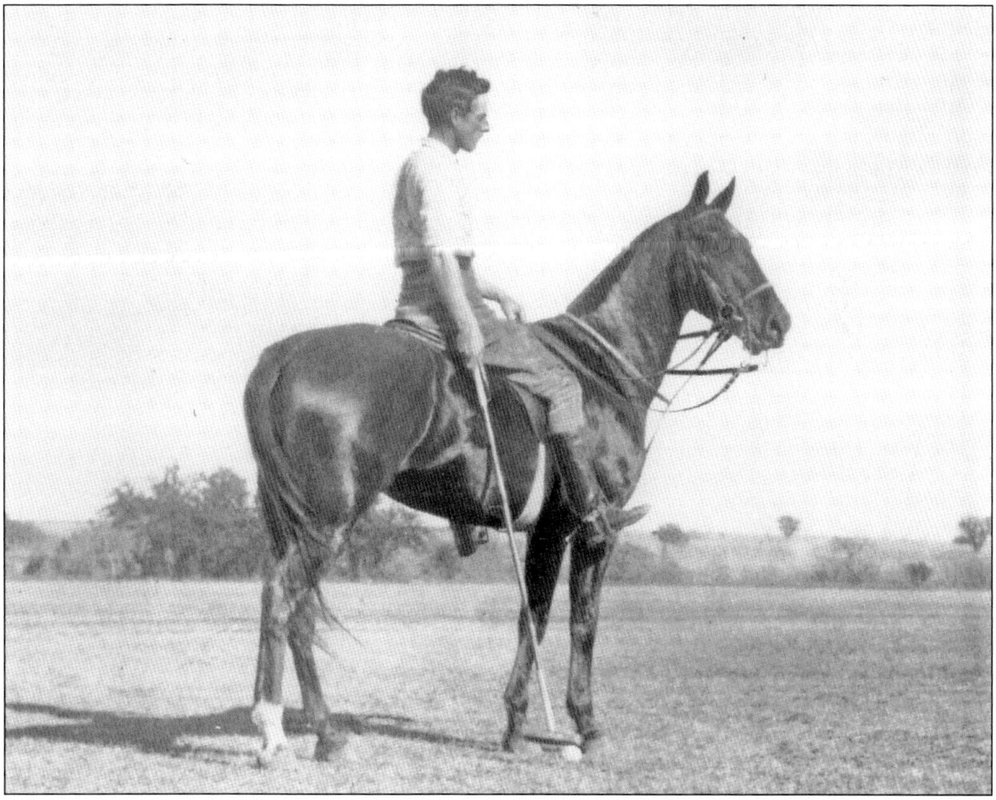

Anson himself played polo, as this photograph attests. Not only did Anson raise horses for the sport, but he also started a strong local tradition of public interest in the game. Polo teams were common around San Angelo, with competitions held locally and beyond the Concho Valley. (FC.)

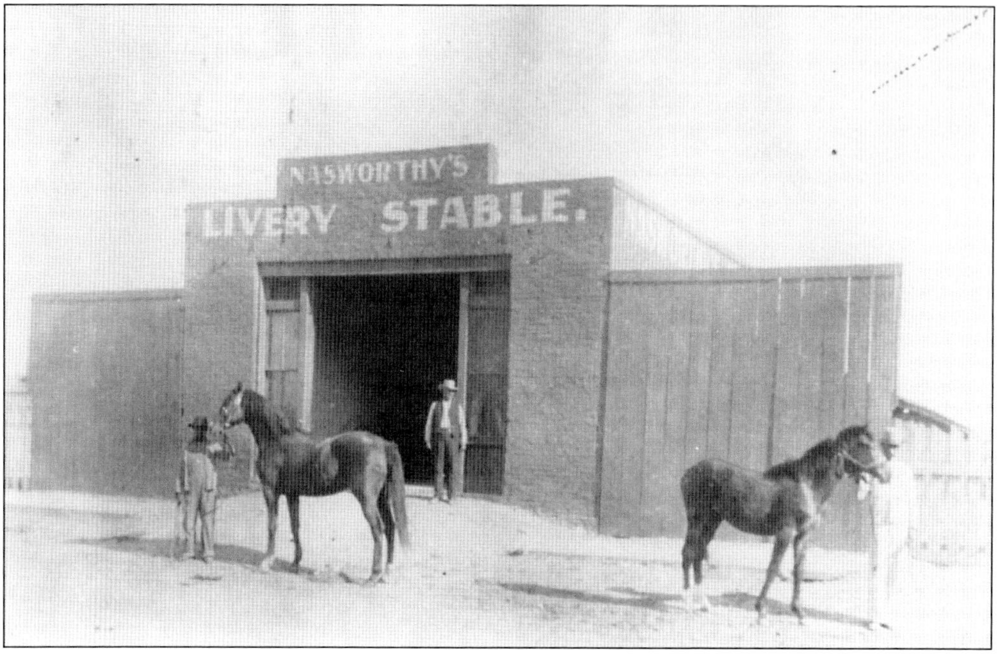

Horse racing was another sport of interest to local citizens and ranchers. Billy Anson also raised racehorses, and he was not alone. This photograph shows Nasworthy's Livery Stable. Tom "Sarge" Nasworthy was a great supporter of horse racing. At one time, San Angelo even had a racetrack where local breeders could show off their prize runners. (FC.)

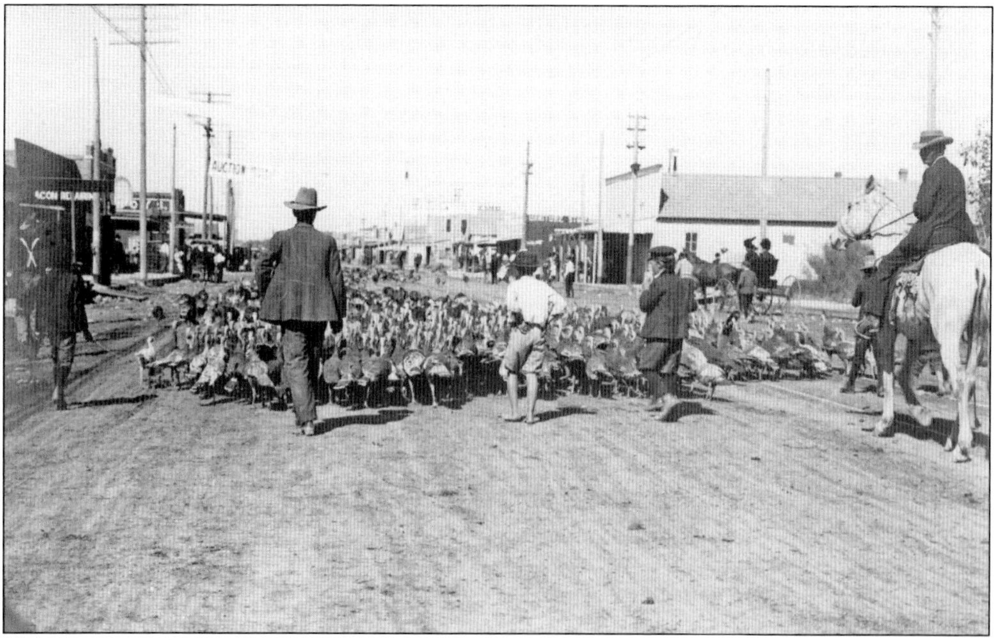

Turkeys were a local crop. This unusual photograph shows a turkey drive through town. It is interesting to note that the men are wearing suits. If the gentlemen had a social or business obligation to attend at the end of the trail, it is a good thing this was not a cattle drive, where dust was always a problem for those bringing up the rear, or riding drag. (FC.)

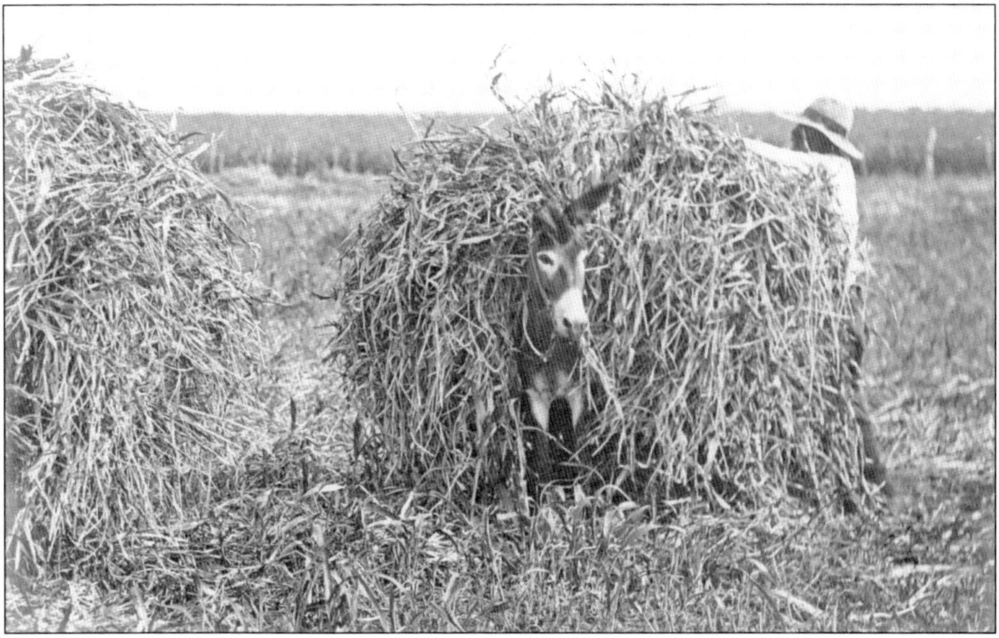

An enterprising individual could make money selling hay. There were large farms that gathered prairie grass on contract with Fort Concho. But there were others in the game as well. This man's problem seems to be that his donkey is not going to last very long. (FC.)

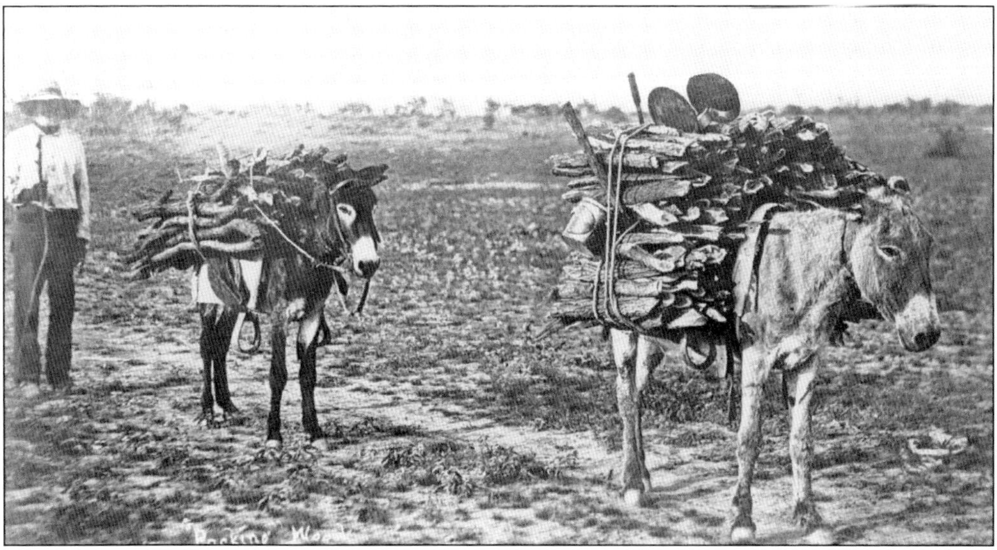

Modern western historians sometimes discuss extractive industries on the frontier. They are referring to such enterprises as mining or the timber business, where entrepreneurs take what is there and do not replace it. Here, an individual is packing wood to town in order to make a living selling what he cut and gathered. There were plenty of agricultural possibilities in early San Angelo if a person did not mind hard work. On this scale, it would be difficult to complain about frontiersmen disturbing the environment. (FC.)

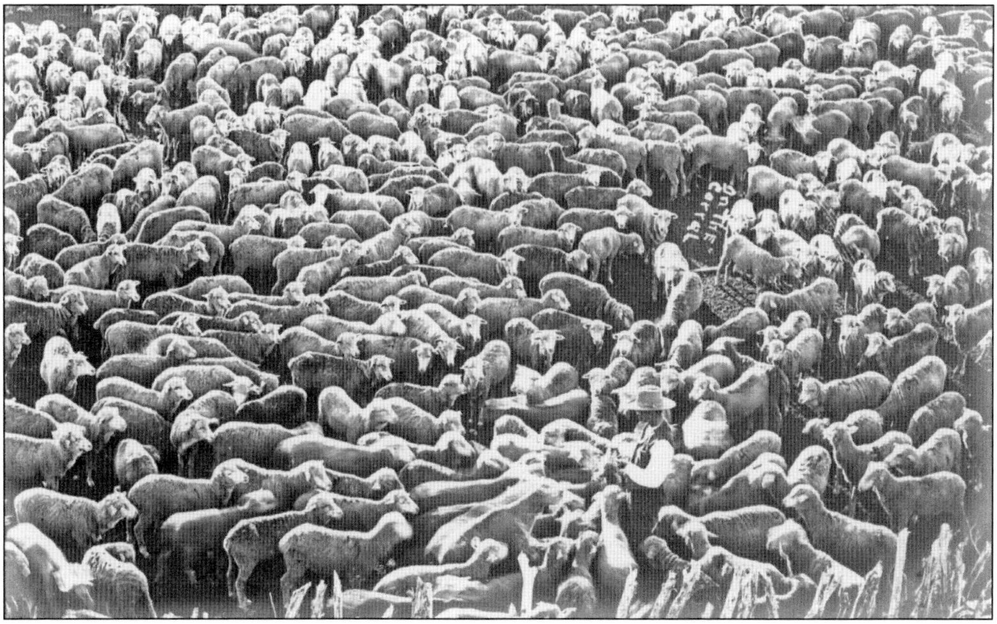

It is hard to know if more Concho Valley livestock producers raised sheep or cattle. Indeed, many people raised both, knowing that these animals did not compete for the same vegetation. The Texas sheep boom was an economic phenomenon in the 1870s and 1880s. The Edwards Plateau is a vast area stretching south and west of the Colorado River all the way to the Pecos River. It turned out to be one of the best areas in the world for raising sheep. By 1880, there were 376,000 sheep on the Edwards Plateau. By 1890, the number was 1,295,000, which represented 37 percent of the production in Texas. San Angelo was the marketing center for most of this vast area, and the town benefited greatly from the sheep boom. (FC.)

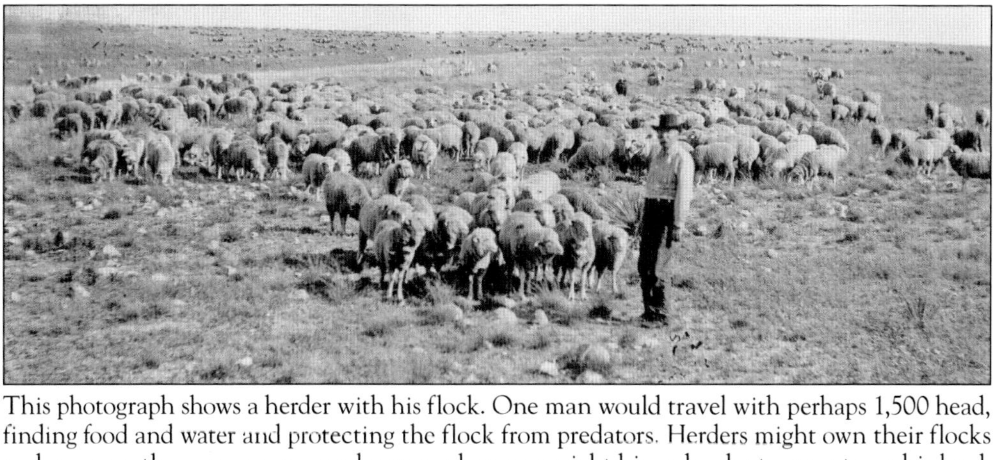

This photograph shows a herder with his flock. One man would travel with perhaps 1,500 head, finding food and water and protecting the flock from predators. Herders might own their flocks and move on the open range, or a large ranch owner might hire a herder to operate on his land. Herding was also a way to get into the business if an ambitious sheep rancher did not have the means to start out on his own. The *partido* system allowed herders to work for a share of the profits, usually paid in sheep. Shepherds were often Basque, German, English, or Mexican. John Loomis raised sheep for 10 years and said in his memoir that he primarily employed Mexicans because they were "faithful, understood sheep, and did not mind the lonely life." He also reported hiring a German college professor, a Spanish nobleman, and a former outlaw who carried a sack of ears taken from those he had killed. (FC.)

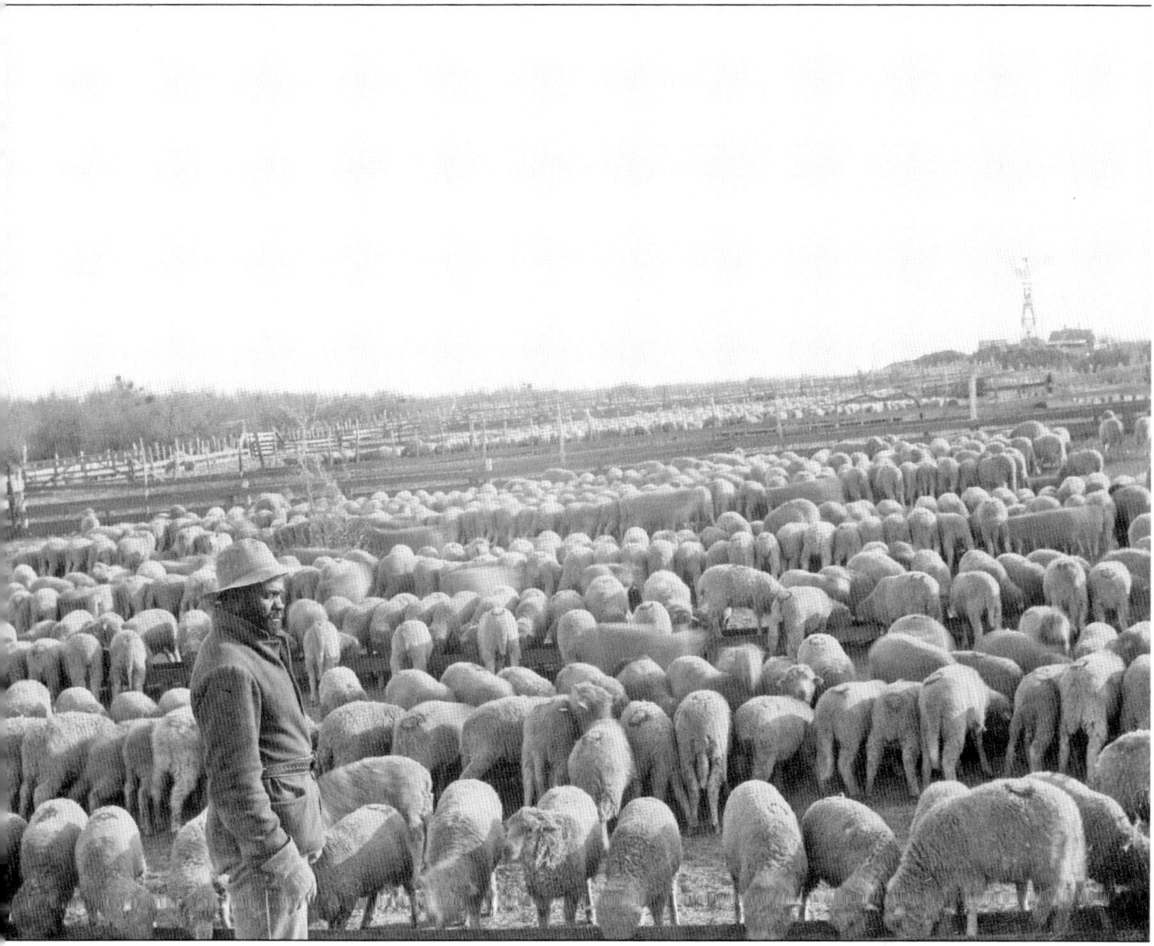

This picture shows a huge number of sheep on the George Richardson Ranch. The demand for sheep was tremendous. When John Loomis decided to go into the business in 1882, his problem was finding sheep to buy. As he told the story in his memoir *A Texas Ranchman*, "There was a boom in the comparatively new sheep business in West Texas at this time. I heard of a bunch of ewes which were for sale in southern Concho county . . . I set out immediately, driving all night in order to reach the ranch before the sheep were sold. I knew I had no time to spare for everyone wanted to buy sheep." He did arrive in time to buy 1,500 ewes at a price of $5.75 a head. To put that price in perspective, he was buying land at the same time for 25¢ an acre. (FC.)

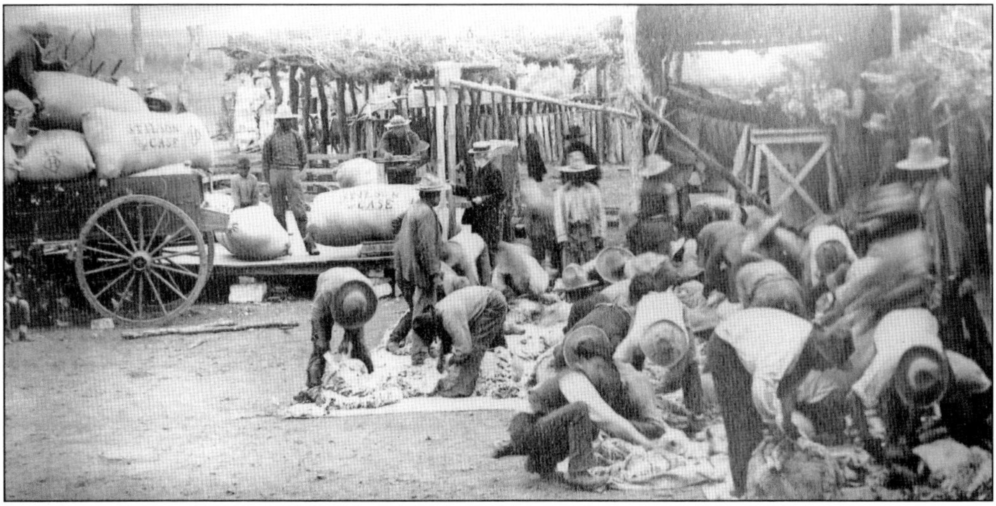

Shearing sheep was a job usually left to traveling crews. In this picture, a large number of people are at work on a sizable herd. Crews were typically comprised of Mexican workers. The person who owned the equipment and hired the men was a true entrepreneur. The labor was difficult and physically demanding. (WTC.)

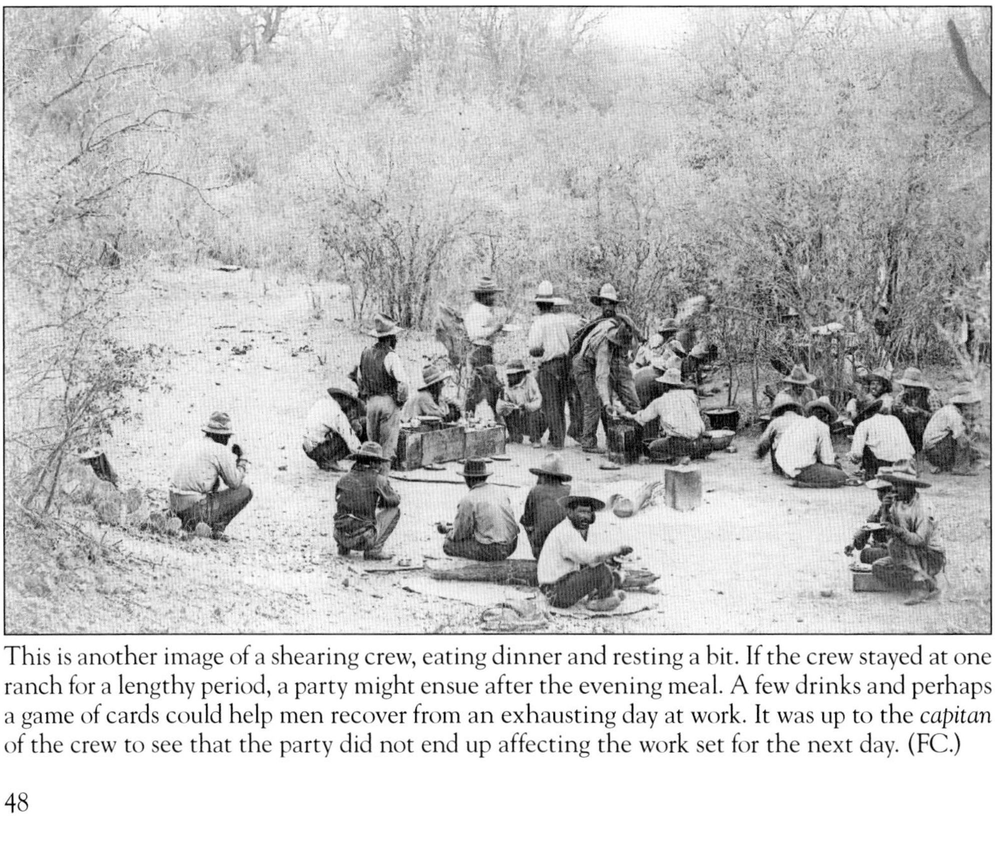

This is another image of a shearing crew, eating dinner and resting a bit. If the crew stayed at one ranch for a lengthy period, a party might ensue after the evening meal. A few drinks and perhaps a game of cards could help men recover from an exhausting day at work. It was up to the *capitan* of the crew to see that the party did not end up affecting the work set for the next day. (FC.)

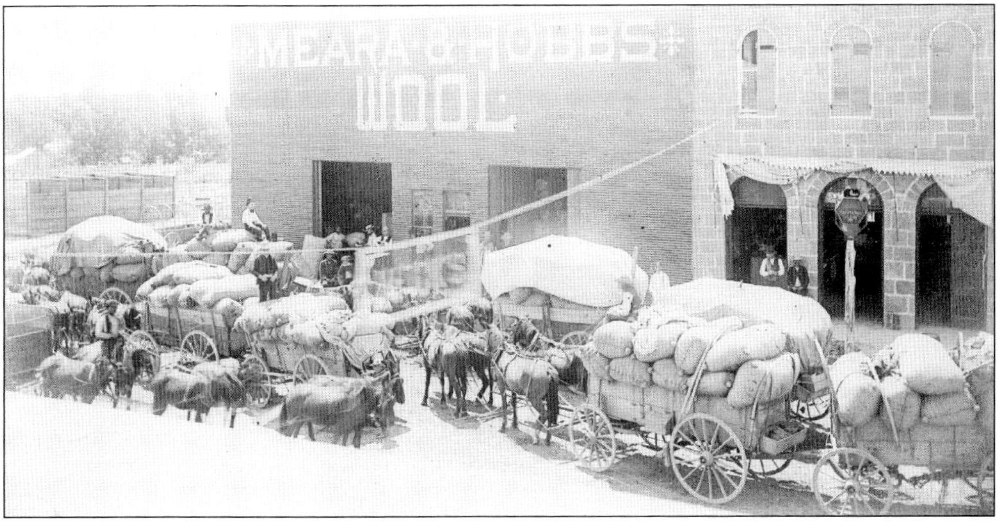

The first wool warehouse in San Angelo was the Meara & Hobbs establishment, which was built in 1888. The warehouse system was a Texas invention. The owners of the wool house served as commission agents for sheep ranchers. Since wool did not deteriorate when it was stored, the warehouses would receive the clip (sheared wool), grade it, and market it at the best time and for the best price. In addition to receiving a commission for this work, the warehouse might loan money and sell supplies for additional profit. It could be a very lucrative business. This photograph shows a rancher delivering his wool to Meara & Hobbs. (FC.)

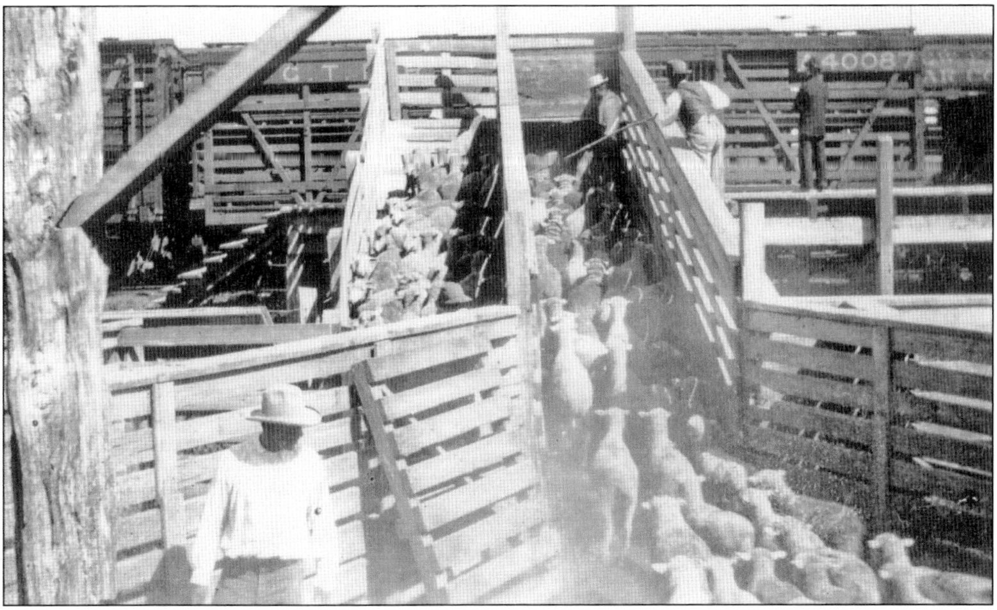

During the sheep boom in West Texas, sheep were raised for their wool rather than for their meat. In 1893, in Menard, William Black tried canning mutton, but it was not a successful enterprise. Sol Mayer, at Fort McKavett, said he shipped the first lambs from San Angelo in 1899, but this did not become a common practice until later. When the Kansas City, Mexico, and Orient Railway came to San Angelo in 1908, it became much easier to ship livestock. This photograph shows lambs being loaded at a state-of-the-art facility located on Chadbourne Street, far from the center of town. Sheep growers could then produce two crops—wool and meat. (WTC.)

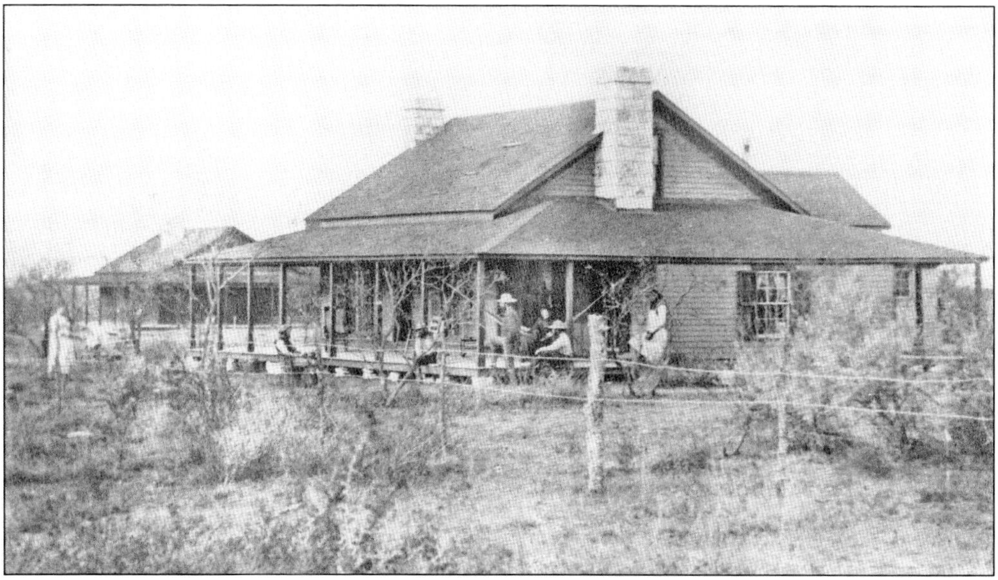

Joseph Tweedy, Morgan and Lawrence Grinnell, and J.B. Reynolds were four young, highly educated adventurers who came from New York to Texas in 1876 to cash in on the sheep boom. They arrived in Galveston with a book about sheep but with very little capital. With the help of a cook who quoted Shakespeare, they became herders in order to learn about the sheep business and make some money. Their first headquarters was an adobe shack with sheets of paper taken from copies of *Harper's Weekly* covering the interior walls. Ultimately, the men established the Knickerbocker Ranch, southwest of San Angelo. This photograph includes family members of all the partners. Eventually, however, the difficulties of the sheep business drove all but Tweedy back to the East Coast. (WTC.)

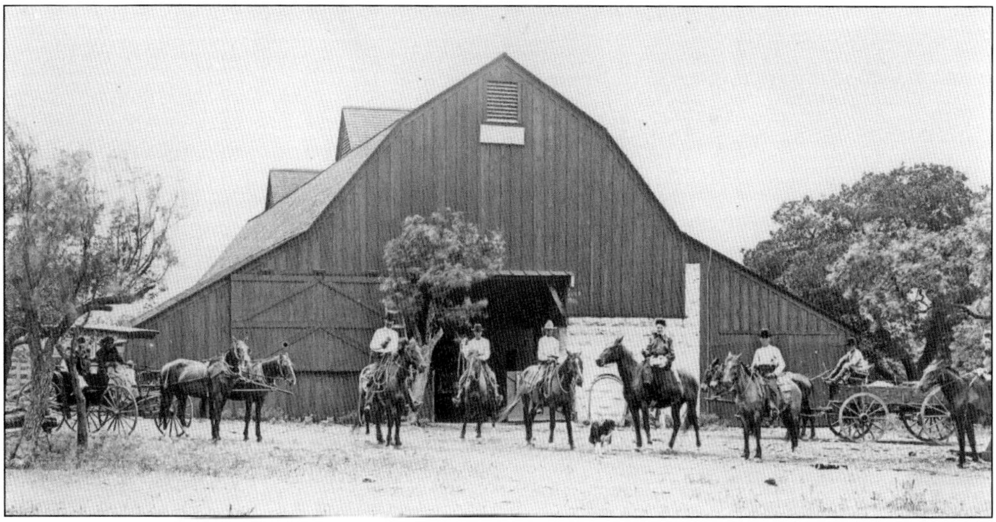

Many sheep ranchers were German immigrants. In 1882, John and Johanna Wilhelm moved with seven children to Menard County, where they established a sheep ranch. After her husband died in 1890, Johanna continued to expand her holdings with the help of her children. She later was dubbed the "Sheep Queen of West Texas" by a Texas newspaper. She ran 10,000 to 15,000 sheep on 100 sections of land. It was clearly possible to cash in handsomely during the boom—even when one started with limited resources. (Private collection.)

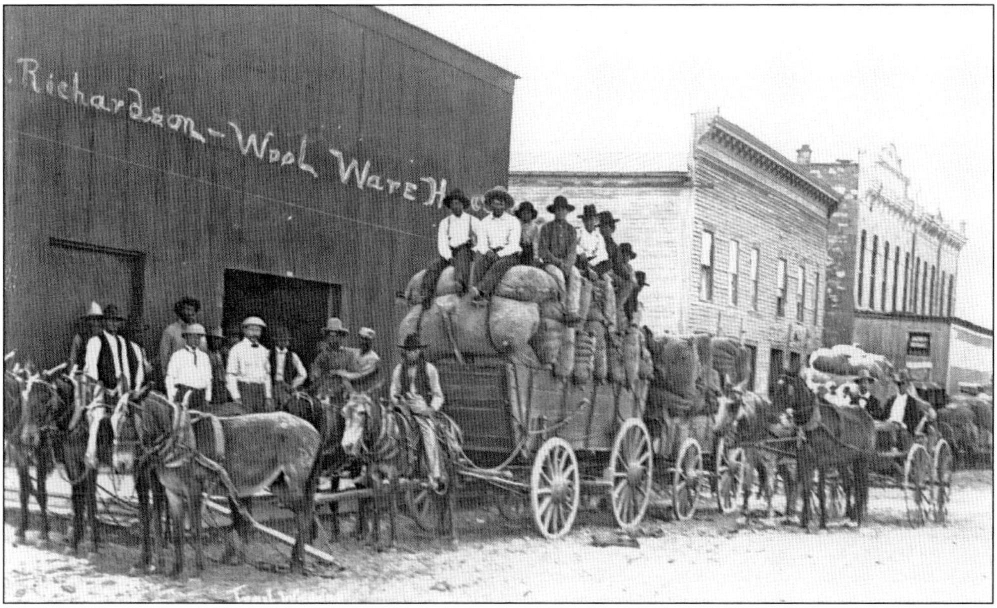

The photograph shows the George Richardson wool warehouse in San Angelo. Richardson was a Scottish immigrant who made a small fortune in the sheep business. San Angelo was the primary marketing center on the Edwards Plateau, and early pictures suggest that the town was absolutely full of wool. (FC.)

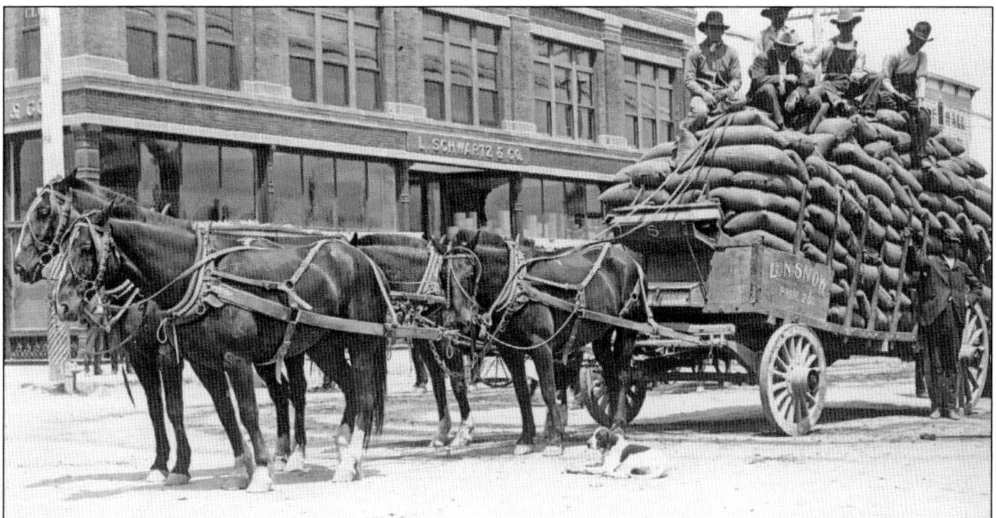

Freighters made a good living during the sheep boom. This picture certainly raises a serious question: how long could a wagon last when loaded this heavily? Perhaps the unidentified men on top were only there for their portrait to the taken. (FC.)

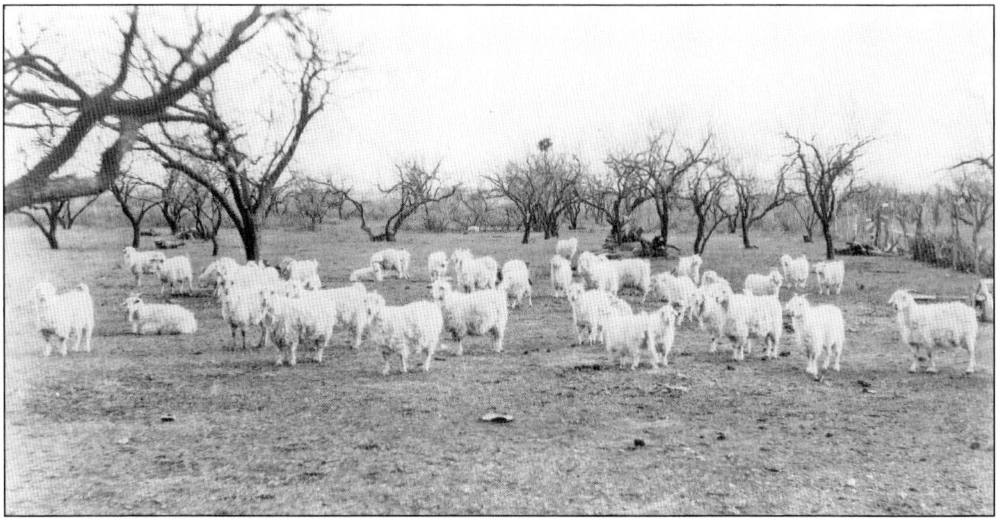

The sheep business had great risks as well as great rewards. A Texas norther could cause the temperature to plummet and kill freshly shorn sheep and newborn lambs. There were screwworms, which would literally eat the sheep alive. Labor costs were high because sheep needed more protection and tending than cattle. Wool prices could fluctuate wildly based on uncontrollable factors such as a national tariff law. For example, wool sold for 20¢ a pound in 1884; in 1885, the price was 7¢. This is a photograph of Angora goats, which were often raised as a hedge against such price fluctuations. Goats thrived on the Edwards Plateau just as sheep did, and San Angelo became the center of the mohair business. In the mid-1920s, an estimated 60 percent of the mohair clip in the United States was sold in San Angelo. (FC.)

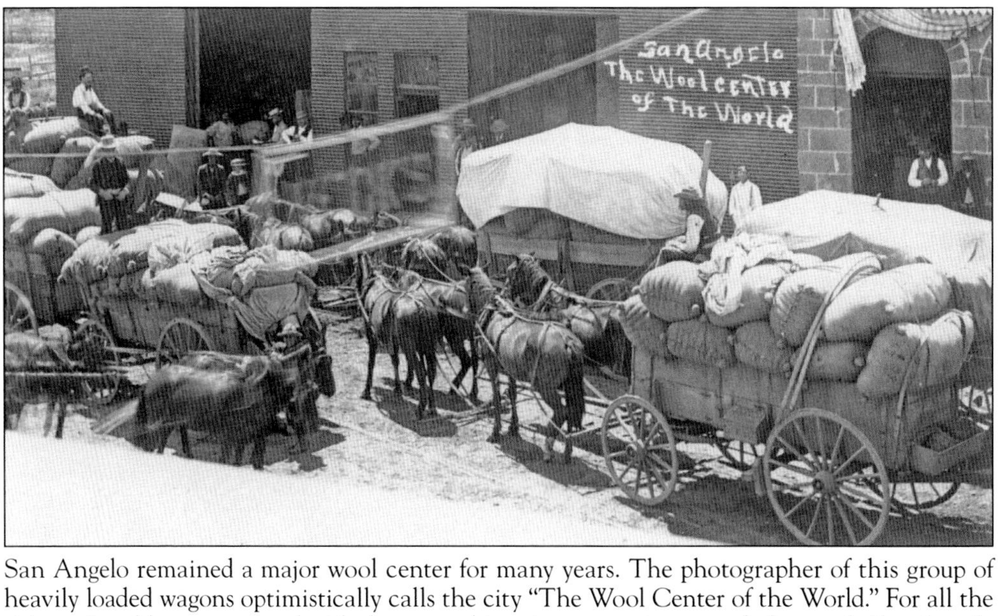

San Angelo remained a major wool center for many years. The photographer of this group of heavily loaded wagons optimistically calls the city "The Wool Center of the World." For all the risks and problems associated with sheep ranching, it was a major part of what made San Angelo an important city on the western plains. (FC.)

Three

Building a City Across the River

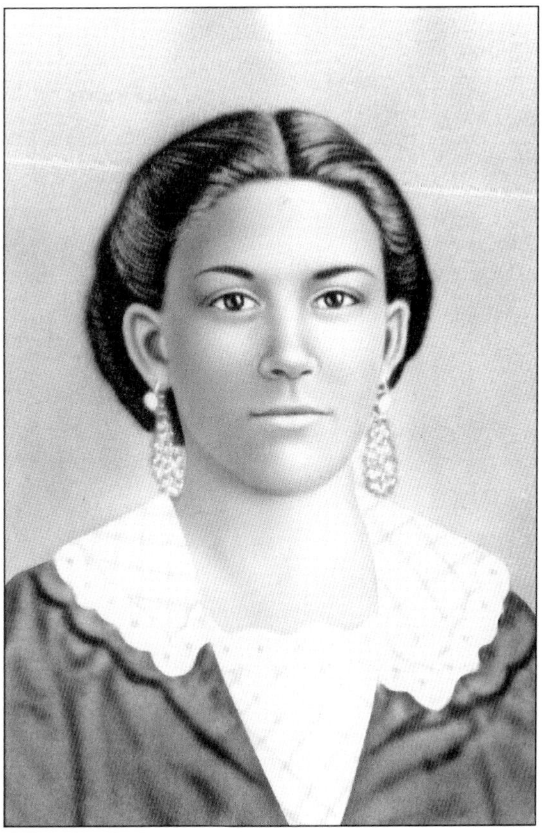

This woman is Carolina Angela de la Garza, for whom San Angelo was named. Her husband was Bart DeWitt. After her death in San Antonio, DeWitt moved west, bought 320 acres of land across the river from Fort Concho, and began to build a town. He developed a plat, named streets, and proceeded to sell town lots. The year was 1870, when just a few dozen people lived at the site. DeWitt sold lots to local worthies such as R.F. Tankersley and W.S. Veck, but otherwise there was not a great demand for his real estate. DeWitt got into financial difficulties before the town began to prosper, and he lost his investment. Family names, however, persist in the city. Magdalen Street was named for his sister-in-law Mother Magdalen, of the Ursaline Academy in San Antonio. The town itself was most often called a variation of Santa Angela, for Carolina Angela. The town had many names before the Post Office Department finally decreed in 1883 that it would be called San Angelo. This narrative uses the final name, San Angelo, throughout. (WTC.)

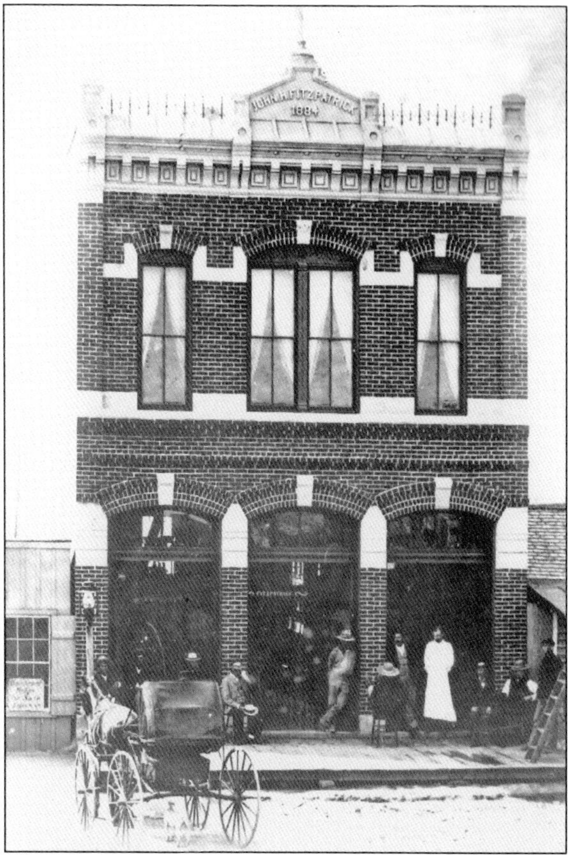

It is a huge irony that San Angelo was named for a saintly woman. The early town was filled with untamed cowboys, buffalo hunters, felons, and prostitutes who patronized the many saloons, gambling dens, and bawdy houses that were there. It was the place where enlisted men at Fort Concho frequently got into trouble but continued to spend their money. This photograph shows John H Fitzpatrick's saloon on East Concho Avenue in 1884. A sharp eye would notice an unidentified Fort Concho Buffalo Soldier on the right. (WTC.)

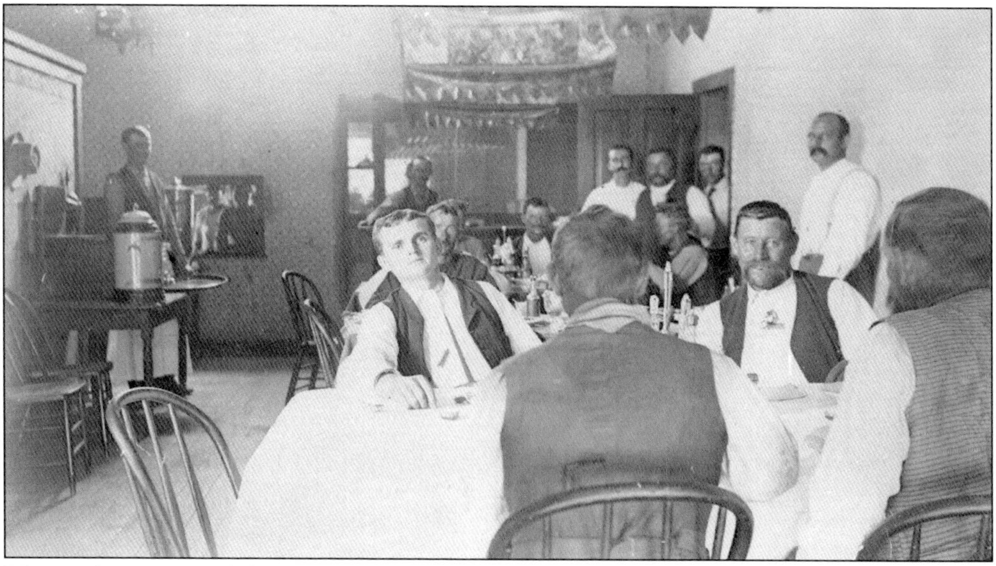

This is the interior of the Star Saloon in 1884. Having a good meal was one of the pleasures of saloon life. Two of the gentlemen pictured here are Albert Hahnswold and Herbert Wolters. Apparently, no one is bothered by being recognized for patronizing this establishment. They appear happy to pose for the photographer. (WTC.)

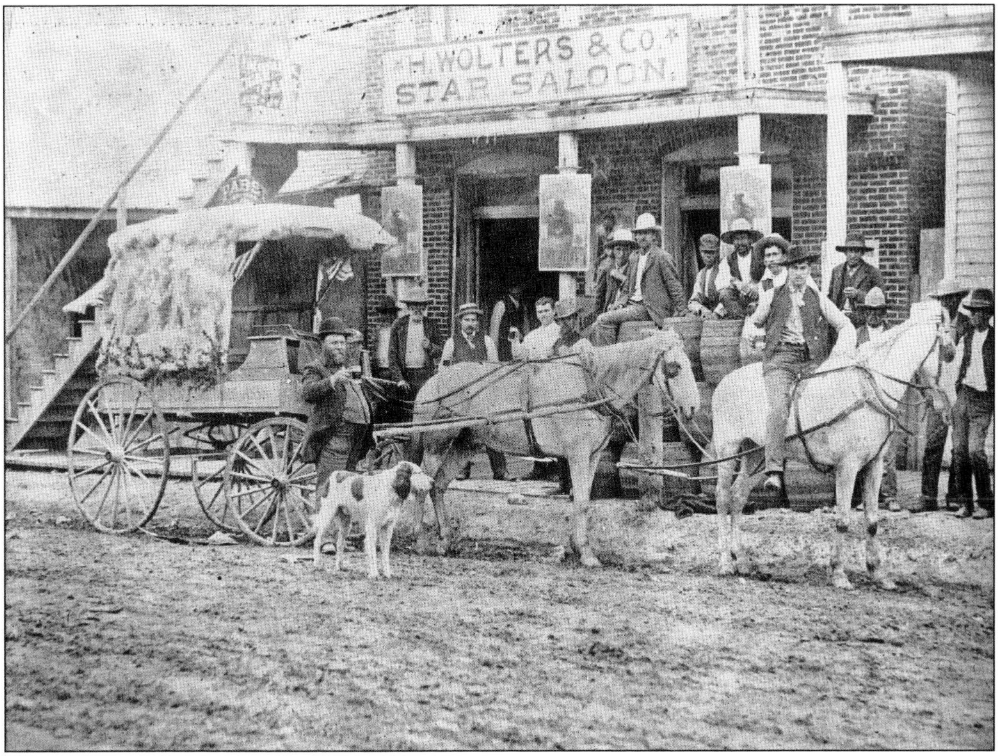

This exterior view of the Star Saloon indicates that the frivolity sometimes spilled into the street. It certainly seems as if a good time is being had by all. (WTC.)

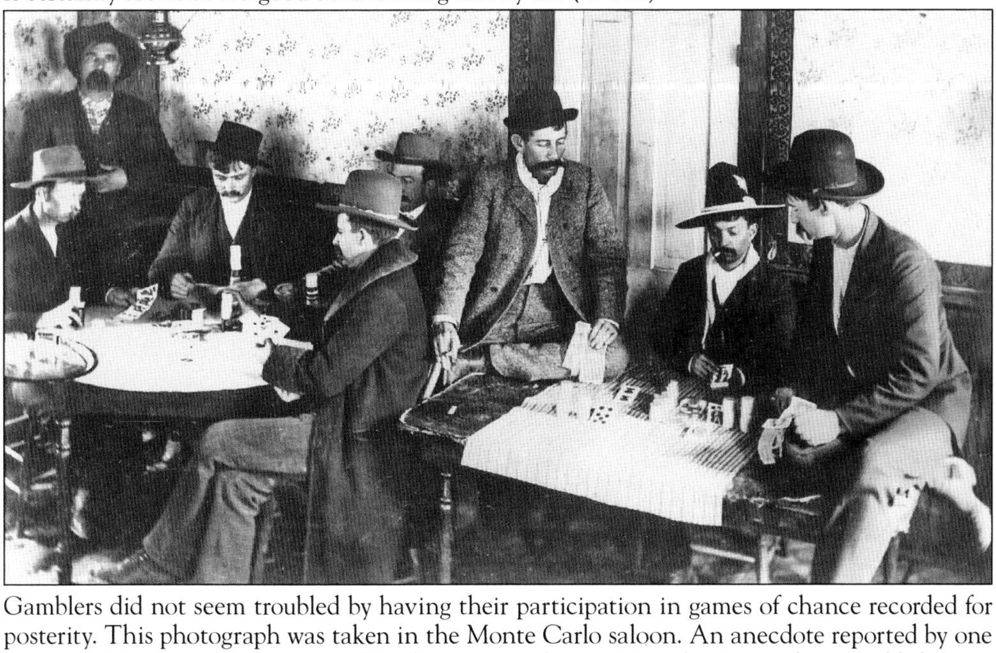

Gamblers did not seem troubled by having their participation in games of chance recorded for posterity. This photograph was taken in the Monte Carlo saloon. An anecdote reported by one historian is interesting. A respected banker was seen by a minister leaving such an establishment. "I am sorry to see you coming out of such a place," said the minister. The unabashed banker replied, "You would not have me stay there all day." (WTC.)

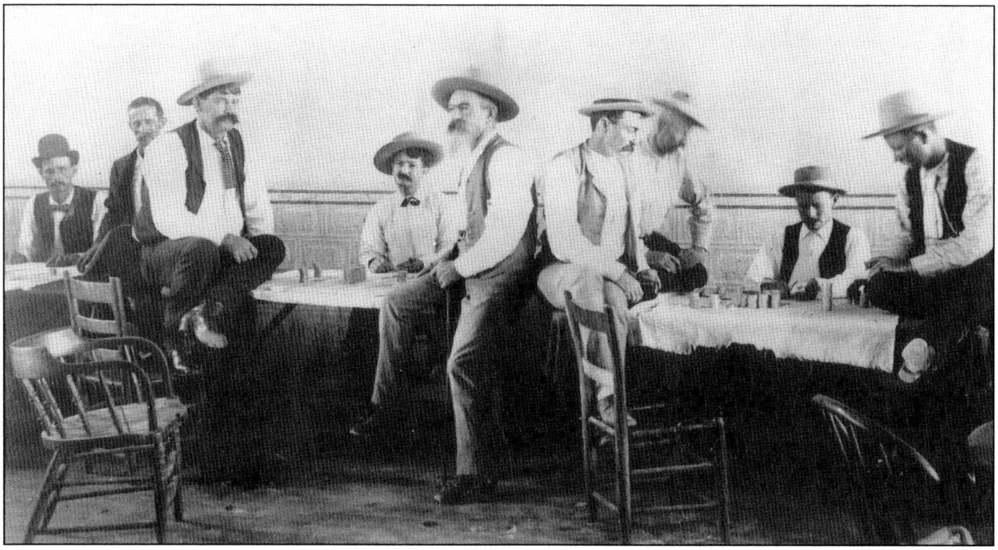

This very similar picture was taken upstairs at the Arc Light Saloon. It is certainly not coincidental that the arrangement of gamblers is the same. Pioneer photographer M.C. Ragsdale took both pictures and included both of them in a series of pictures he sold entitled *Views of the Concho Country*. Ragsdale obviously figured gambling was an interesting feature of life in early San Angelo. (WTC.)

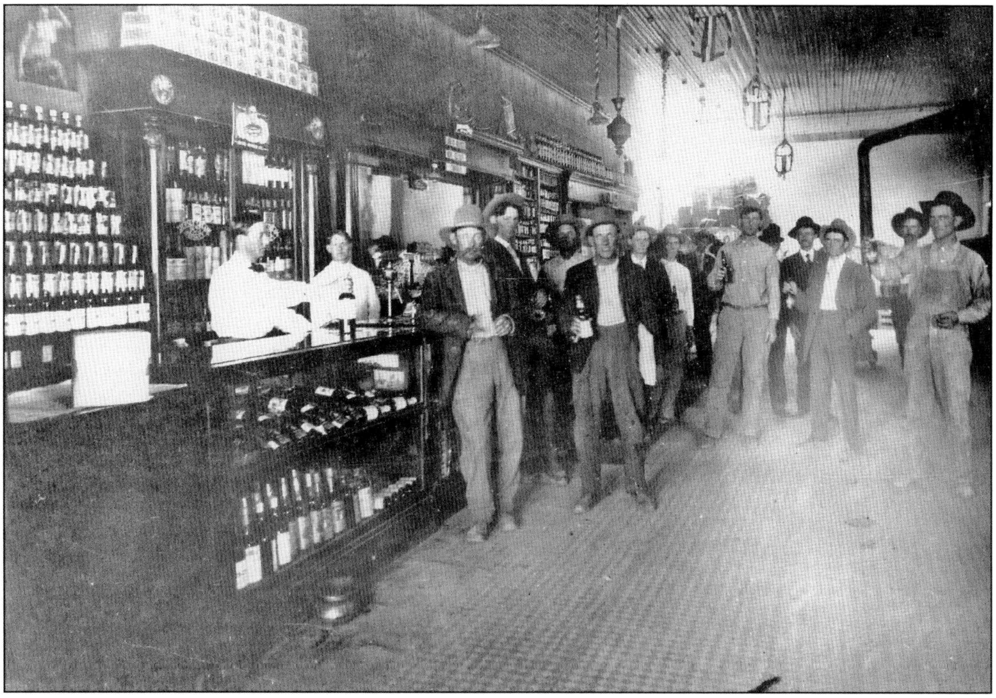

This picture of the interior of the Bank Exchange Saloon hints at some of the other pleasures available in San Angelo. The art at the top left of the photograph is very suggestive. Dr. S.L.S. Smith wrote that the town was full of "human sharks" trying to get the soldiers' money. He also reported that his time at the fort was often spent treating wounds, injuries, and venereal diseases. (WTC.)

The saloons in early San Angelo even had their own minister. Parson Potter had been a fearless fighter and gambler before his conversion to the Methodist faith. Afterwards, he was by all accounts equally fearless and driven to preach the Gospel. Carrying his gun with him to protect the congregation from any rowdy behavior, Potter held services in saloons and gambling houses. Even those who did not go to his services respected him for his sincerity and determination. (WTC.)

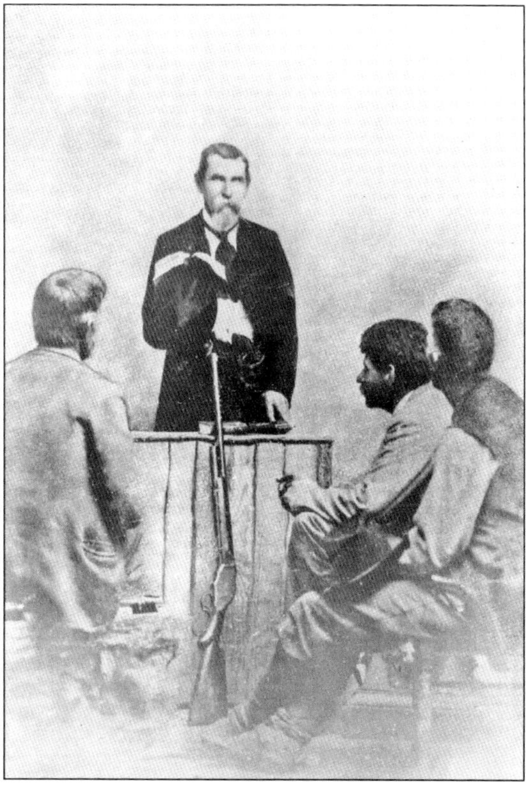

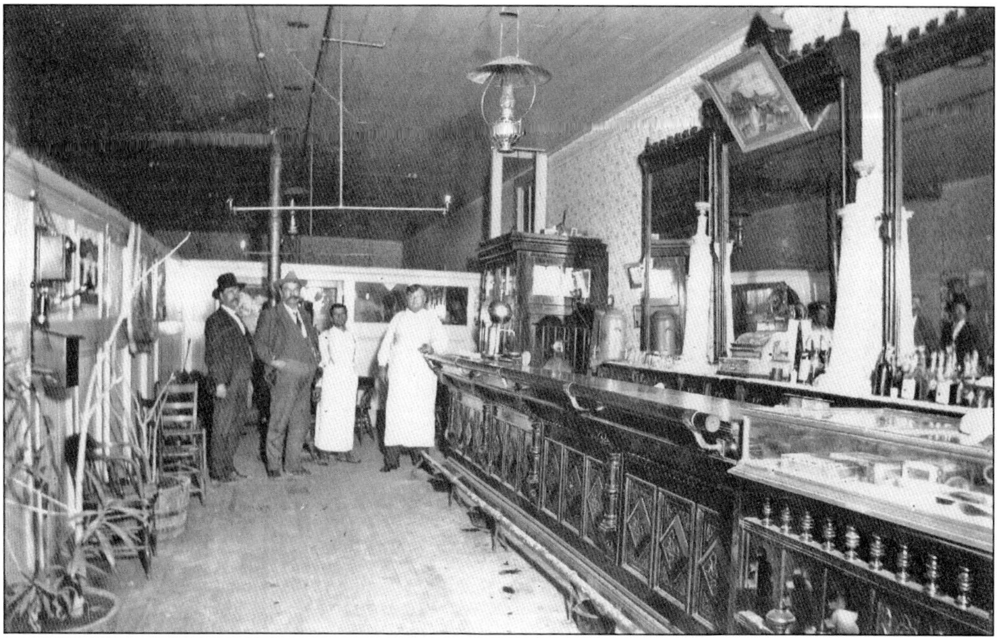

Not all saloons were equally rambunctious. This picture of the Legal Tender Saloon shows the local constable, Dick Runyon, on the left, with the owner, Jim Crenshaw, to his immediate left. Not only was the law comfortable here, but patrons could also enjoy potted palms in this relatively classy establishment. (WTC.)

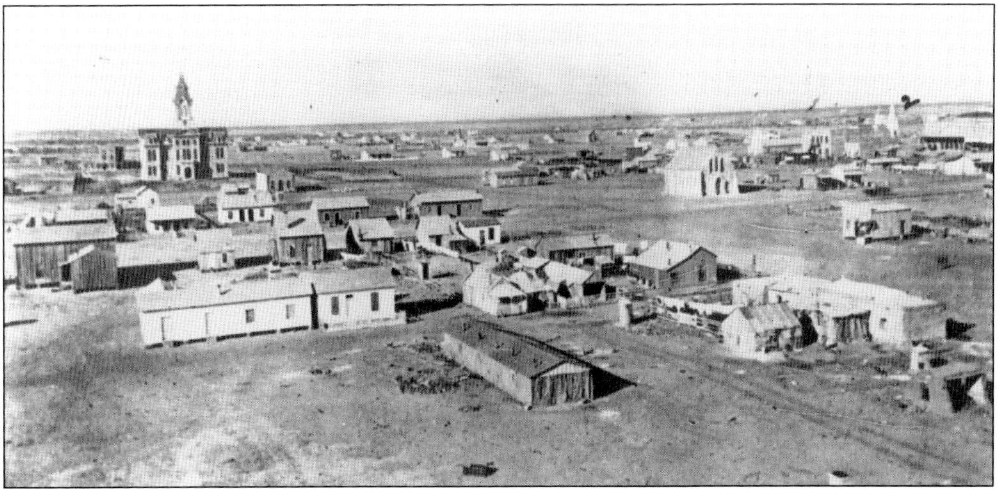

There were other places to spend money in San Angelo. This early photograph shows a long building constructed of pickets in the foreground. It was a dance hall, which featured an entertainer named Bess, a woman acclaimed by cowboys far and near. By tradition, none other than Billy the Kid was once a patron here. (FC.)

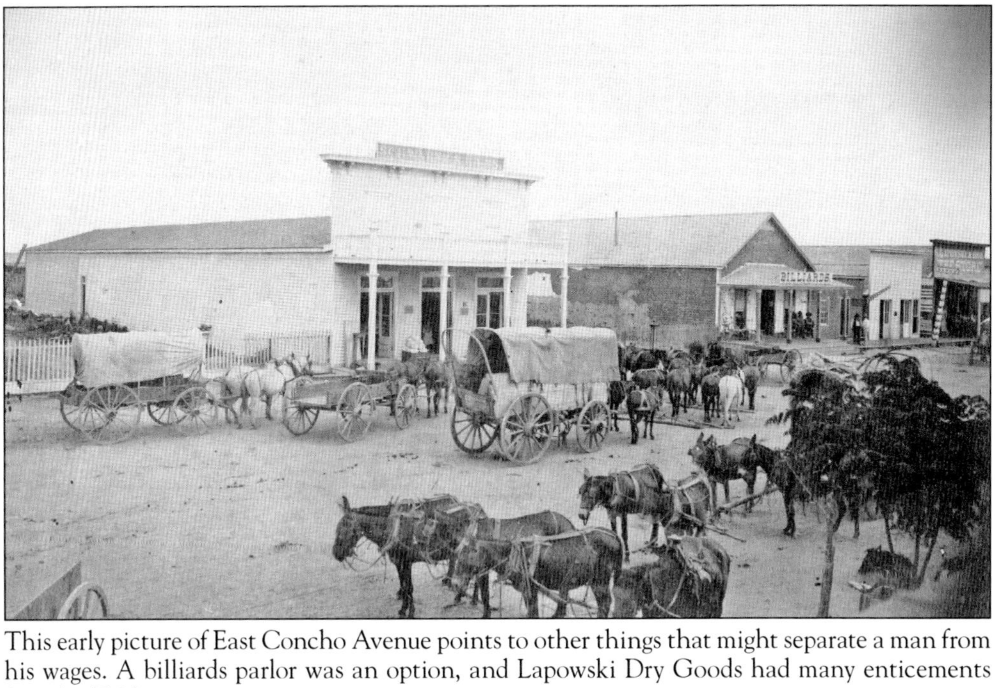

This early picture of East Concho Avenue points to other things that might separate a man from his wages. A billiards parlor was an option, and Lapowski Dry Goods had many enticements for sale. (FC.)

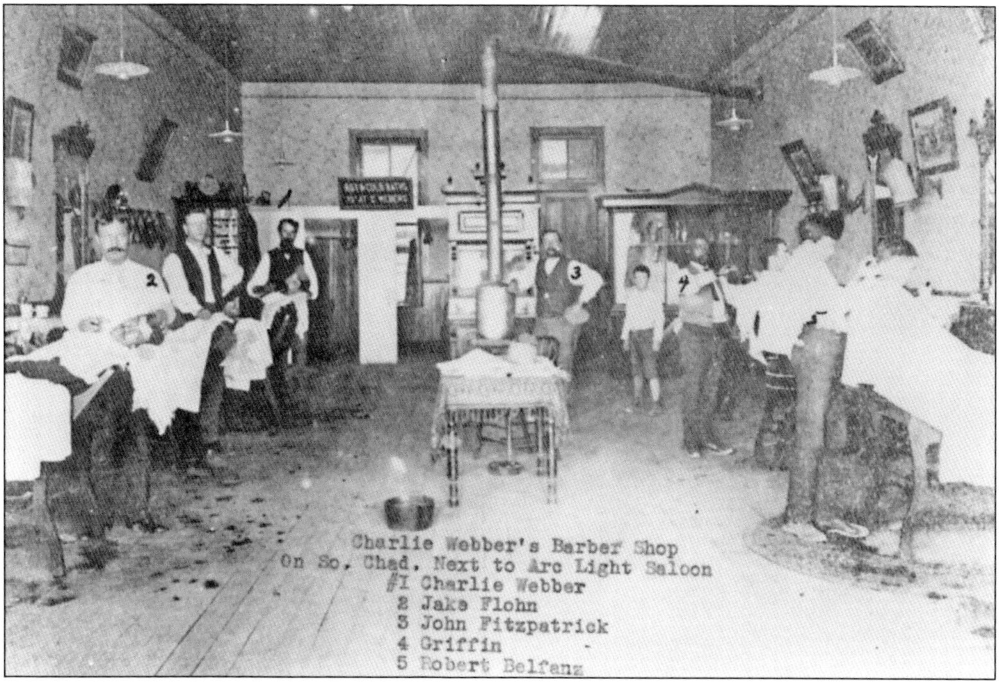

It was also comforting to get a shave or a haircut. Charlie Webber's Barber Shop, on Concho Avenue next to the Arc Light Saloon, was the first in San Angelo. Robert Balfanz is the barber cutting hair on the far right. He would soon open his own shop down the street. (Private collection.)

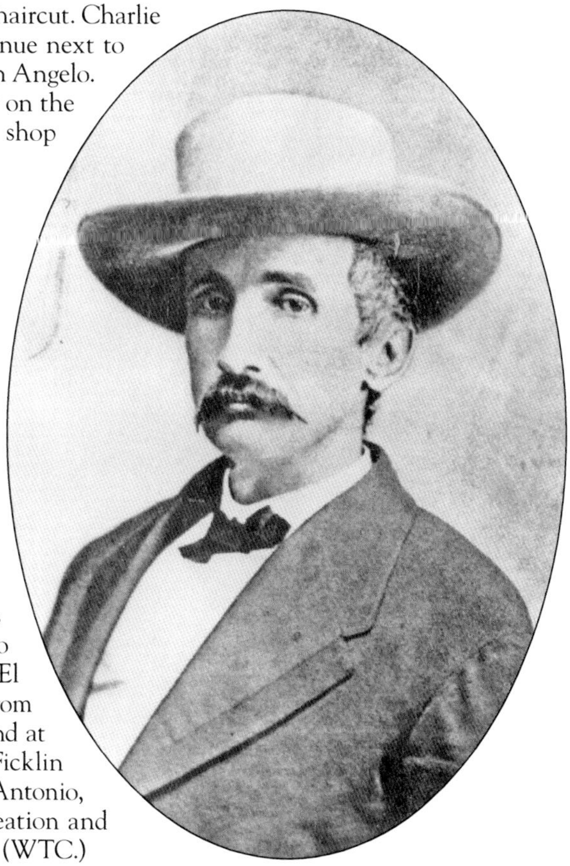

This dashing Virginia gentleman was Benjamin F. Ficklin, one of the most fascinating characters associated with the early history of the Concho Valley. He helped establish and run the Pony Express in the 1850s. After the Civil War broke out, Ficklin was a Confederate blockade-runner and later a suspect in the Lincoln assassination. Despite his Southern ties, Ficklin had enough friends in Washington to procure a contract to deliver mail between San Antonio and El Paso. In 1869, he bought land three miles from Fort Concho and established a stage stand at a crossing of the South Concho River. Ficklin maintained his primary residence in San Antonio, but he came to the stage stand for recreation and hunting with his pack of 50 greyhounds. (WTC.)

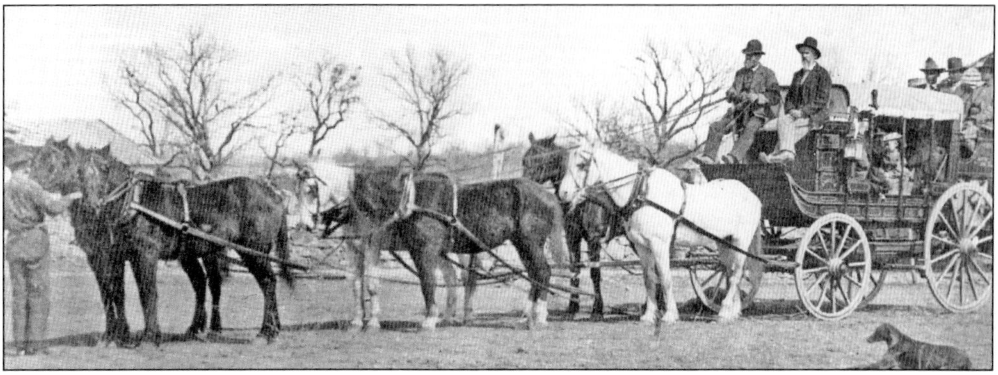

This stagecoach was one of the vehicles used on the San Antonio–to–El Paso mail route. Travel by stage was not cheap. It cost $75 to travel the whole route and took six days to complete the trip. For a shorter trip, from Ben Ficklin to San Antonio, the fare was $25. Ficklin spent only $1 an acre to buy the land for the stage stand, which puts these fares in perspective. Ficklin's fabulous career ended abruptly in 1871. He was in Washington lobbying for his interests when he dined on a piece of fish at the elegant Willard Hotel. A bone lodged in his throat and killed him. Back at the stage stand, his good friend and trusted associate Francis Corbett Taylor, pictured here holding the reins to the stage, took charge and dedicated himself to creating a town named Ben Ficklin, which would be a proper monument to his dead friend. (WTC.)

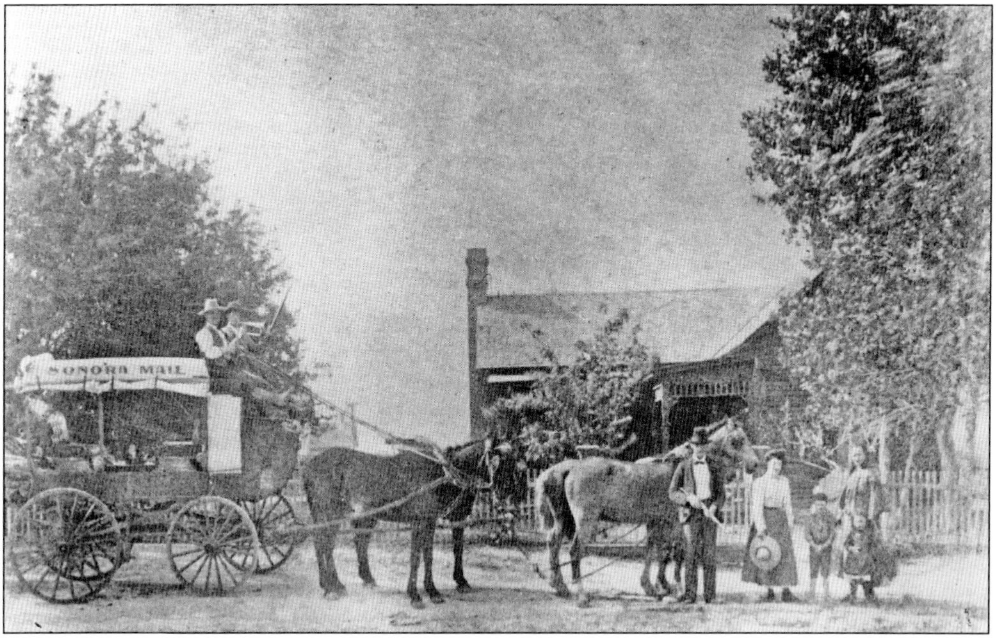

F.C. Taylor was a skilled politician as well as a good businessman. The town of Ben Ficklin would be a formidable rival to San Angelo for the political and financial control of Tom Green County. Ben Ficklin continued to be a transportation hub in the era of stage travel; pictured above is the Sonora Mail arriving in town. Ranchers, professional people, merchants, and many solid citizens moved to the site because it was a proper and safe place to live. In 1875, Taylor pulled off a major coup when voters in Tom Green County chose Ben Ficklin to be the county seat rather than San Angelo. Though more people lived in San Angelo than in Ben Ficklin, Taylor rounded up many rural people and brought them to the polls. Some contend that Mexican American workers were the people who decided this issue by a 65-vote margin. (FC.)

Floods were a fact of life in the Concho Valley. In another tremendously ironic twist, the good people of Ben Ficklin suffered from an epic flood in 1882, while the rougher crowd in San Angelo escaped major damage. The South Concho River was swollen with torrential rains and roared downstream at a pace that swept up people, livestock, and houses. People on rooftops in Ben Ficklin, trying to escape the torrent, watched neighbors floating by to their deaths. Finally, the river, which had been two or three miles wide in spots, subsided. The losses were terrible; 65 people drowned, and property destruction was devastating. This dead cow had been swept into the upper branches of a tree by the floodwaters. The 1882 tragedy marked the end of Ben Ficklin as a rival to San Angelo. (FC.)

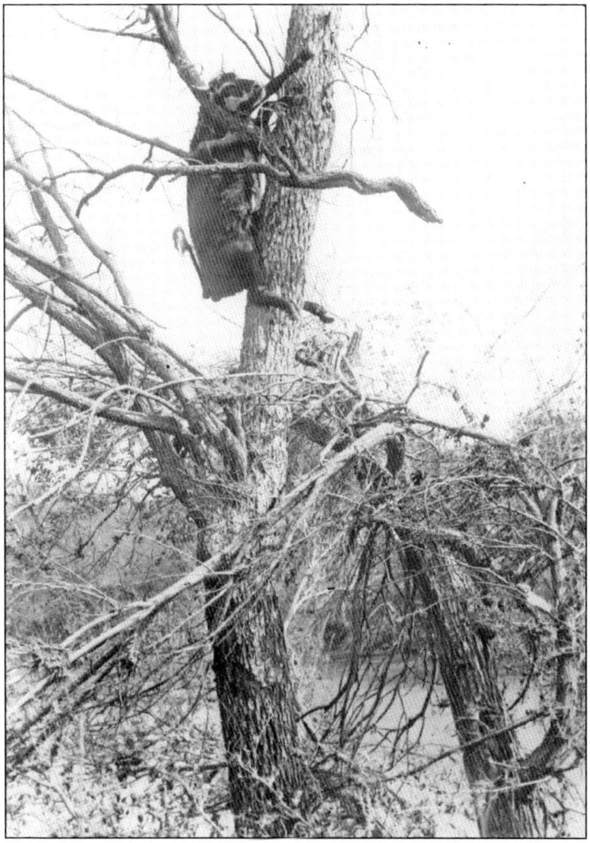

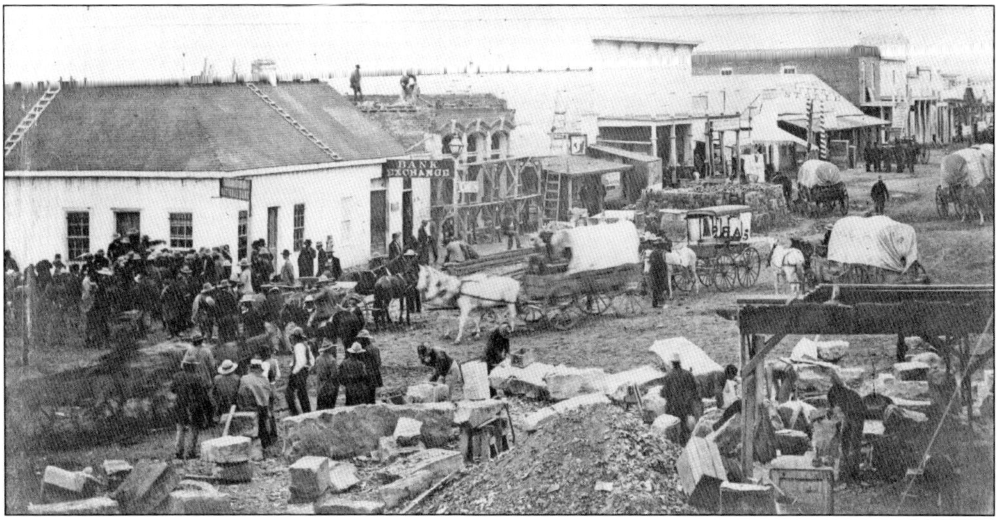

One person's tragedy is another person's opportunity. San Angelo entered a boom period after the flood. The respectable citizens of Ben Ficklin moved to San Angelo as did businesses and the county seat. This picture suggests the feverish pace of building in San Angelo in 1883. Here, the Concho National Bank is under construction, right next door to the Bank Exchange, which was a saloon. Having the bank built next to a saloon is highly symbolic of the huge changes taking place in the city. (FC.)

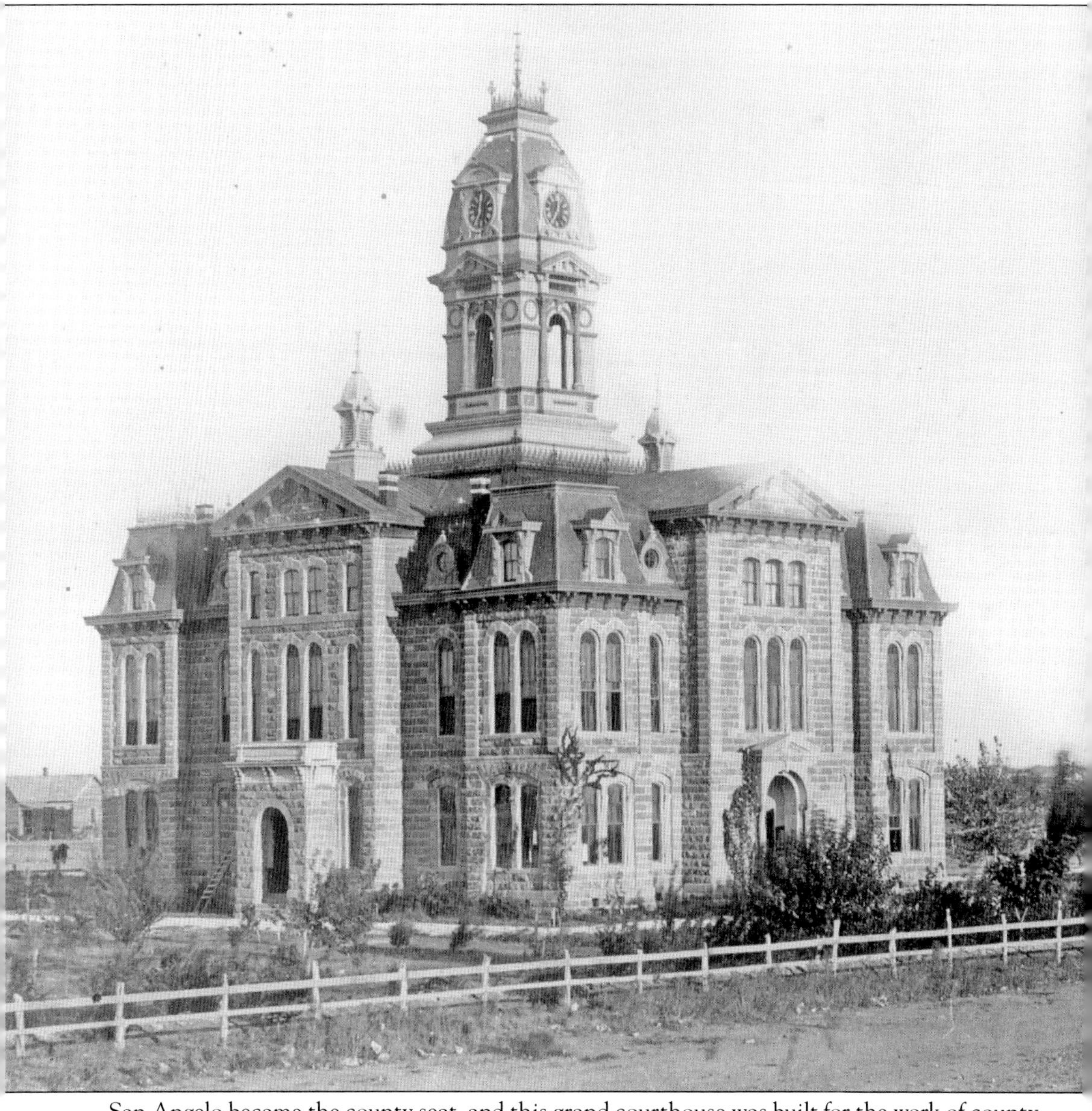

San Angelo became the county seat, and this grand courthouse was built for the work of county officials. The structure dwarfed all other buildings in the area, and it is a clear statement of the optimism residents felt about their city. The supervisor of construction was Oscar Ruffini, who came to San Angelo in 1884 for the job. The elegant courthouse was completed at a cost of $18,000. The stone, again ironically, was quarried just above Ben Ficklin, and the lumber came by wagon from Abilene. In May 1887, the original cupola was destroyed by a tornado, and another was built with a four-sided clock, which chimed every hour. (FC.)

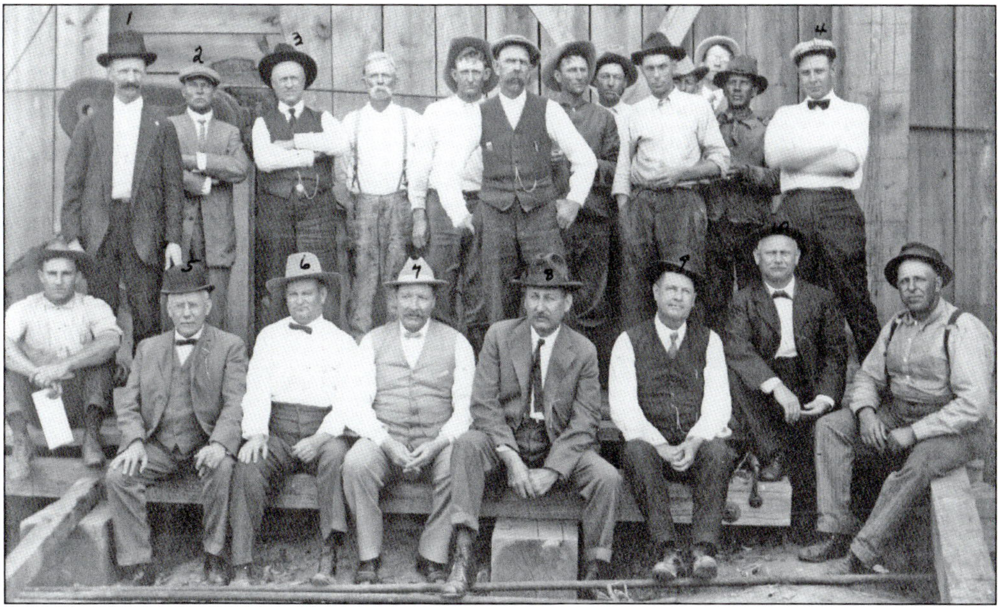

Oscar Ruffini (seated second from right) came to do one job, but he ended up living in San Angelo for the remainder of his life. The climate suited him. In 1884, he had a lung condition that was expected to kill him. Ruffini started breathing the dry West Texas air and stopped smoking his customary 25 cigars a day. He lived to be 98, dying in San Angelo in 1957. Ruffini also liked the business climate in the booming city. He invested in land and other businesses and left a considerable estate. Few frontier towns had a professional architect to guide the building of a city. Ruffini left his mark on San Angelo and many surrounding communities as well. The image above shows him with a group of civic leaders. (WTC.)

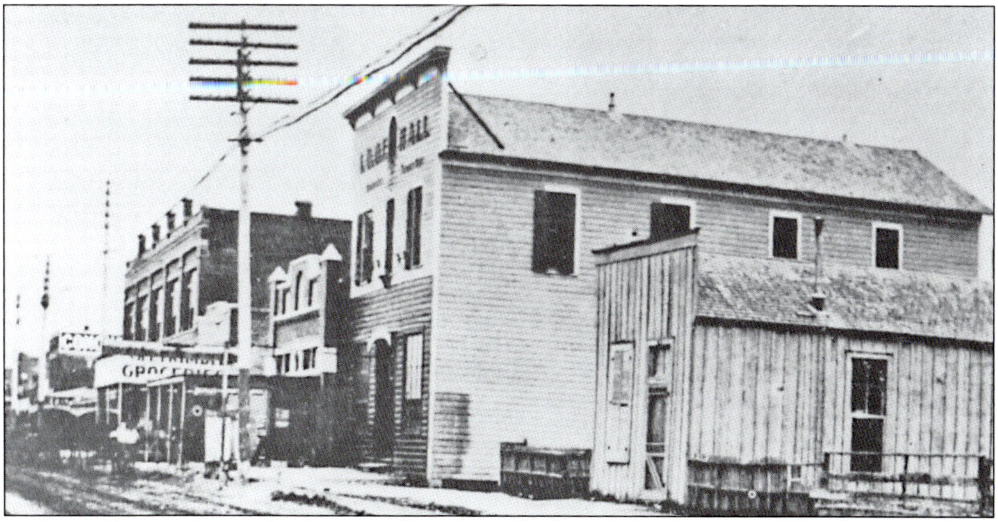

Oscar Ruffini was somewhat eccentric. He always wore a black suit, a black tie, and a black hat. He ate the same meal everyday at the same time and in the same place. And he was quite frugal. This photograph shows his studio and home at the far right of the picture. These were quite unassuming digs for a prosperous architect. In later years, San Angelo civic leaders did everything they could to force him to destroy what they considered to be an eyesore. Ruffini did not respond to the pressure. (WTC.)

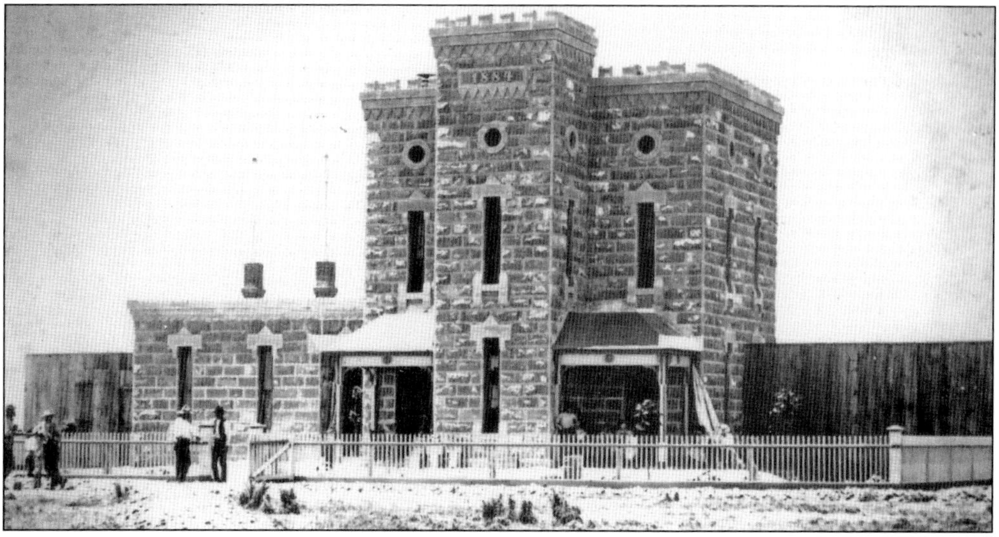

One of Ruffini's early designs was a new jail to replace the primitive picket building that was holding wrongdoers. This structure was located very close to the courthouse. It would seem that the design was very closely aligned to the function of the building. The ornament made the building look like a medieval castle or fortress where prisoners could be kept safe and secure. (WTC.)

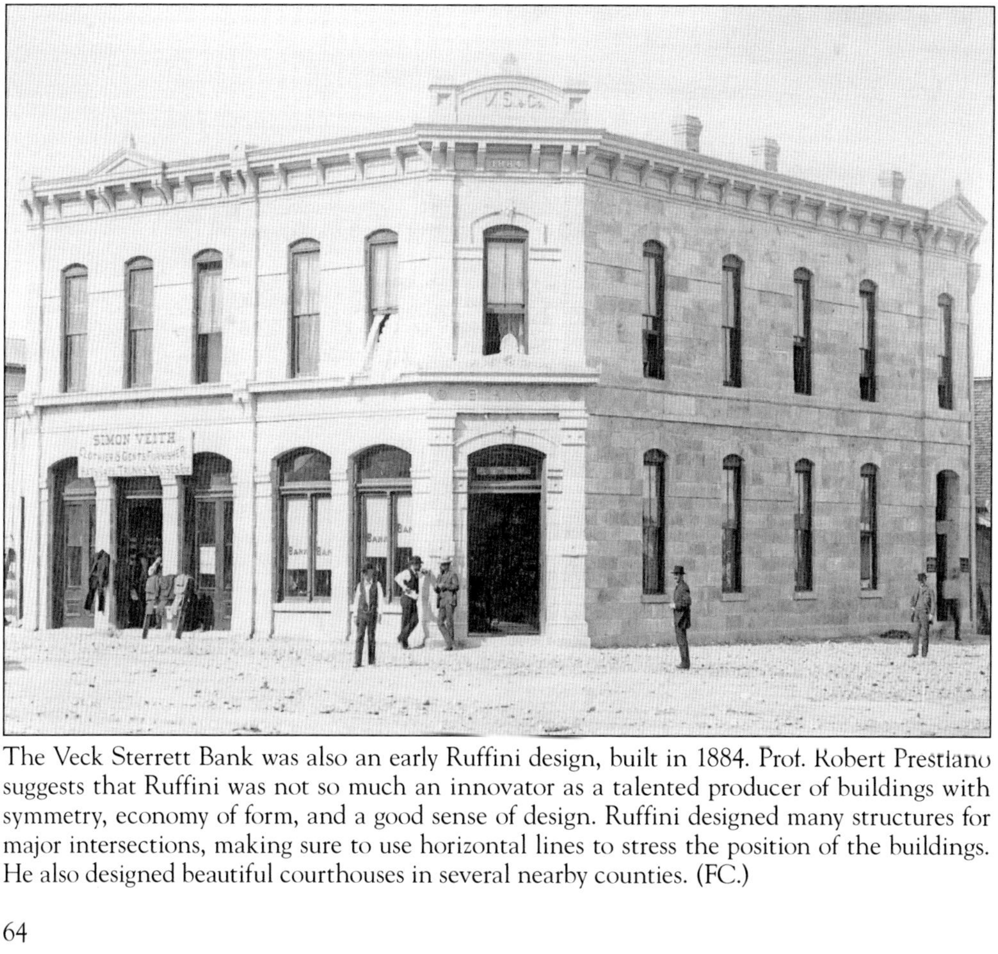

The Veck Sterrett Bank was also an early Ruffini design, built in 1884. Prof. Robert Prestiano suggests that Ruffini was not so much an innovator as a talented producer of buildings with symmetry, economy of form, and a good sense of design. Ruffini designed many structures for major intersections, making sure to use horizontal lines to stress the position of the buildings. He also designed beautiful courthouses in several nearby counties. (FC.)

A professional photographer arrived in San Angelo in 1874. McArthur Cullen Ragsdale was born in South Carolina and moved with his family to Texas in search of business opportunities. He opened a photography shop in San Angelo, but he worked as an itinerant photographer for a number of years. As San Angelo grew, he stayed closer to home. This portrait shows Ragsdale in his later years, when he still was a resident of San Angelo. This narrative makes extensive use of his work. Ruffini and Ragsdale provided a sophisticated and artistic element to the growth of the city. (WTC.)

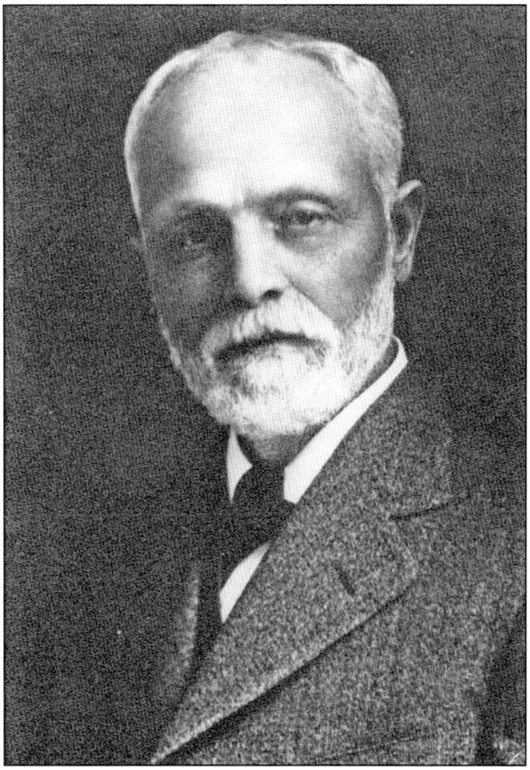

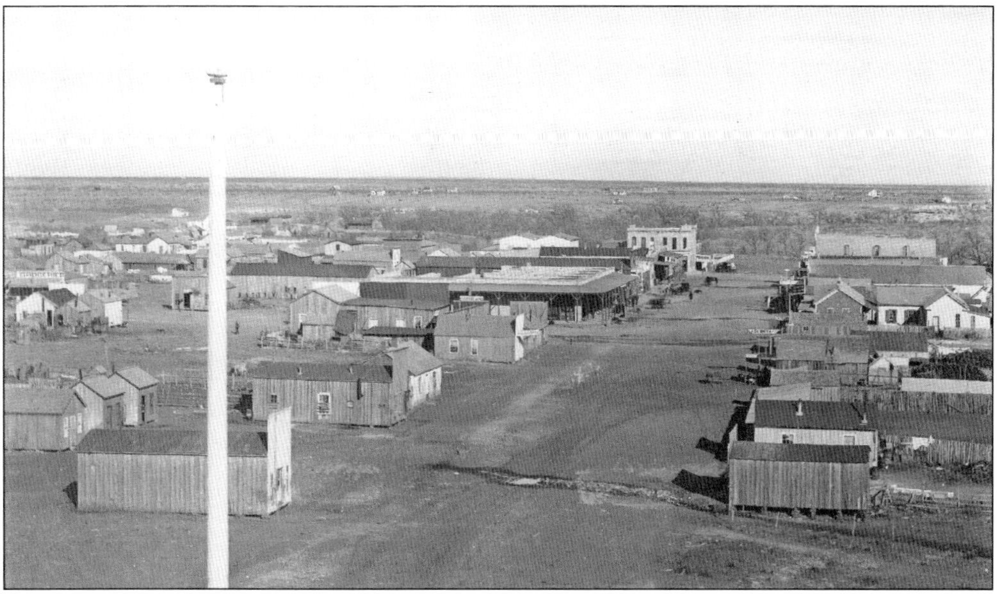

This is a view of East Concho Avenue in 1885. There is the appearance of an orderly city here, and there are many growing enterprises. In addition to the saloons and restaurants, there are several Chinese laundries, a printing press that was publishing a newspaper, a blacksmith shop, and several mercantile establishments. Quickly built picket-style buildings prevailed. But at the end of Concho Avenue is the Veck-Sterrett Bank, an elegant Ruffini design, which was a harbinger of good things to come in terms of San Angelo architecture. (WTC.)

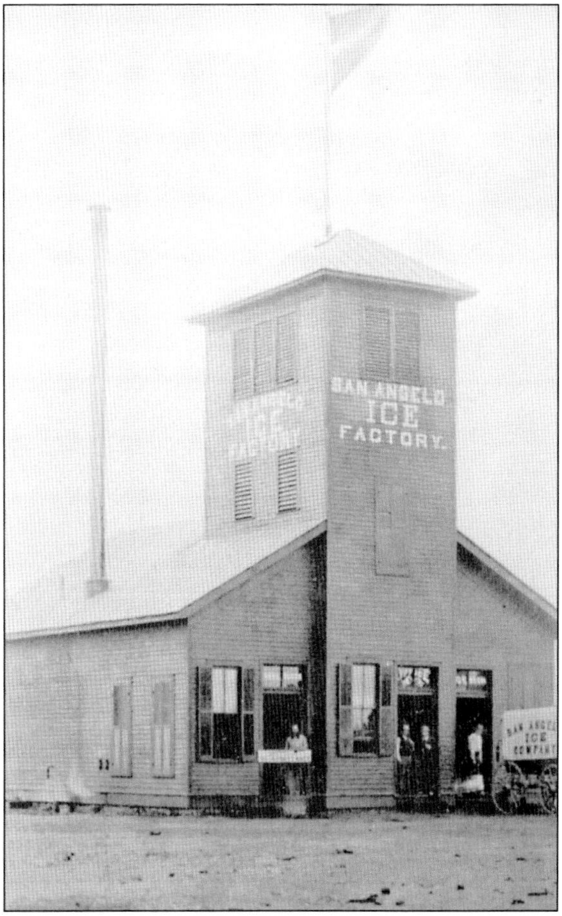

Many town builders worked on the infrastructure of the town in the 1880s. J.L. Millspaugh, formerly the Fort Concho sutler, devoted his efforts to improving San Angelo as well as to making money. In 1884, he built this factory. A steam engine powered a generator to create the electricity necessary to make ice. When the equipment was idle, the factory provided electricity to individuals. In 1890, Millspaugh created the first full-time power company for the growing city. (WTC.)

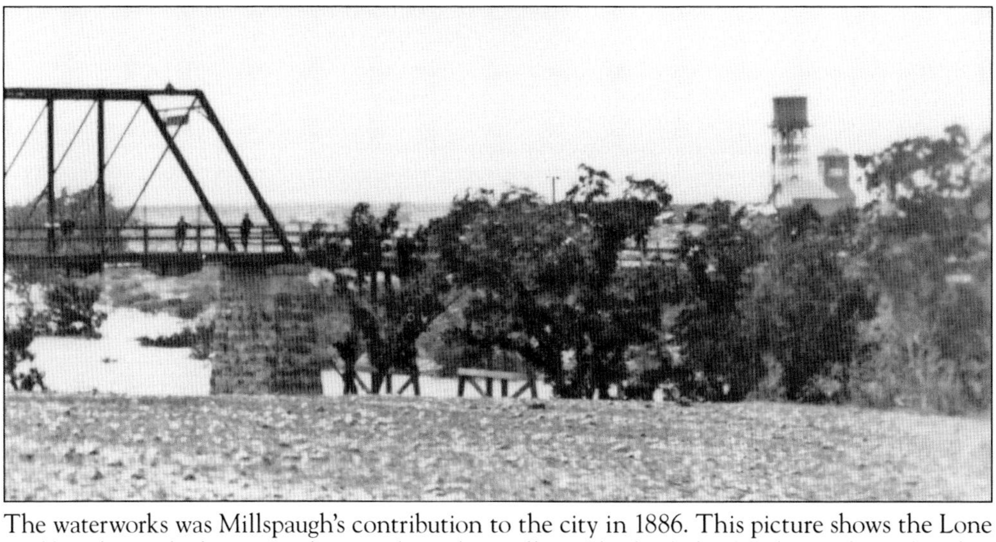

The waterworks was Millspaugh's contribution to the city in 1886. This picture shows the Lone Wolf Bridge with the water plant to the right. Millspaugh also helped to bring the railroad to town, and he was involved in other projects and political decisions that were important to the growth of the city. (FC.)

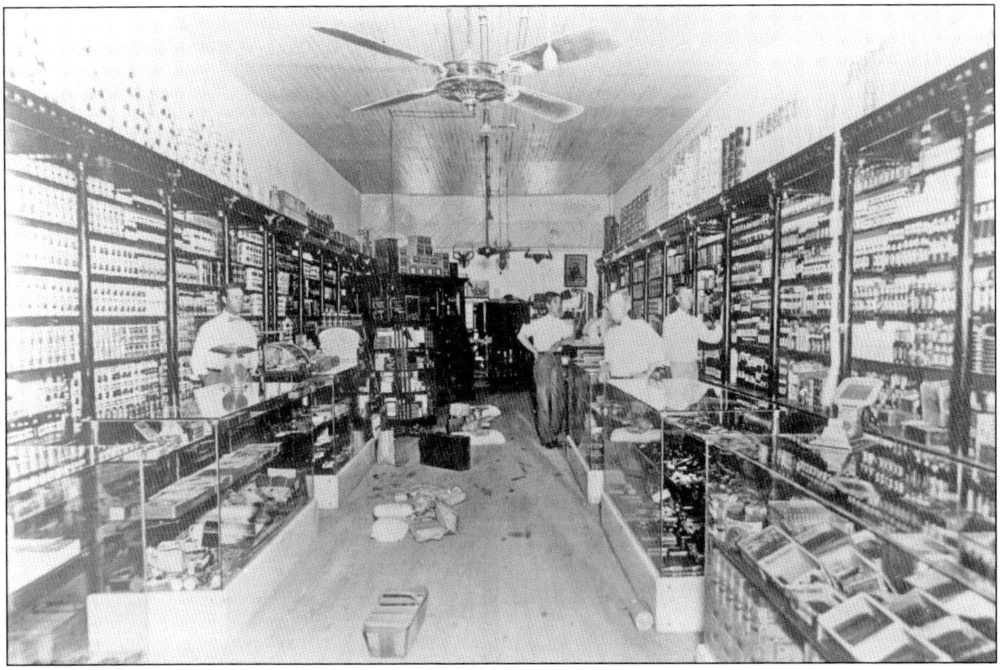

Retail establishments were often very large in San Angelo. Not only was the town growing dramatically after the tragedy at Ben Ficklin, but San Angelo businesses also served a very large rural area. Agriculture was the basis of the local economy, and many people traveled long distances to San Angelo to purchase what they wanted and needed. This picture shows the interior of the Silas Keeton Grocery Store with a sizable stock and many employees. (FC.)

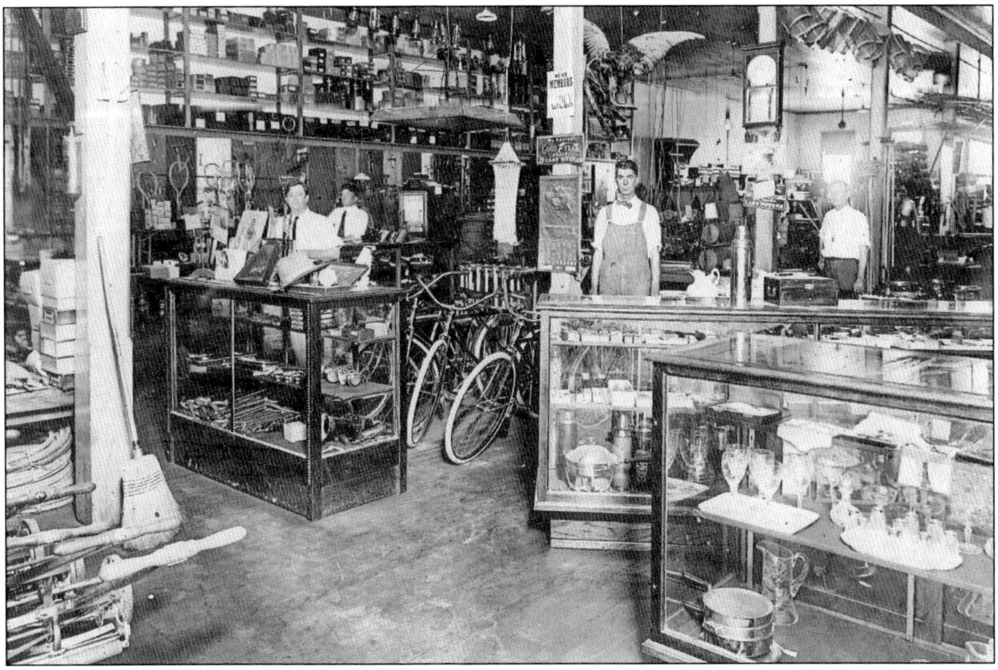

This photograph depicts the interior of the Johnson and Taylor Store on East Concho Avenue and shows an eclectic array of merchandise for sale. (WTC.)

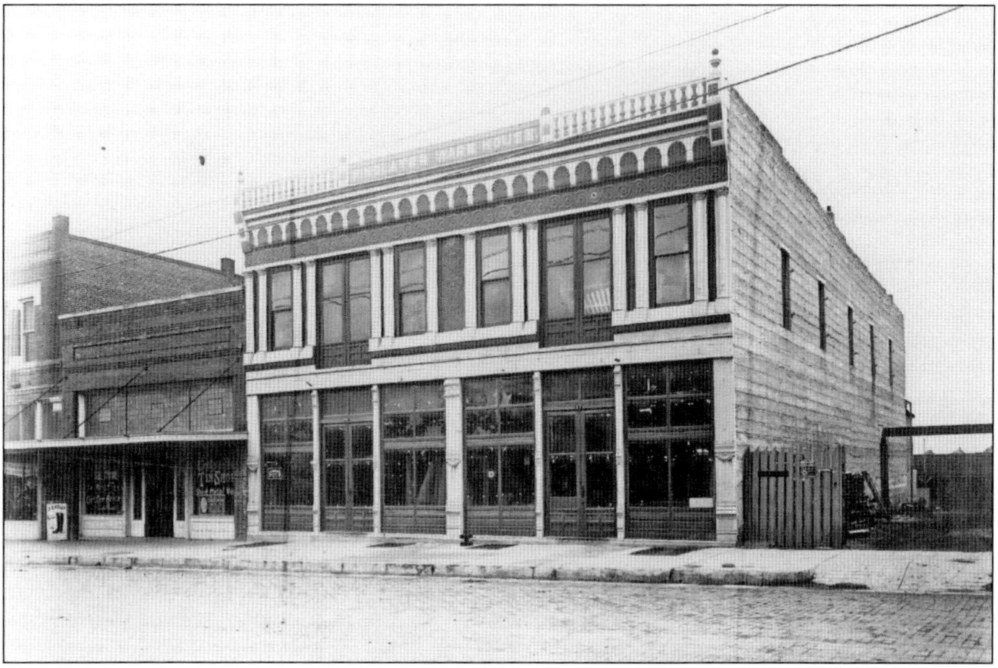

Findlater Hardware was another substantial business built in San Angelo in this period. As the retail sector of the city grew, it also became more specialized. (FC.)

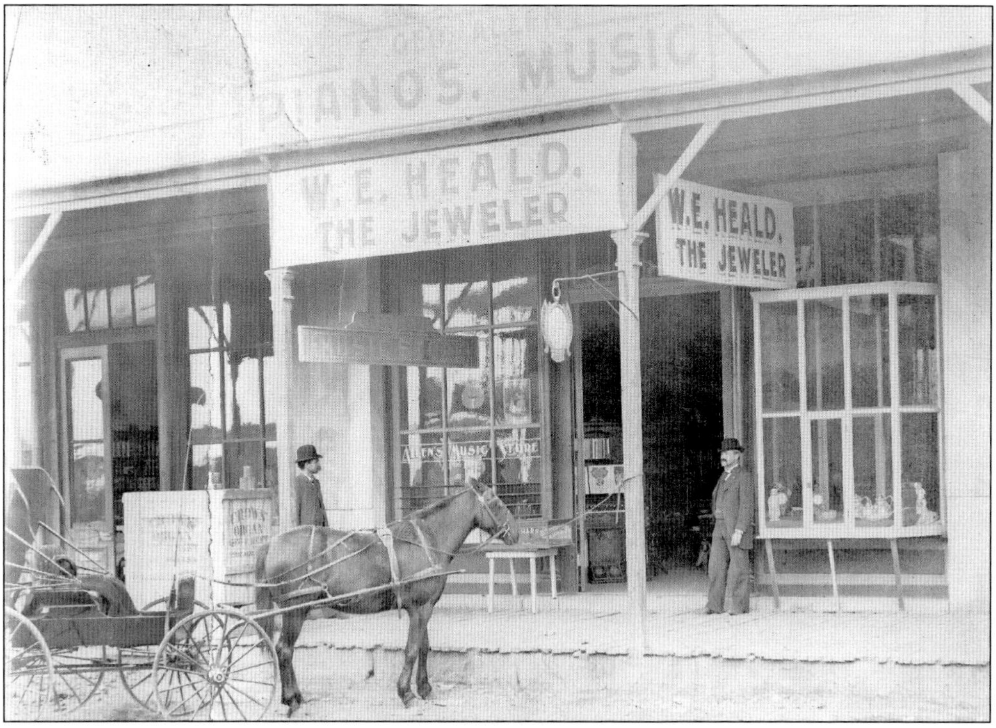

There were luxuries available as well. This photograph shows the W.E. Heald Jewelry store located next to Allen's Music Store. The elegant buggy and driver waiting outside of these establishments indicates a growing affluence and sophistication in San Angelo. (FC.)

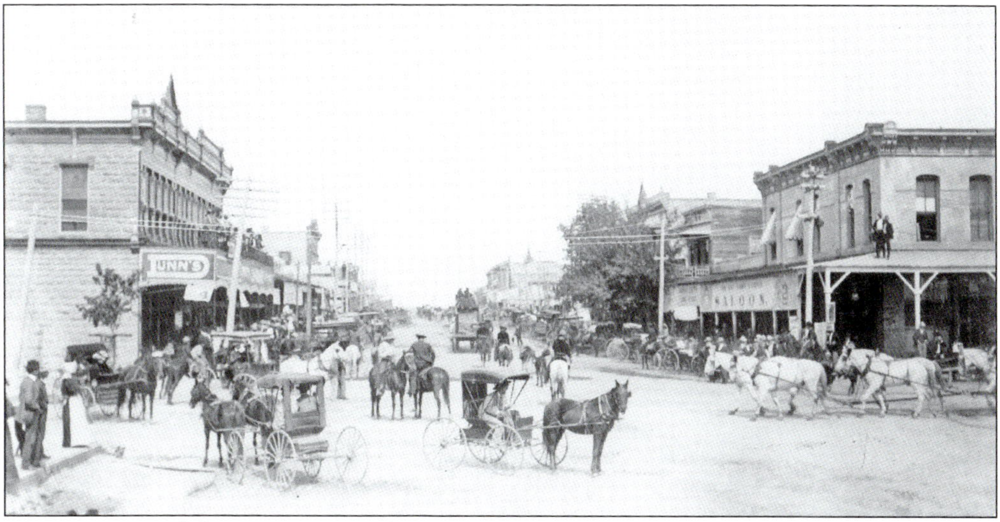

This is a view of the intersection of Concho Avenue and Chadbourne Street taken in 1895. Compared to the urban scene taken 10 years before, there are dramatic changes in this image. People crowd the streets. The buildings are varied and substantial. The Arc Light Saloon is a prominent feature of the downtown district, but saloons do not dominate. Telephone poles and electric lines destroy the beauty of the scene, but they certainly are signs of progress. This photograph may depict a parade. (FC.)

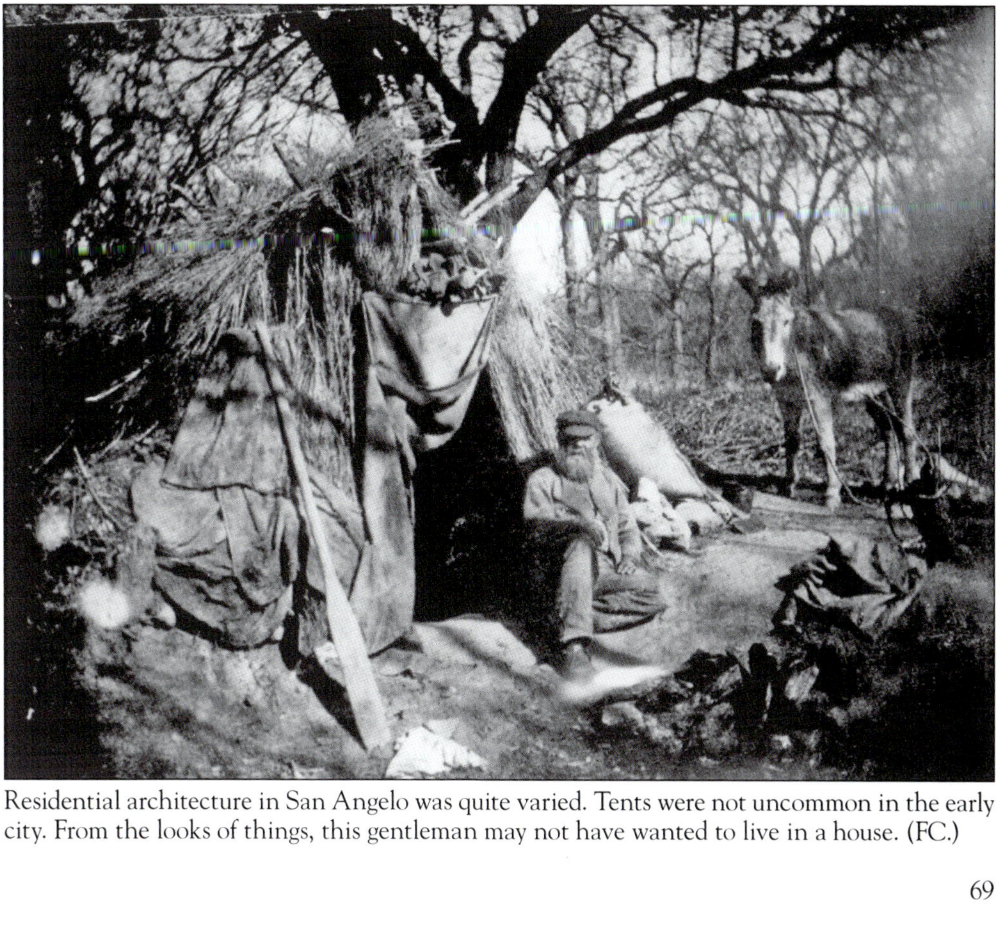

Residential architecture in San Angelo was quite varied. Tents were not uncommon in the early city. From the looks of things, this gentleman may not have wanted to live in a house. (FC.)

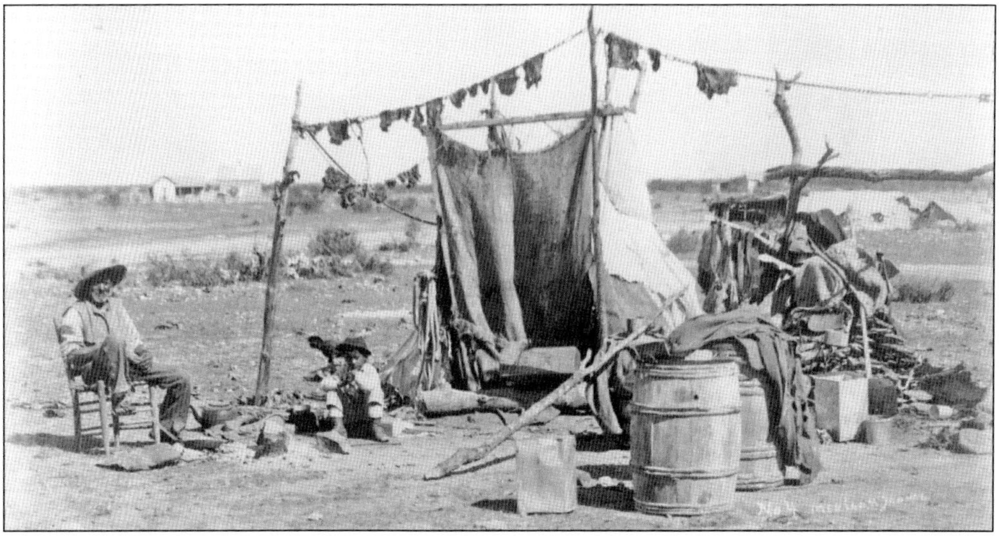

This is another tent home with a few refinements, such as a child, a chair, water barrels, and jerky drying on the line. The name of this man is unknown, but stories were told about him. He never wore shoes and had a small bag of money, which he used to pay for what he bought. The rumor around town was that he was wealthy. In 1886, he was murdered and his money bag stolen. No one knows what happened to the child. (Private collection.)

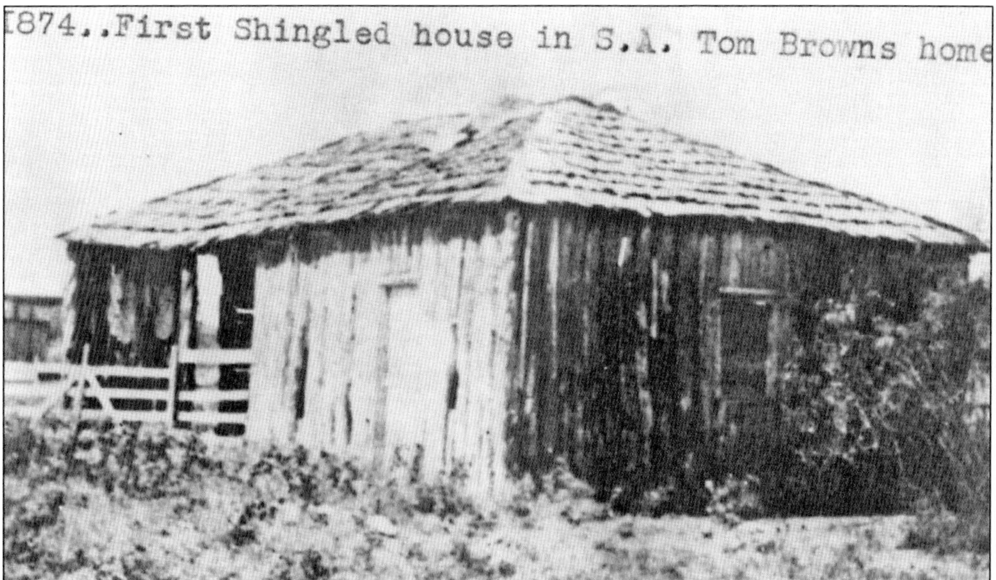

According to the caption on this photograph, this is the first shingled residence in San Angelo, owned by Tom Brown. The date on this picture is 1874. The picket construction of the house itself was a typical feature of early business establishments and houses. (FC.)

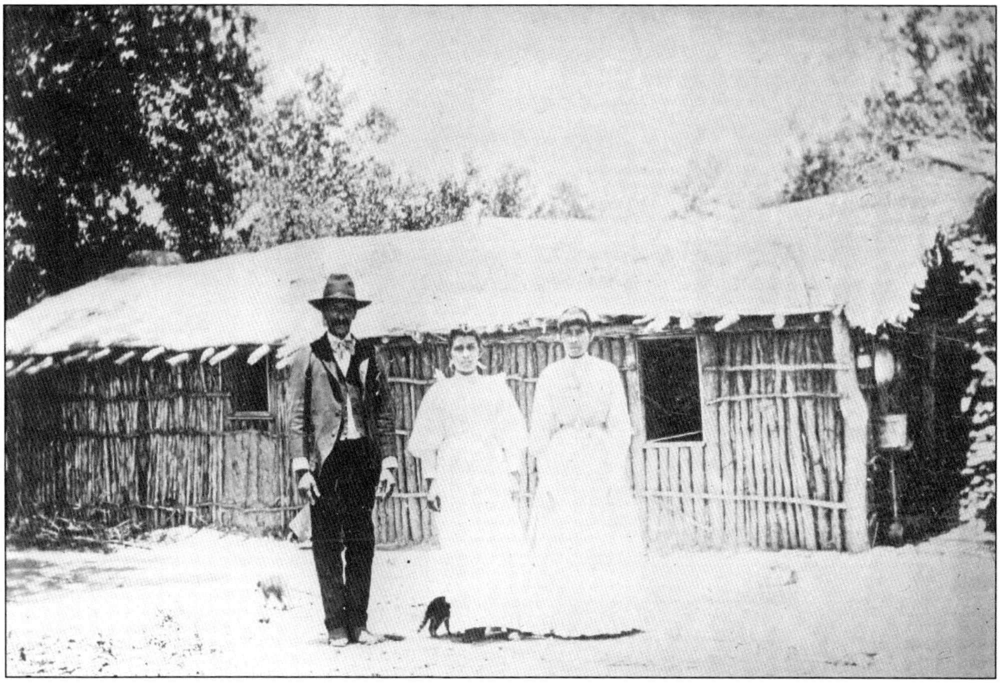

This early dwelling has some interesting features. The picket construction was common enough, but this dwelling has a roof made of buffalo hides. Hides were also used to cover the windows when the weather made it necessary. (WTC.)

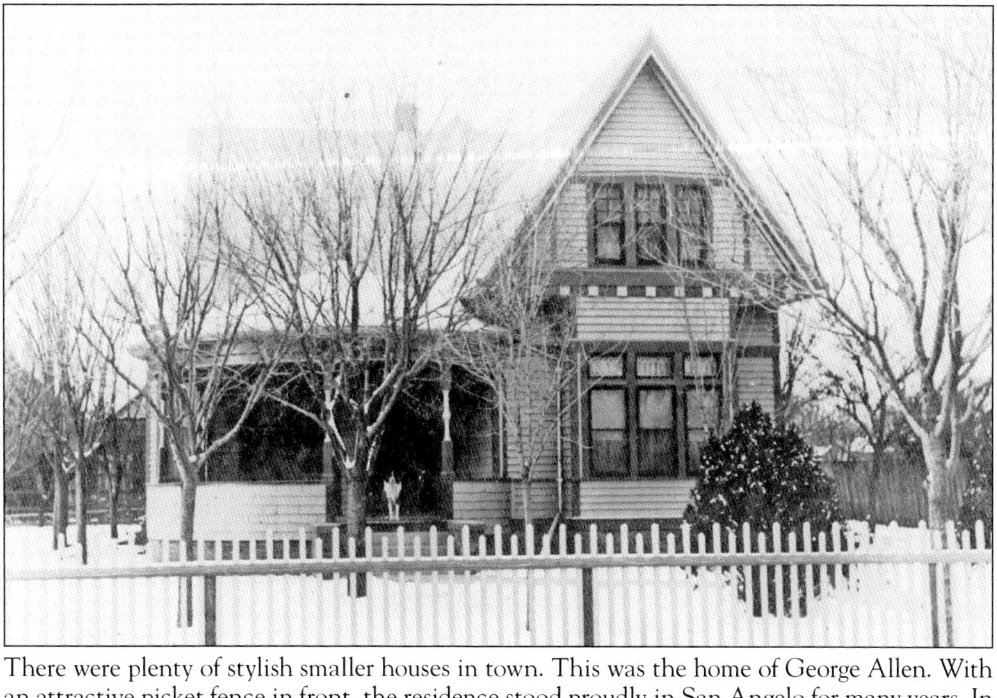

There were plenty of stylish smaller houses in town. This was the home of George Allen. With an attractive picket fence in front, the residence stood proudly in San Angelo for many years. In the latter part of the 20th century, the house was moved to a ranch, refurbished, and moved again to a heritage park near Fort Concho. Today, it serves as an architect's office. (FC.)

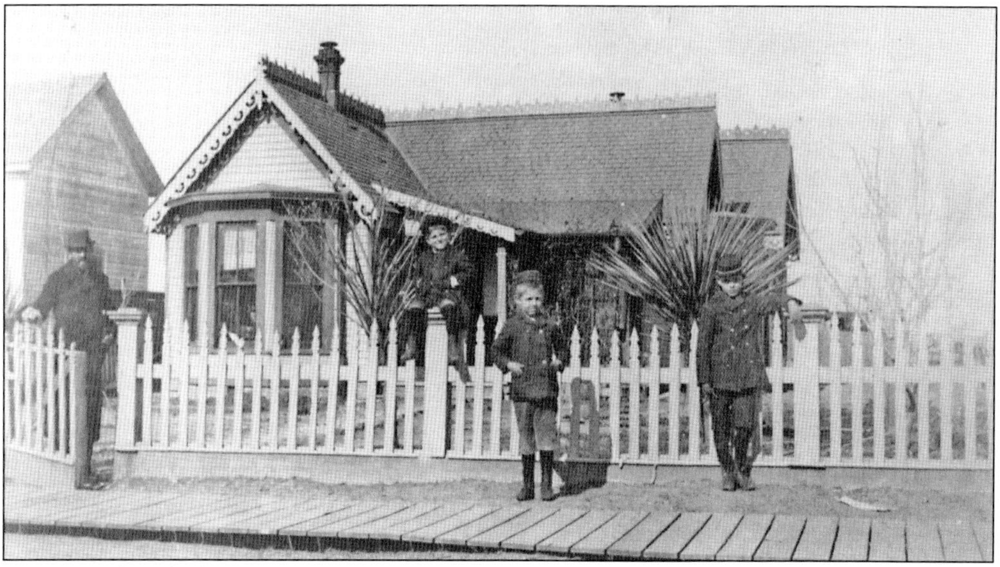

Some ranchers had houses in town to use for shopping trips or other purposes. The Tweedy family of Knickerbocker owned this tidy dwelling. The people in front of the house are family members. (WTC.)

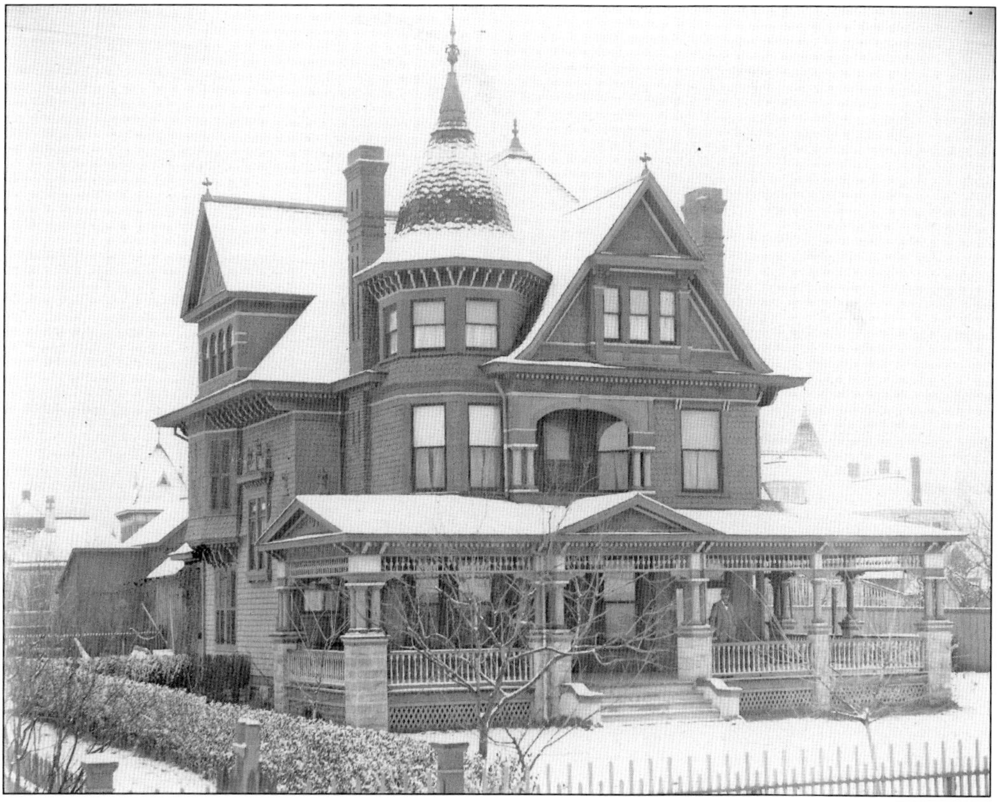

A sure sign of the growing affluence of San Angelo was the large number of very large houses built by local business leaders. This beautiful winter scene shows the home of John W. Harris, located close to the downtown area. (WTC.)

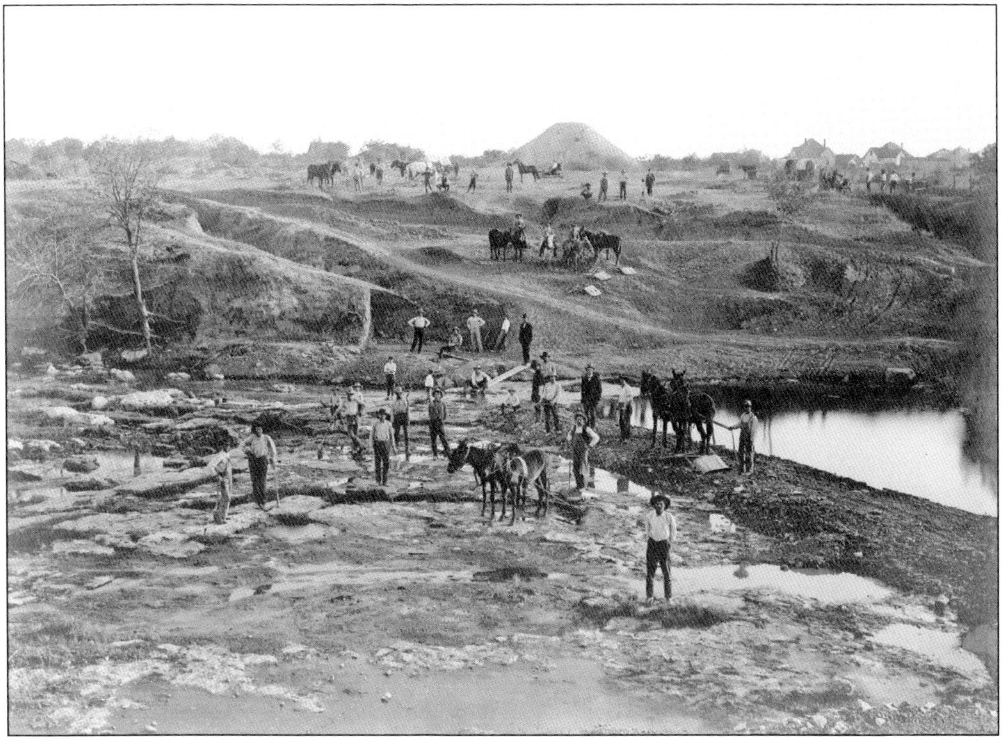

Population growth expanded the city in many directions. This is a photograph of the opening of Angelo Heights, a subdivision across the winding Concho River in an opposite direction from Fort Concho. Many of the larger houses were built on a tall bank overlooking the river, which minimized the danger from flooding. The views are very good also. (FC.)

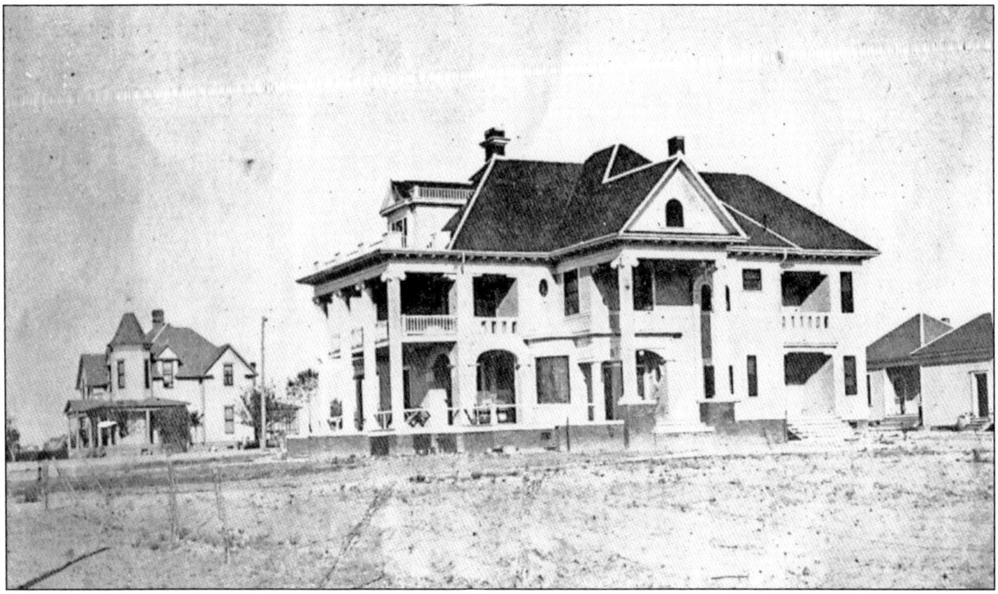

These beautiful houses are still standing in the Angelo Heights area of the city. They were two of the most impressive structures in the new suburban area. This photograph was taken when the house in the foreground was built in 1907. (WTC.)

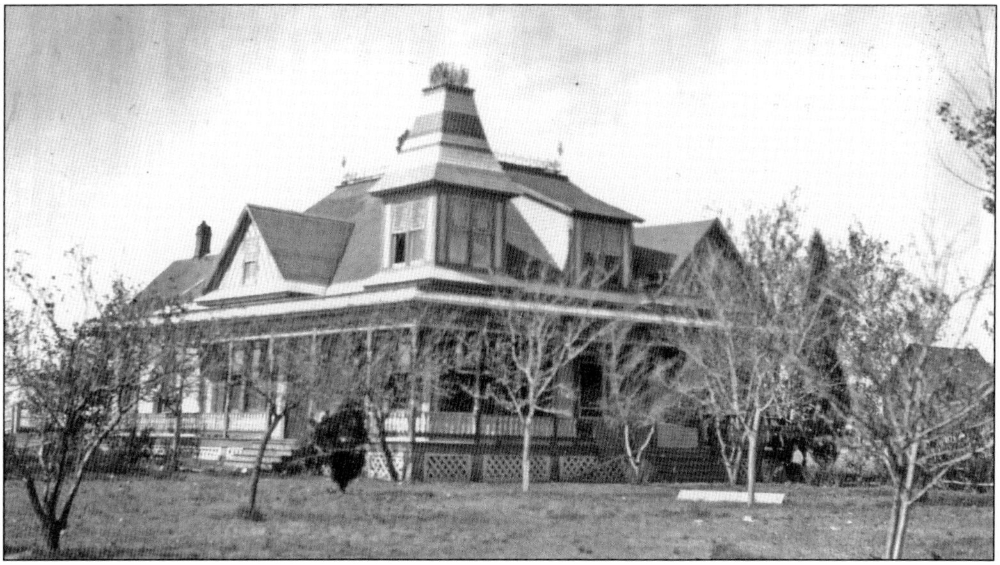

This residence was identified as the Lapowski House. Brothers Sam and Jake Lapowski owned a chain of dry goods stores in West Texas, including the largest such business in San Angelo. Sam and his family left San Angelo in 1903. They decided to Americanize their name to *Dillon*. Sam's grandson C. Douglas Dillon was later US ambassador to France in the Eisenhower administration and treasury secretary under presidents Kennedy and Johnson. (WTC.)

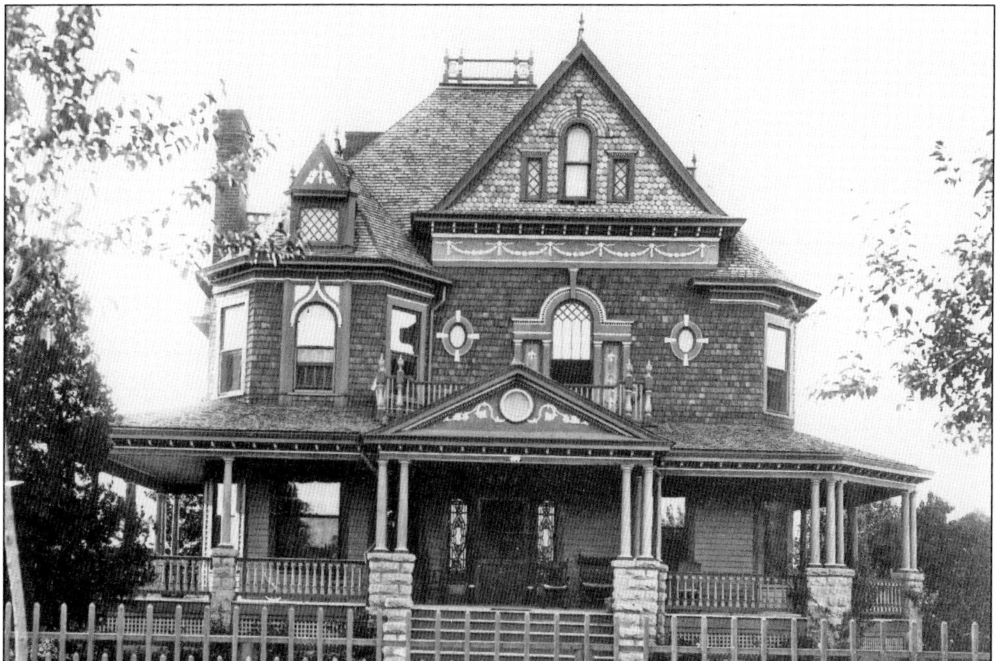

This ornate mansion probably was built by a New Englander named George Bird. He came to San Angelo and got involved in ranching and other livestock enterprises. Bird was a partner of Mortimer Mertz in many of his businesses. Residential architecture in San Angelo clearly showed that substantial profits were to be made in the Concho Valley. (WTC.)

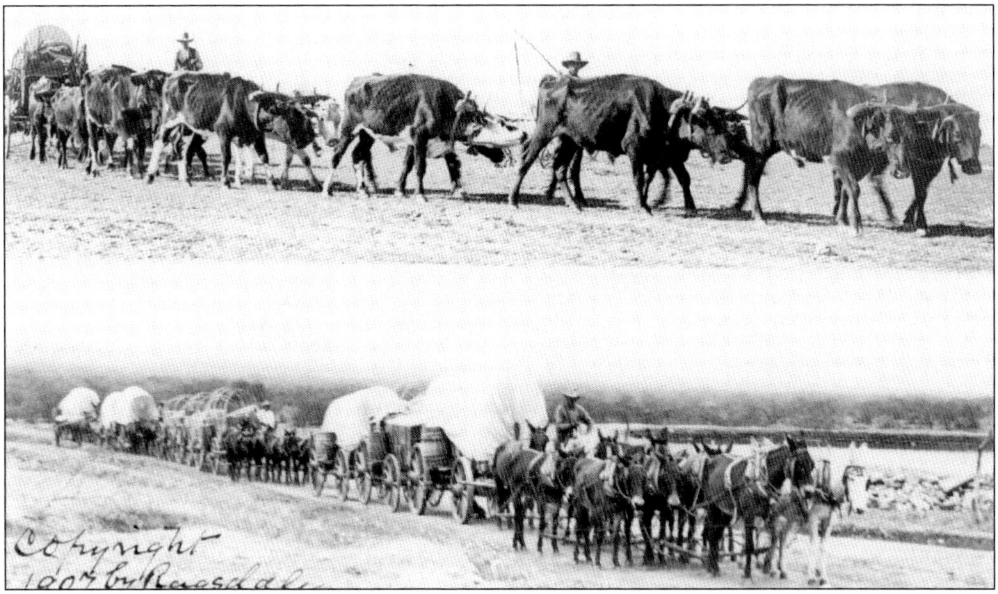

Transportation remained a big issue in San Angelo. Stagecoaches and freight wagons, such as the ones in this photograph, could only bring so much to town in an economical fashion. Building materials were scarce in the Concho Valley, and merchants needed to offer citizens competitively priced merchandise. Local producers needed markets without huge costs. San Angelo needed a railroad, or it would surely fall behind other West Texas cities in growth and development. (FC.)

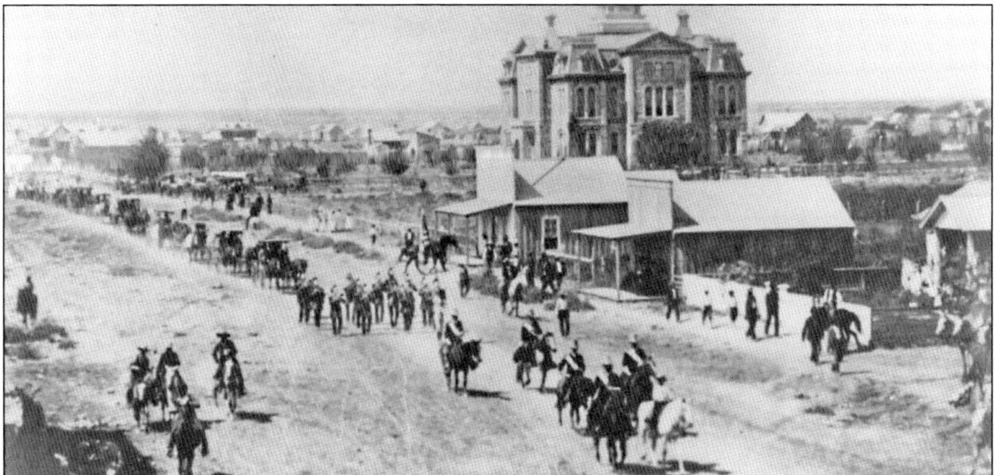

The town finally got a rail link in 1888, when the Gulf, Colorado, and Santa Fe Railway arrived from Ballinger, Texas, 35 miles to the east. The town provided a graded right-of-way as an incentive to entice the Santa Fe to build to San Angelo. Citizens rejoiced at this achievement. On September 17, San Angelo held a celebration. Thousands of citizens met the first engine at the station. The parade pictured here lasted an hour and a half and kicked off other festivities. Later, there were speeches, the firing of cannons, a barbecue dinner, and a street dance that lasted until the early-morning hours. The local newspaper was ecstatic about this development, praising the men who had worked on this deal, which would, the paper claimed, "place San Angelo Ahead of all other Cities in Western Texas." (FC.)

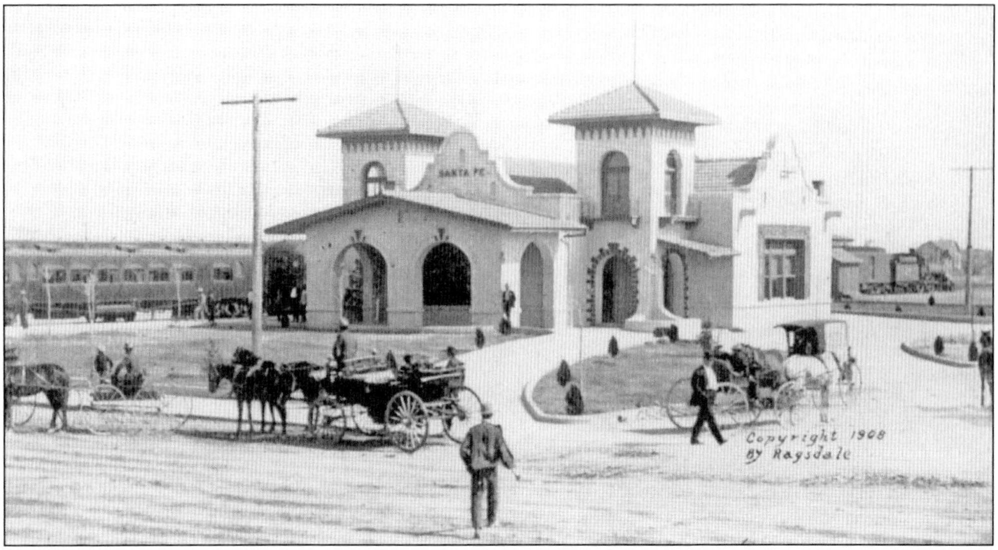

This photograph shows the Santa Fe passenger depot. There is no question that this rail link dramatically changed the town. The population tripled in the next 20 years. San Angelo became a city. (FC.)

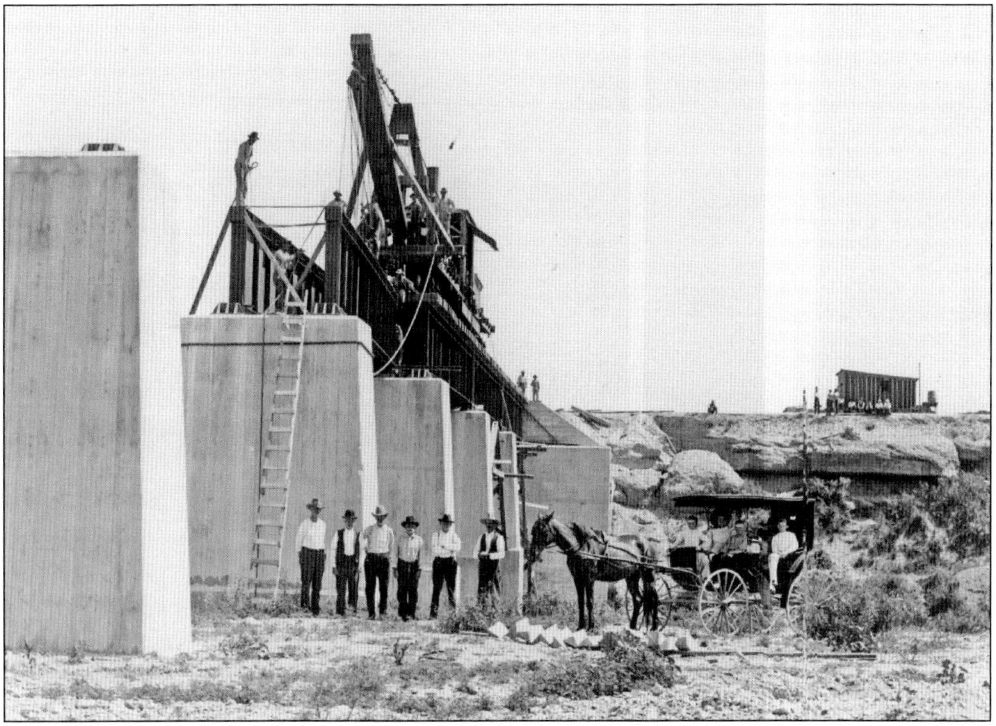

In 1909, a second railroad, the Kansas City, Mexico, and Orient Railway (Orient), came to town. The line originated in Kansas City and ran to Topolobampo, on the western coast of Mexico. San Angelo again donated some right-of-way to make sure the train would not bypass the city. This photograph shows the construction of a railroad bridge across the Concho River. It took many years to complete the line, but this railroad meant much better freight opportunities for local merchants as well as healthy competition and cheaper rates. (FC.)

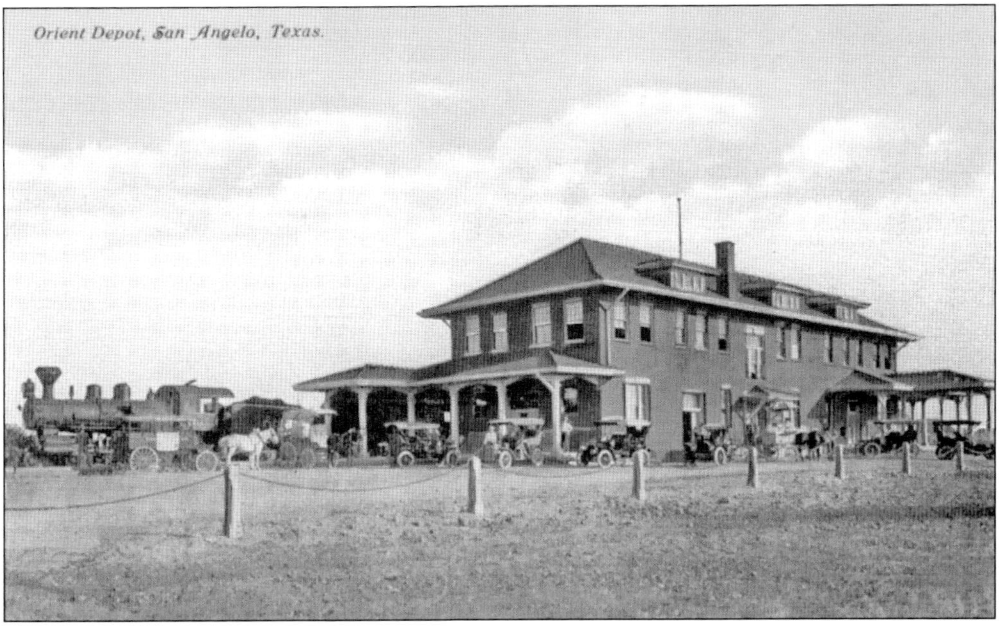

The Orient located the Texas headquarters of the railroad in San Angelo and built this large depot to handle both train traffic and commercial matters. It was the second largest building in San Angelo. In 1928, the Orient sold out to the Santa Fe, and this became the Santa Fe depot. (FC.)

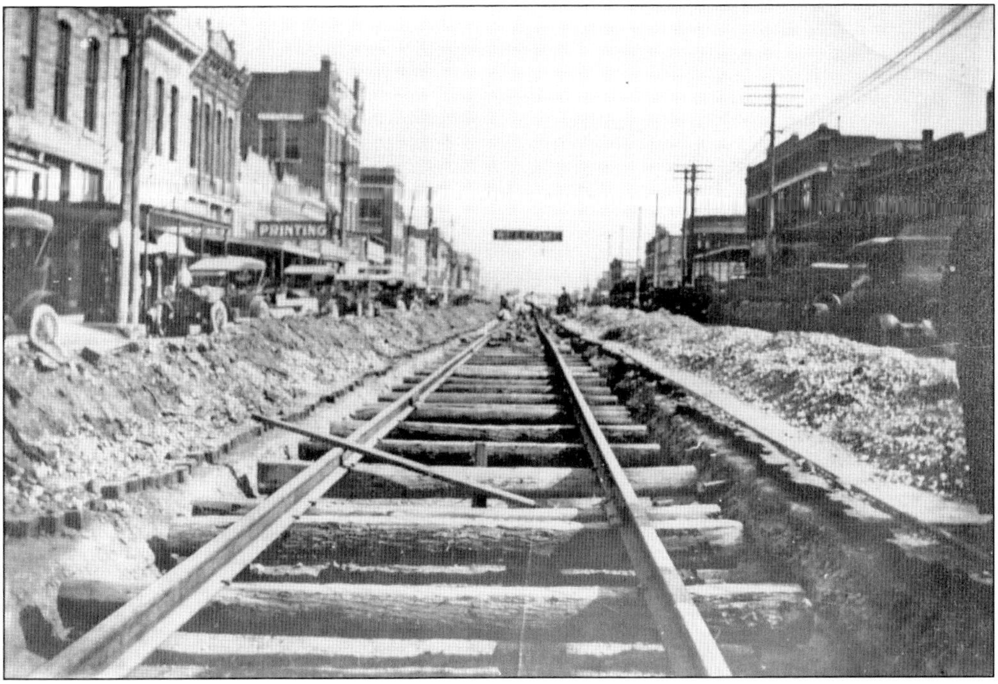

For a brief period, San Angelo had rail transportation within the city. The San Angelo Power and Traction Company received permission from the city government to build a streetcar system. It started at the Landon Hotel downtown and ran three miles north on Chadbourne Street to the fairgrounds and the Lakeview subdivision. Here, the rails are being laid through the town. (FC.)

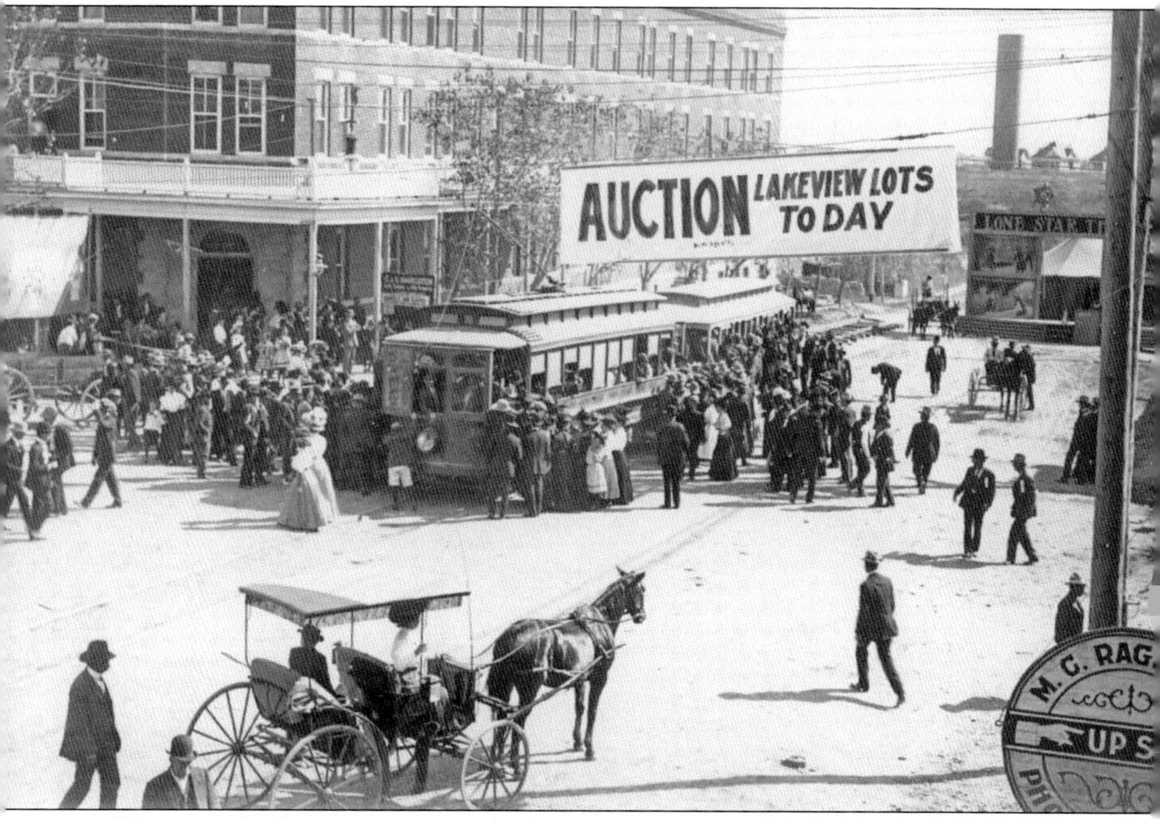

The motive for this project was to make the Lakeview subdivision seem closer and more desirable. Real estate developers were eager to sell more lots, and many in the city considered the construction of such a transportation facility to be a matter of public pride. This photograph, dating from 1908, shows the excitement of the citizenry over this new form of transportation and the land that it opened for development and sale. (FC.)

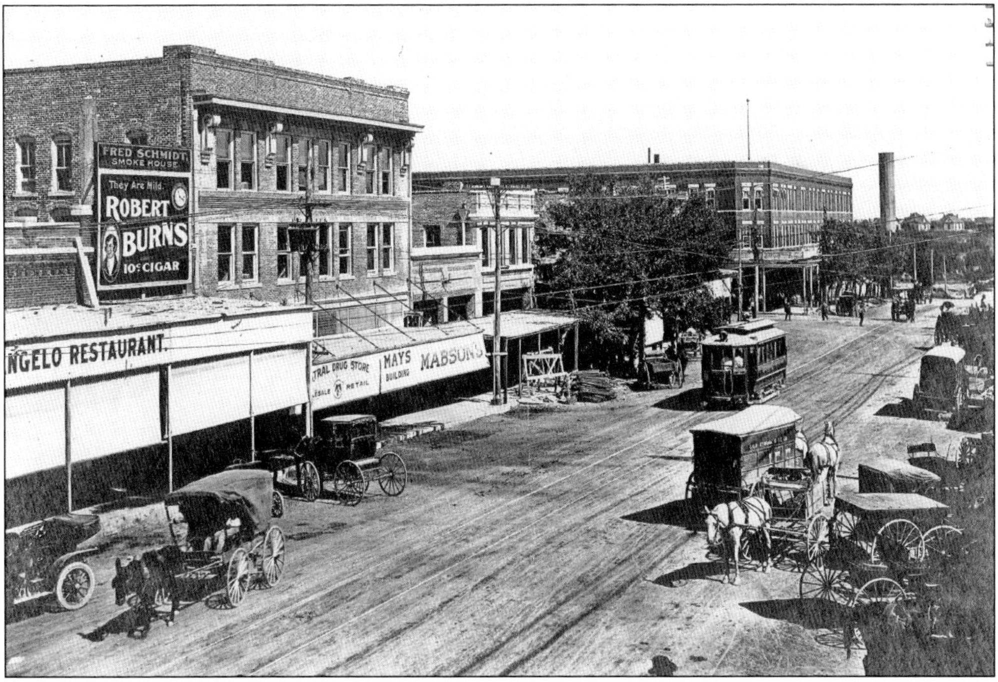

Unfortunately, there was not enough business to make the streetcar company profitable. On a regular day, such as the one pictured here, the car went quietly on its way with very little demand for its seats. The original company failed, reorganization took place, and new lines were added. After a few years of service, the streetcar ceased to operate, and the rails were paved over. (WTC.)

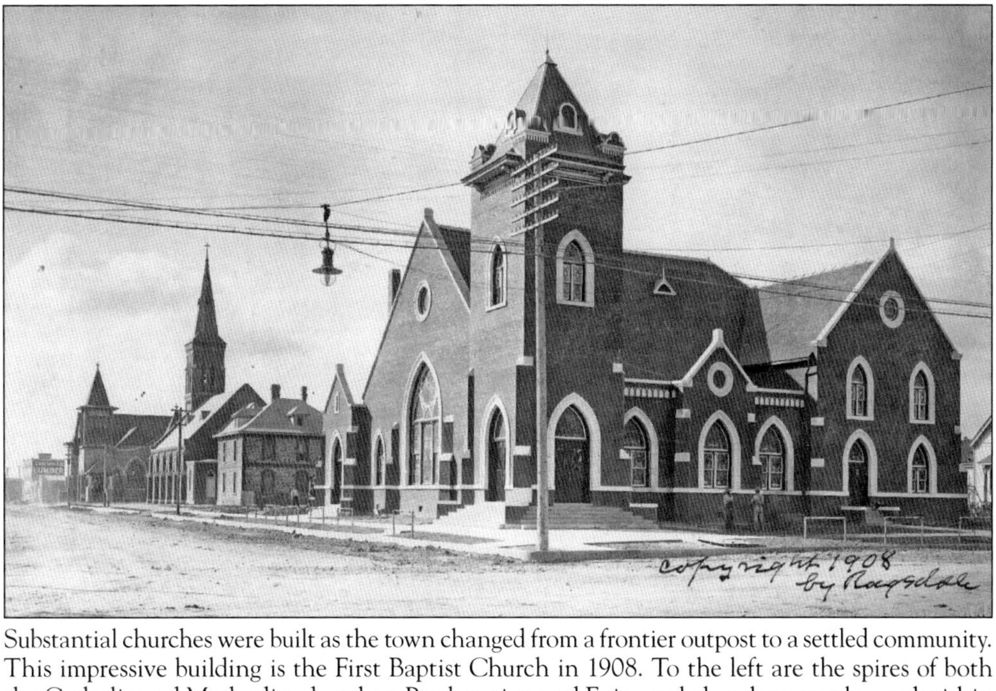

Substantial churches were built as the town changed from a frontier outpost to a settled community. This impressive building is the First Baptist Church in 1908. To the left are the spires of both the Catholic and Methodist churches. Presbyterian and Episcopal churches were located within two blocks. (FC.)

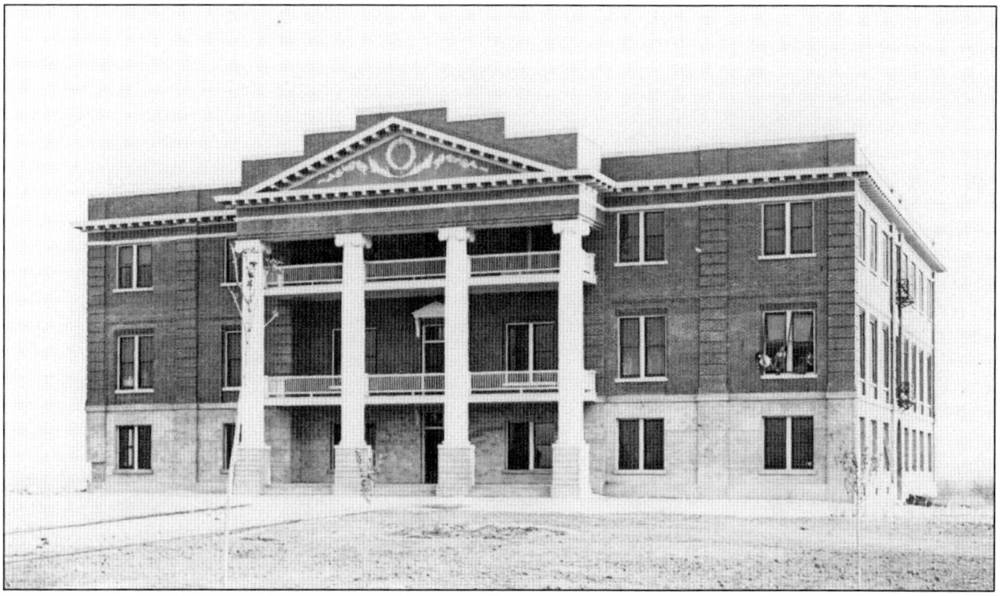

Education was also very important to the community. In the fall of 1885, public schools opened to supplement the many private educational efforts in town. By 1909, the city even offered college classes at the San Angelo Collegiate Institute. (FC.)

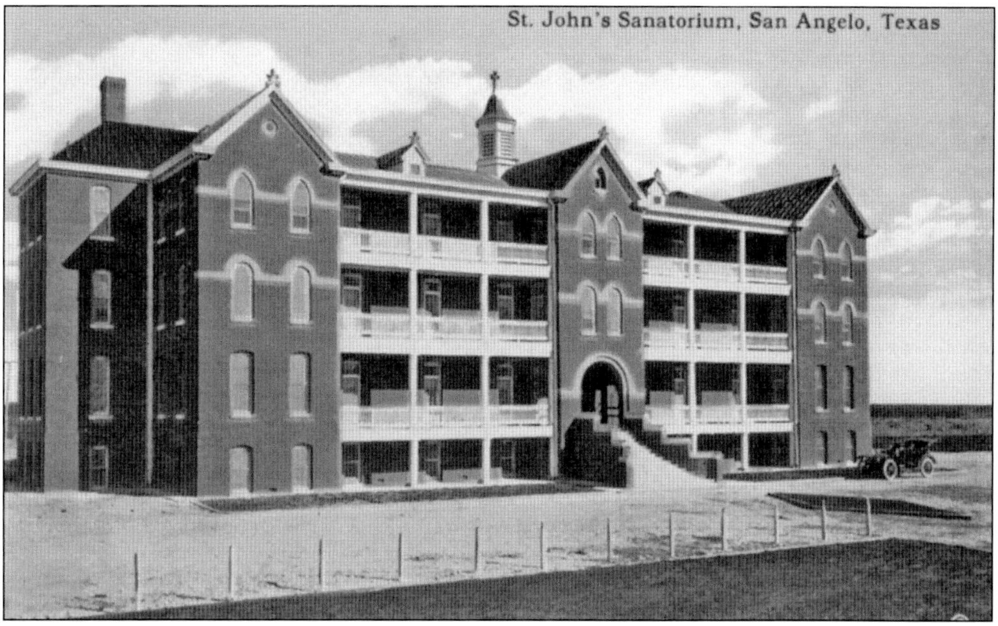

In 1910, St. John's Hospital opened. Dr. S.L.S. Smith worked hard, along with the Sisters of Charity of the Catholic Church, to bring a modern medical facility to town. Before this development, medical care was only available at Fort Concho, local drugstores, and doctor's offices. St. John's had 30 beds, surgical facilities, and dedicated nuns who were trained as nurses. It was the only hospital between San Antonio and El Paso, and it became extremely important for patients in a vast geographic area. (FC.)

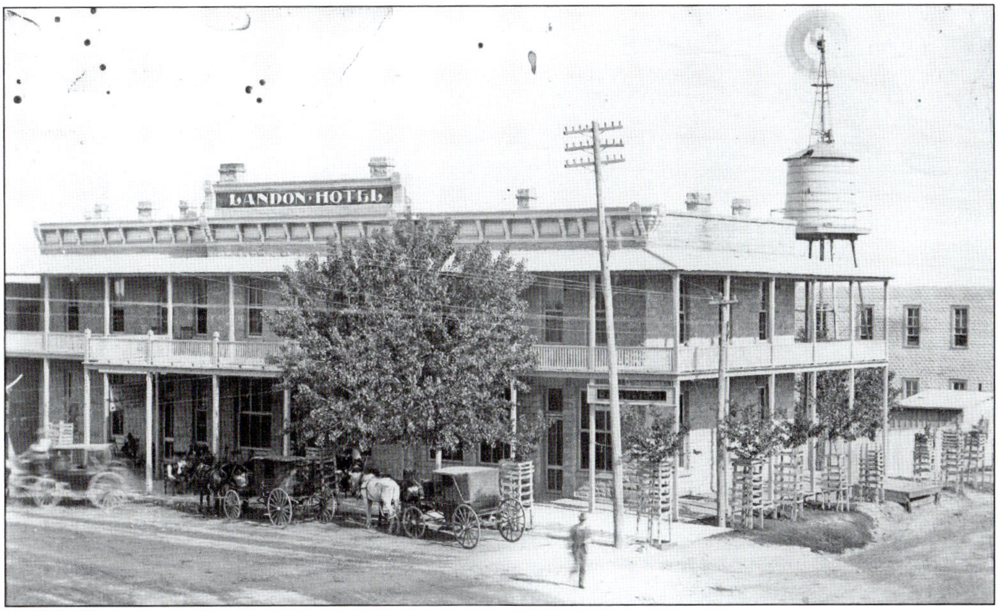

The Landon Hotel was a large, fashionable hotel built in 1899. Oscar Ruffini designed this structure, which was located on Concho Avenue. It was the starting point of the streetcar route to the distant fairgrounds. If a family wanted an elegant dinner in a formal setting, this was the appropriate destination. (FC.)

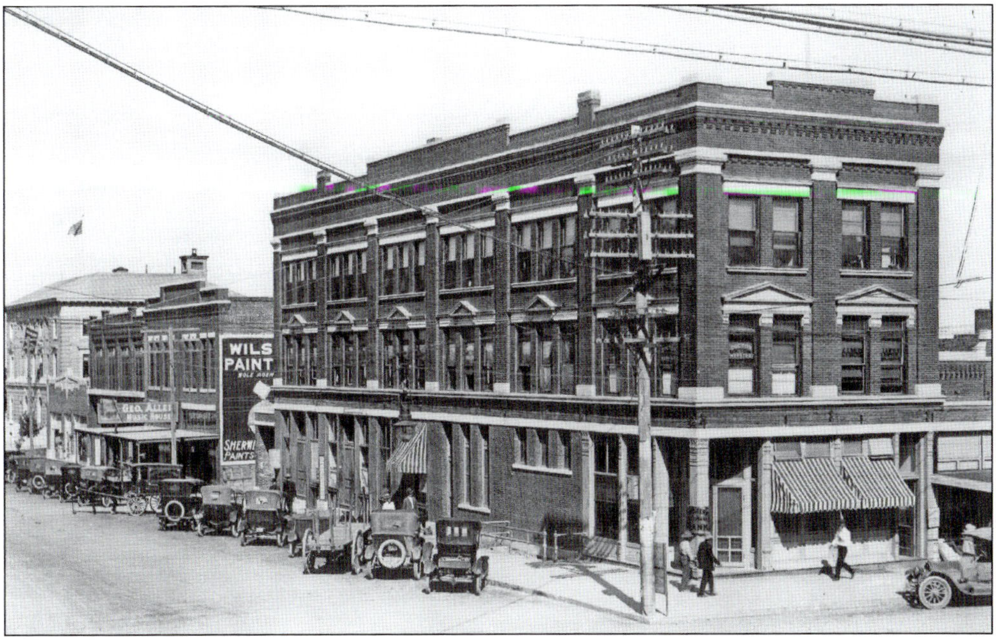

The Guaranty Bank Building pictured here was designed and built by Oscar Ruffini in 1908. It is the largest of Ruffini's buildings left in modern San Angelo. The location is the corner of Chadbourne and Twohig Streets, which led to familiar elements in the design. There are classical decorations on the facade, and there is a strong linear quality in the plan that defines the intersection where it is located. The picket buildings of 1885 were being replaced with substantial and pleasing urban architecture. (WTC.)

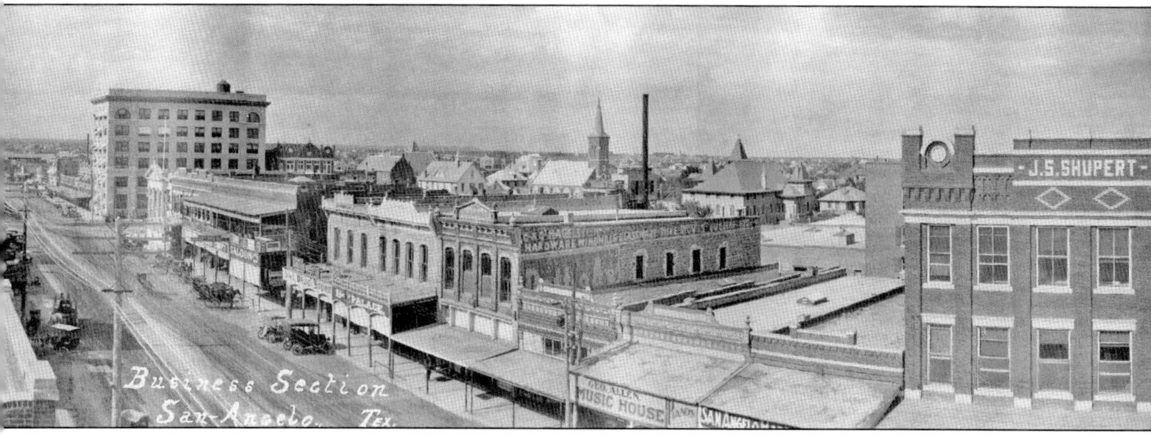

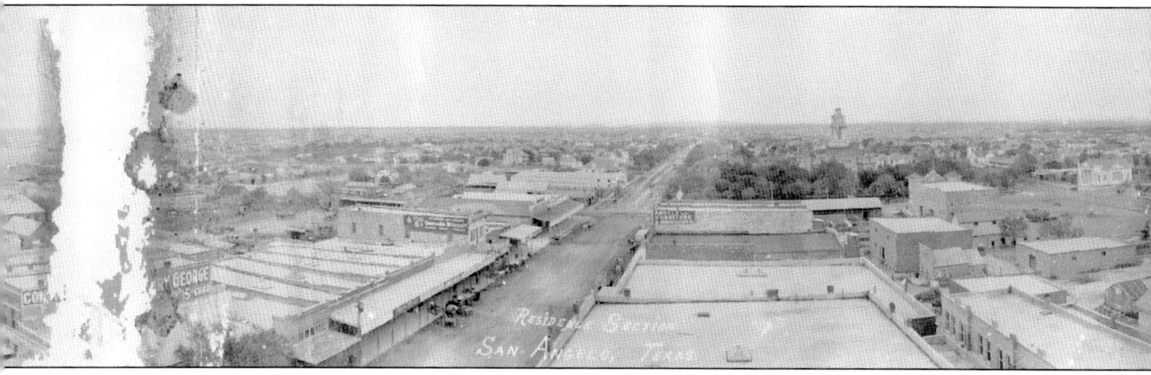

These panoramic views were taken for the chamber of commerce in 1911. (WTC.)

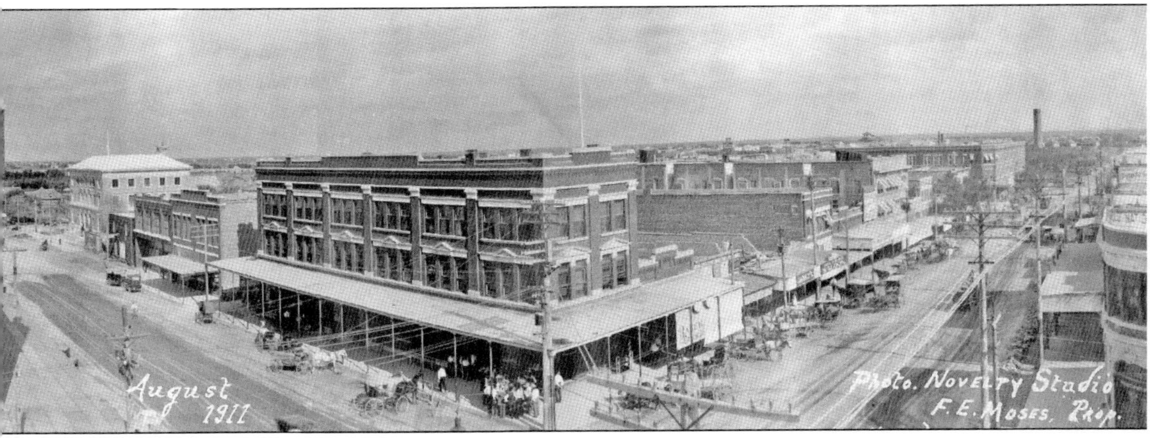
August
1911
Photo. Novelty Studio
F.E. Moses, Prop.

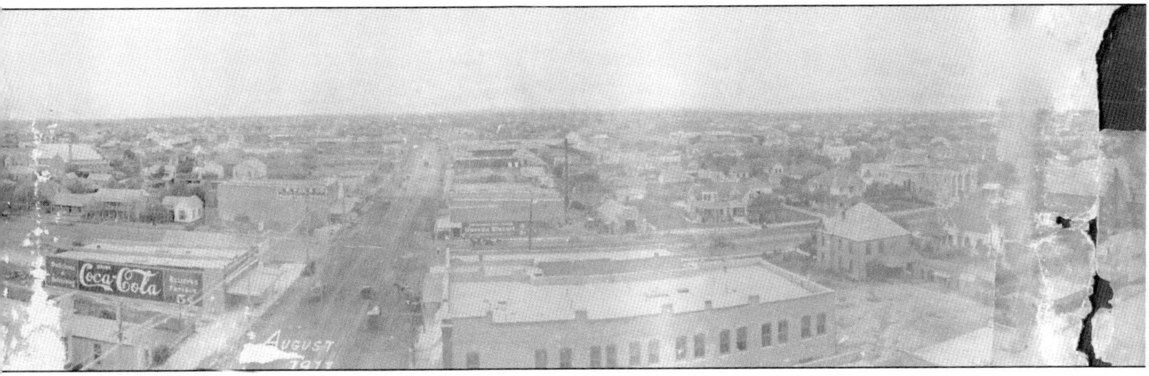
Coca-Cola
August

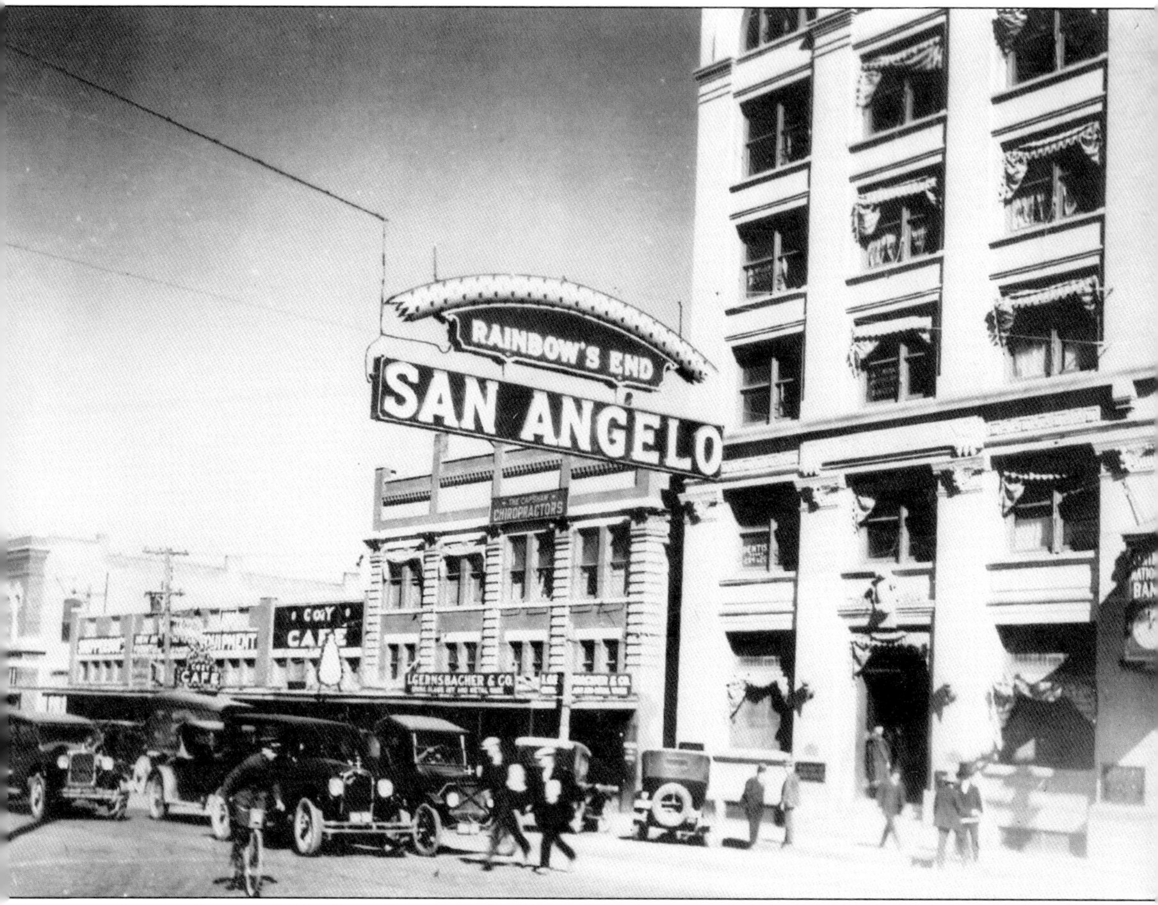

It is understandable that the citizens of San Angelo were optimistic about their city. From 1870 until 1920, San Angelo developed from a rough and raucous frontier outpost to a substantial city. For many years, this banner stretched from the Central National Bank building across Chadbourne Street to proclaim San Angelo the "Rainbow's End." A promotional booklet of this period called the city "The Metropolis of the West in the heart of the Concho Country." The growth of San Angelo was based on agriculture well before oil became an important part of the economy of the region. Boosters, health-seekers, adventurers, town builders, soldiers, visionaries, investors, risk takers, and hard workers of all types made this happen. No one thought the city would fail, and they were correct. (WTC.)

Four

The Rich Tapestry of a Frontier City

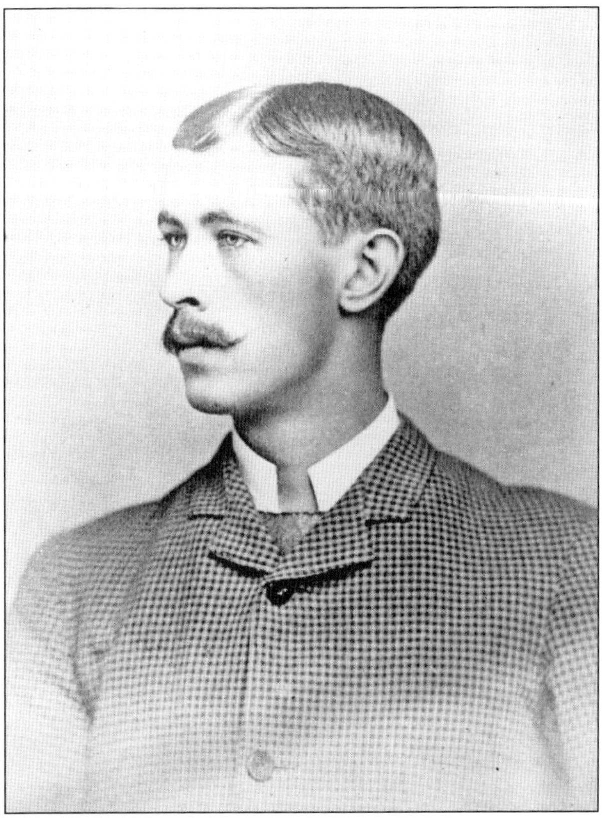

The American West attracted a variety of people who produced a unique community in every town and city. John Loomis, pictured here, came from Syracuse, New York, to the Concho Valley in order to ranch. In his memoirs, he called San Angelo "a picturesque place with its strange mixture of people. Such an assortment could only be found near an old frontier post. White and black, soldiers, gamblers, gunmen, cowboys, ranchmen and business men composed its cosmopolitan population. Men had come from all over the United States and foreign countries. There were the educated and those who could not read. . . . I always had the feeling that I was at the jumping off place, near a little known or entirely unknown country, a delightful feeling." (WTC.)

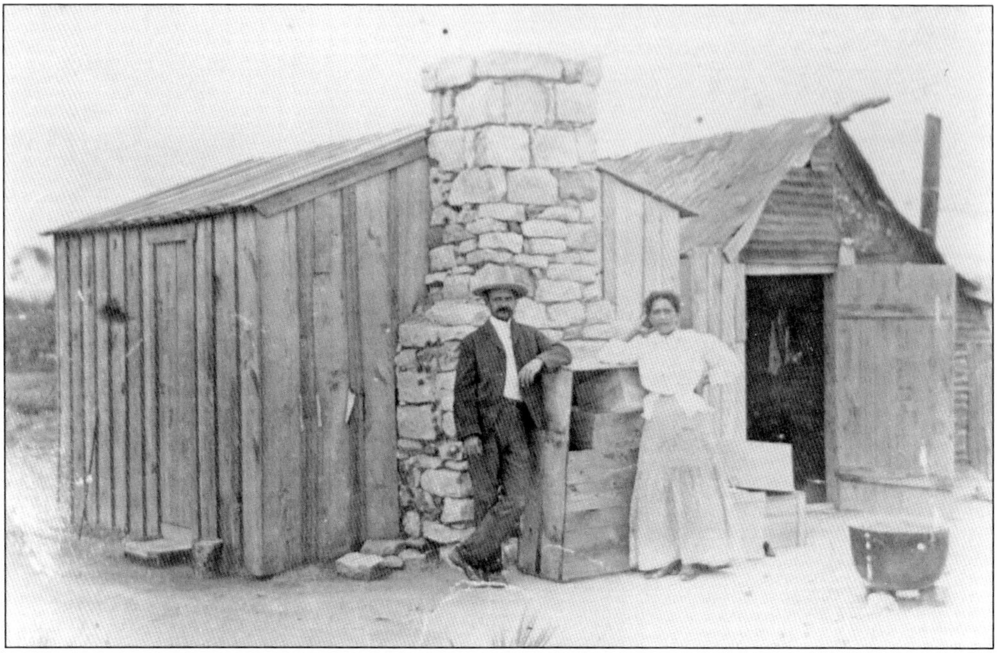

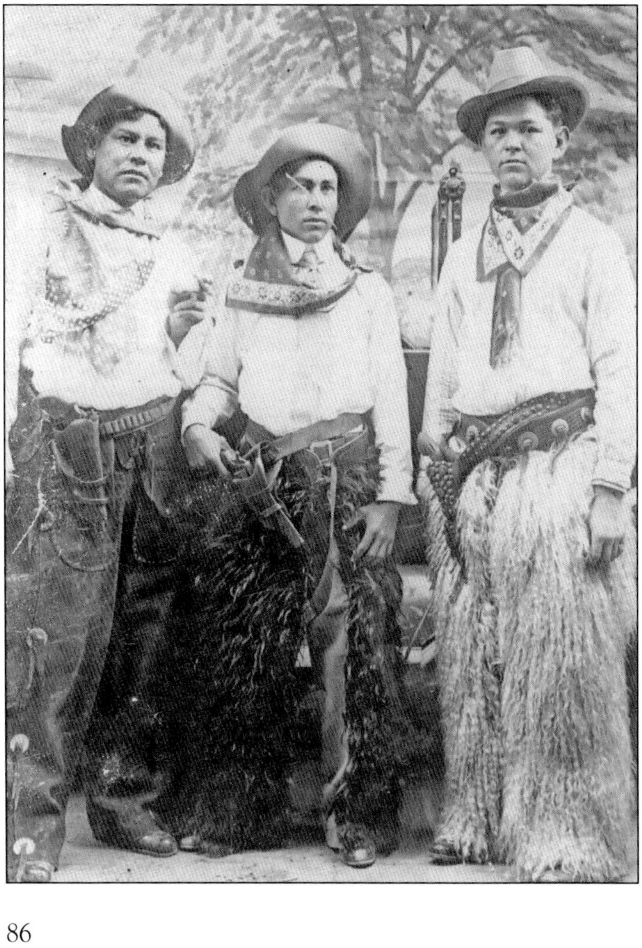

Large numbers of people of Spanish or Mexican heritage came to the Concho Valley searching for work and prosperity. The 1880 Census figures show that 24 percent of the population of 3,609 people had Hispanic surnames. Mr. and Mrs. Manuel Morales can be seen in this picture posed outside of their house. (FC.)

There were many Hispanic cowboys and sheepherders in the area; indeed, many of the ranching methods in Texas were derived from Spanish and Mexican traditions and practices. In this photograph are three proud cowboys coming to the Ragsdale studio to have a portrait made, a practice common to cowboys all over the West. Hispanics worked on the Bismarck Farm and did many other agricultural jobs in the Concho Valley. San Angelo could not have developed as it did without their labors. (FC.)

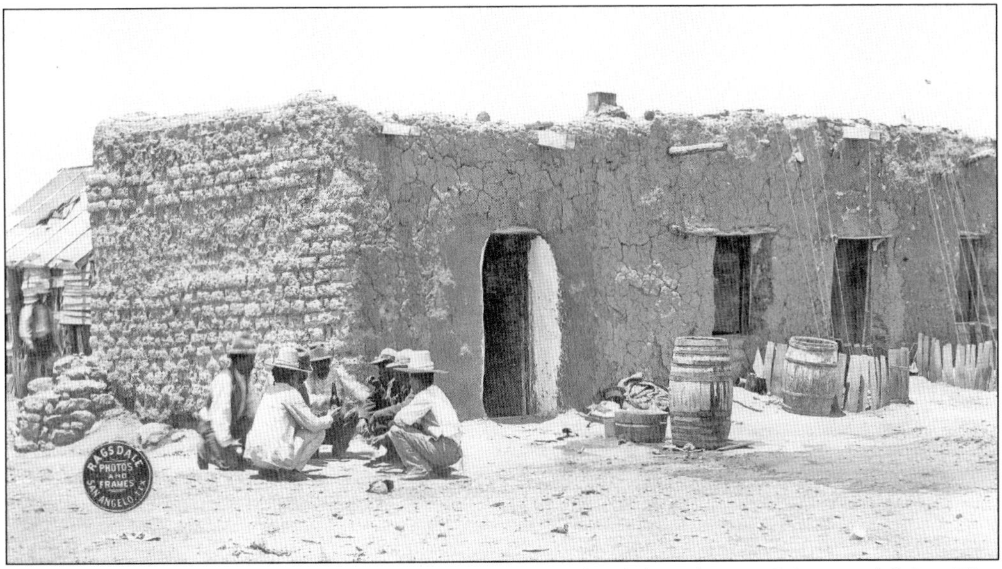

The photographer M.C. Ragsdale titled the photograph of these houses *Mexican Adobes*. The adobe architectural tradition came with the Hispanic population. These homes were inexpensive to build and a bit rough, but one can clearly sense that there was a vibrant Hispanic community residing there. (FC.)

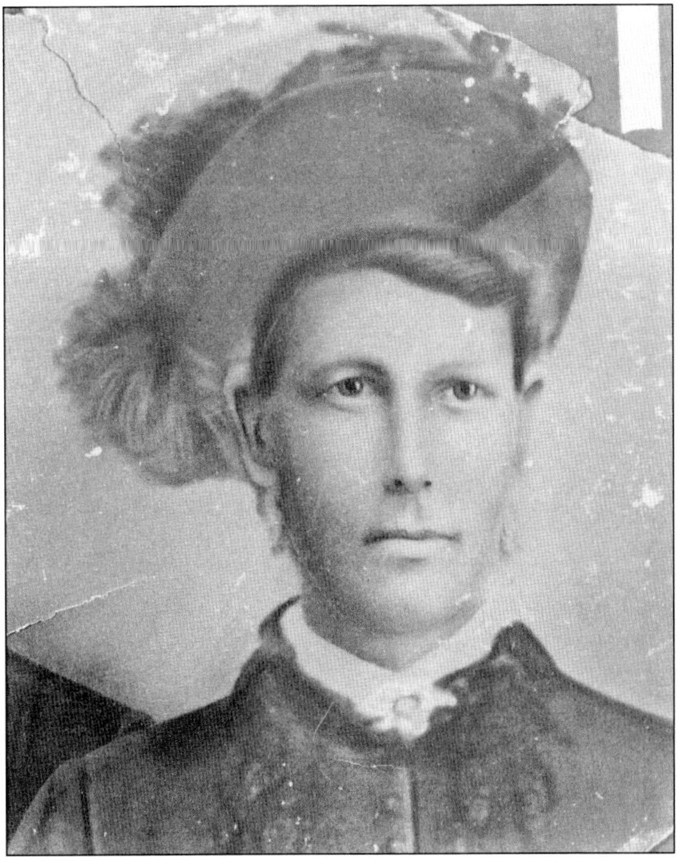

Many of the Latinos in San Angelo purchased land and established businesses. Pablo Alderette came to San Angelo from New Mexico and bought a farm consisting of several hundred acres. He served on the first Tom Green County Commission, and he was a justice of the peace. In addition to political influence, Alderette was socially prominent in San Angelo. He married Ramona, pictured here, the widow of a wealthy San Antonio German. His stepdaughter Catalina Wuertemberg married W.S. Veck in 1872. The Alderette family was definitely bicultural. (WTC.)

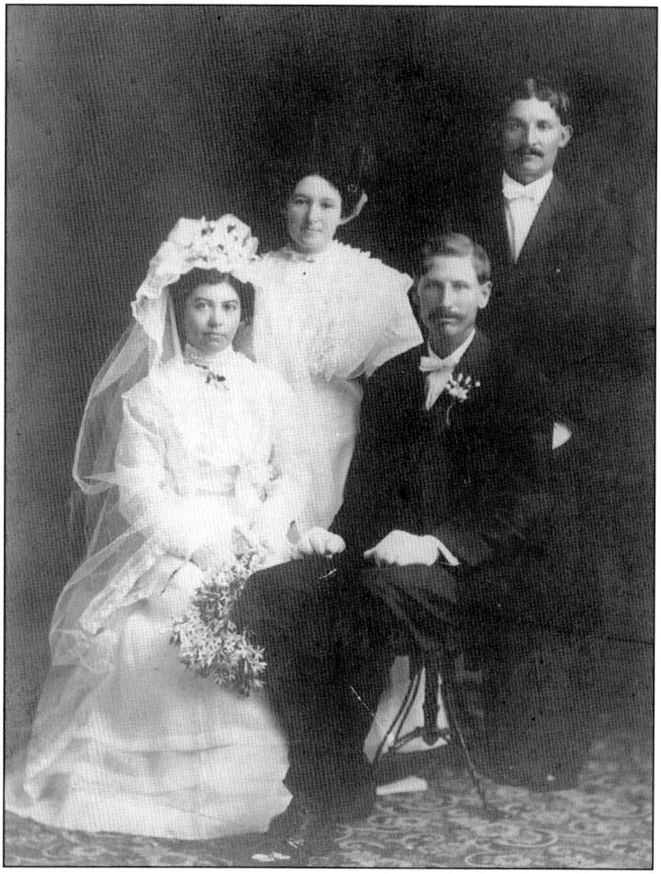

Raymond Camunez Jr. and Josefa Lara were married in 1909. The Camunez family originally came to San Angelo from New Mexico. Reynaldo Camunez Sr. worked at Bismarck Farm, formed a truck farm with several Chinese partners, sold supplies to Fort Concho, and started a freighting business, which operated throughout West Texas. When he was old enough, the junior Camunez worked with his father in these enterprises. Raymond Jr. and Josefa's daughter Eva was born in 1911. She would work as a teacher and a school principal and ultimately become one of the most respected philanthropists in the history of San Angelo.

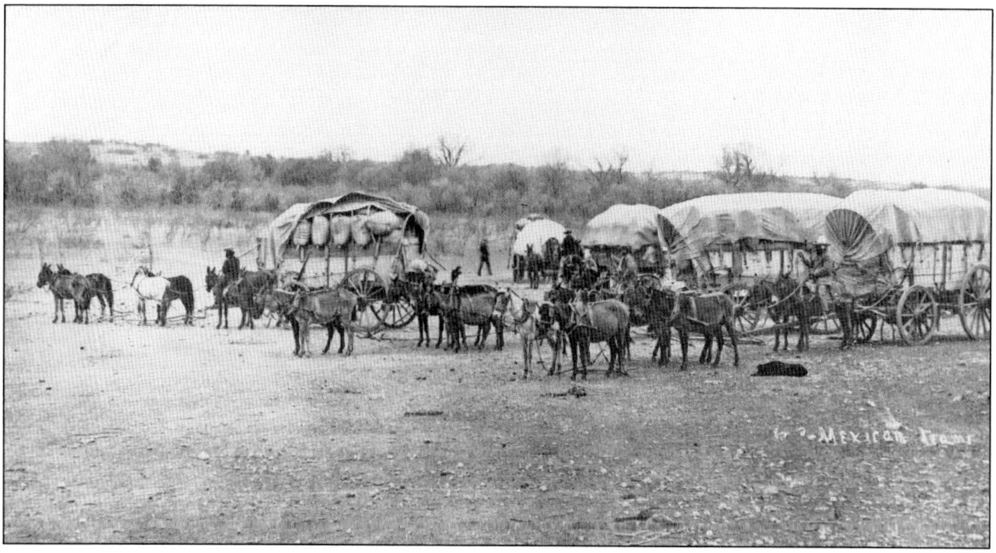

Hispanic entrepreneurs were common in the transportation business, as this photograph of "Mexican Teams" suggests. Shearing crews, saloons, and other businesses in town were Hispanic owned. Opportunities abounded in San Angelo for those formerly living south of the Rio Grande River. (FC.)

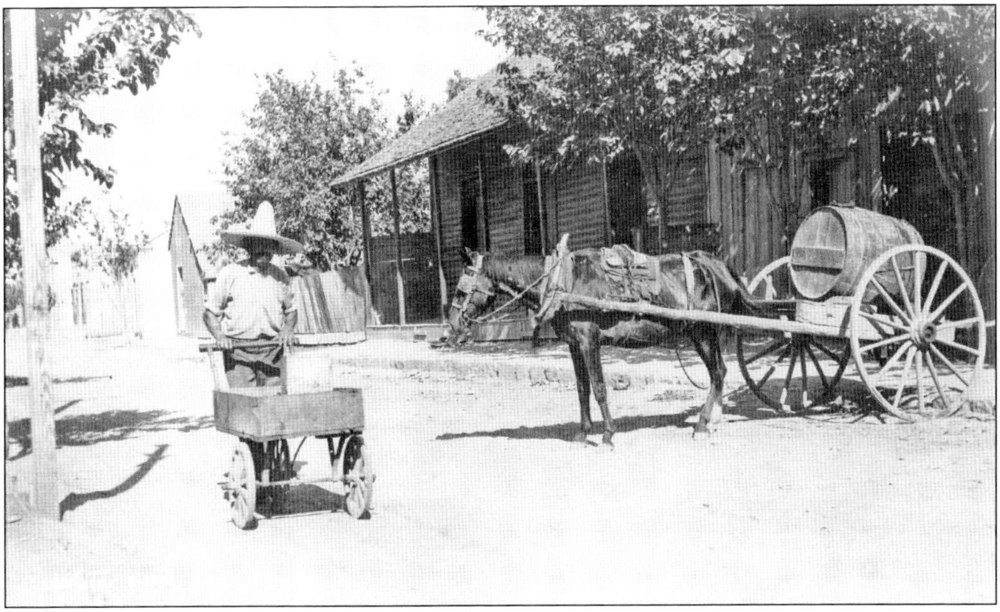

In this photograph, the pointed hat worn by the gentleman pushing the ice cream wagon strongly suggests that the vendor was Hispanic. On the right is a water wagon. Many small businesses were created by individual operators selling items such as wood, hay, or food. (FC.)

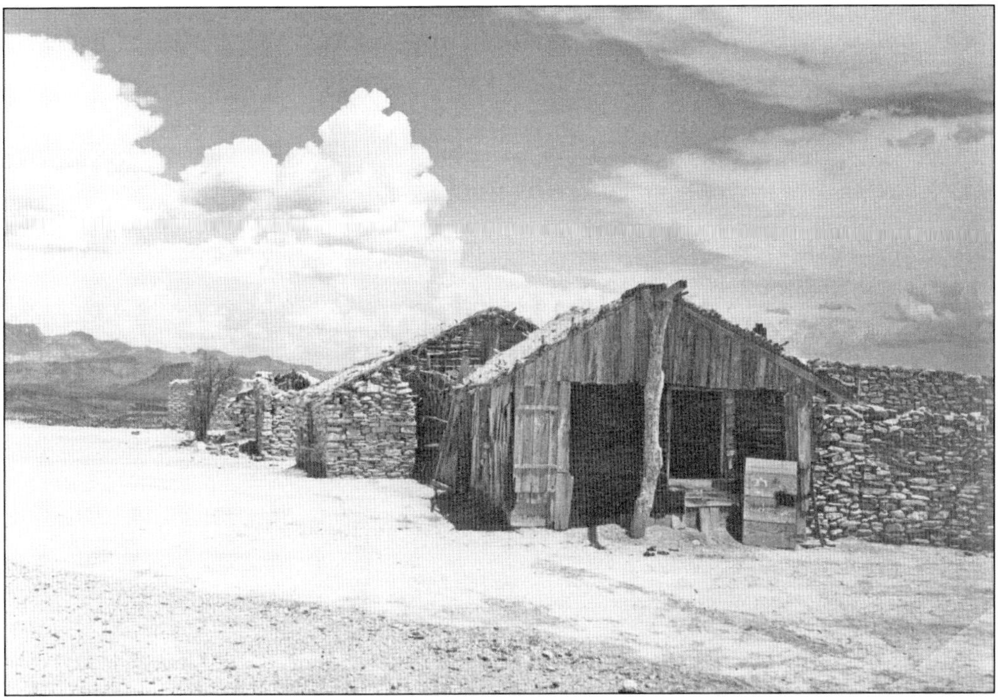

This photograph is titled *Mexican homes near Fort Concho circa 1895*. These structures were located close to the Oak Street Bridge on the same side of the river as Fort Concho. In his book *San Angelenos*, Prof. Arnoldo DeLeon writes that Hispanics in early San Angelo would lose political rights and live in more segregated settings as time passed by and the city population increased. (FC.)

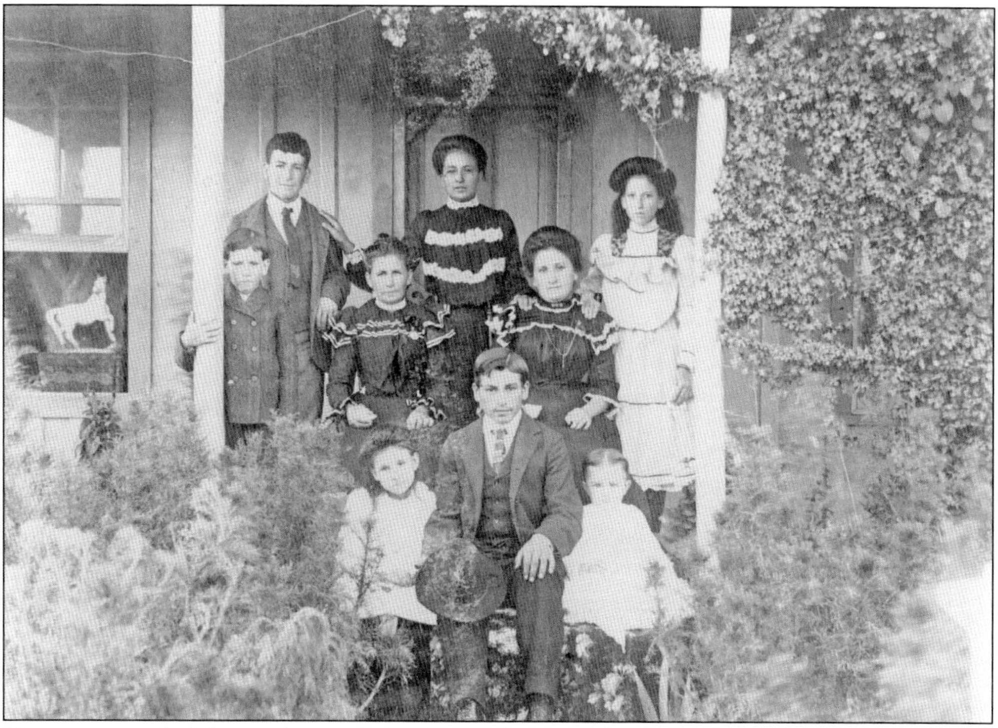

Here, one sees the Thomas Bastardo family members posed in front of their home. The Hispanic population in the Concho Valley faced hardships, but many Latinos were substantial citizens who made a good life for themselves. The census data from 1910 and 1920 indicates that residents with Hispanic surnames composed a smaller percentage of the population than was the case in 1880. They were still a significant part of the demographic tapestry of San Angelo and continued to make major contributions to regional development. (FC.)

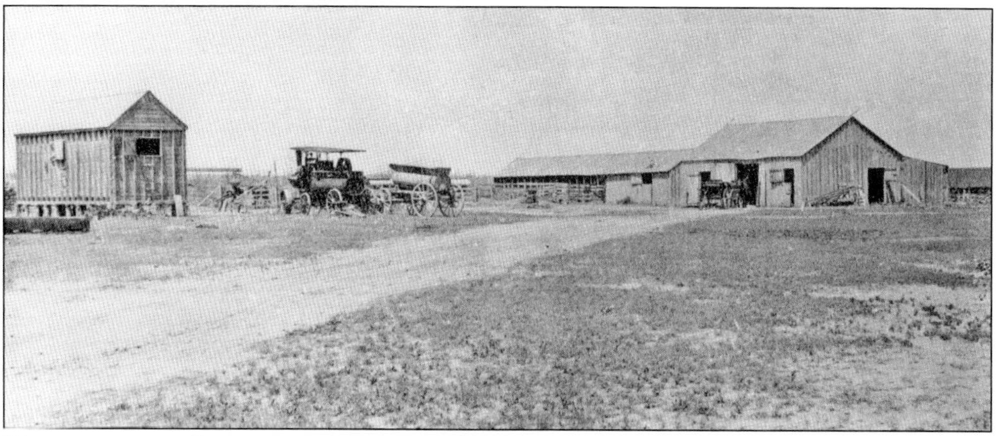

There were many European immigrants and European traditions that were important in early San Angelo. A large number of German Texans ranched in the Concho Valley and beyond. The stone buildings at the fort were the work of German stonecutters from San Antonio and Fredericksburg. Established to provide fresh produce for Fort Concho, the Bismarck Farm was founded by Jacob G. Marshall, Gustav Schleicher, Gustav Hoffman, and Abijah Bayless. The business was named Bismarck in honor of Otto von Bismarck, the so-called "Iron Chancellor of Germany." This picture shows several buildings on the farm. (WTC.)

George Richardson was one of the most important businessmen in the Concho Valley. He owned a very large sheep ranch, a wool warehouse, and a commission agency. Richardson was from Scotland. The traditional dress he is wearing in this portrait livened many parties in West Texas. (WTC.)

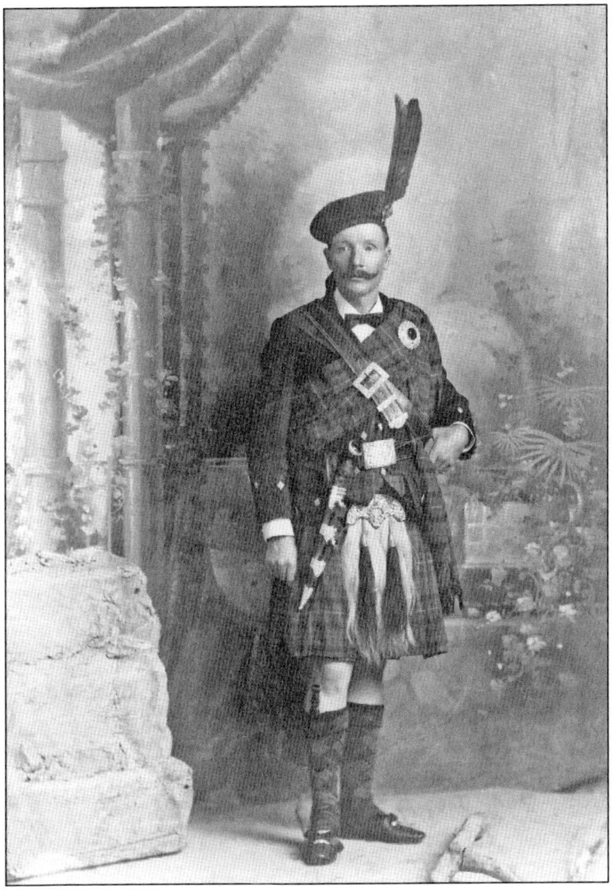

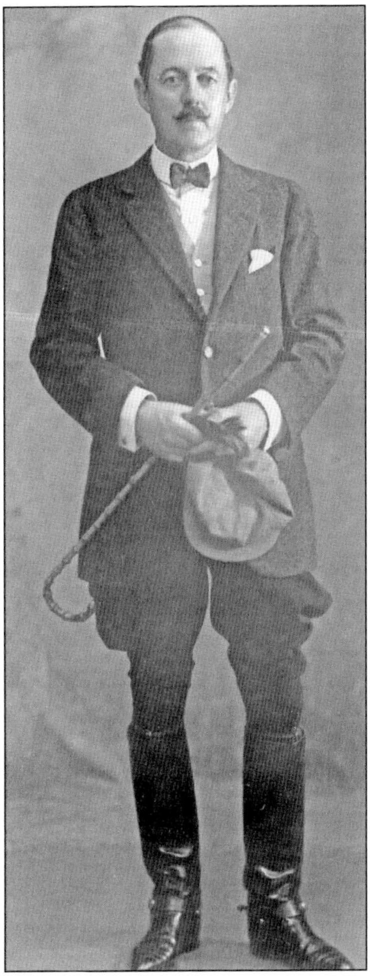

William Anson and his brothers brought the traditions and civility of the English nobility to the Concho Valley. The Ansons were very popular with area residents. (FC.)

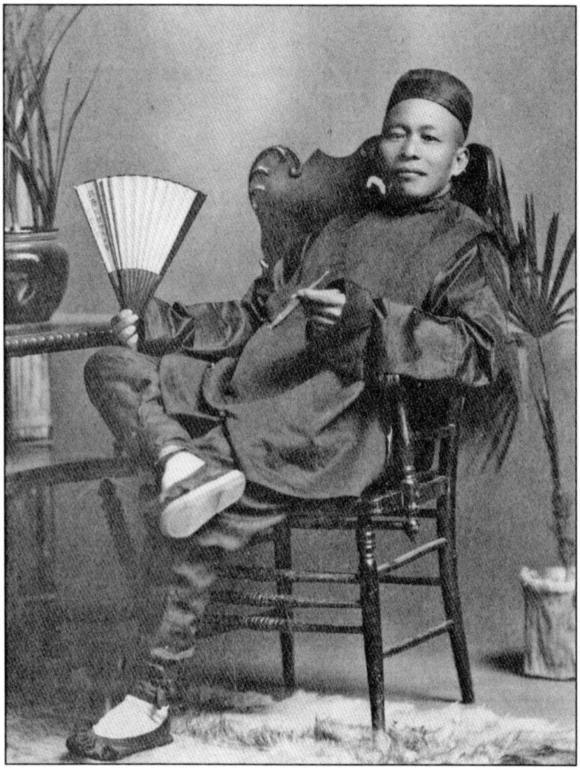

Ali Saru is the gentleman in this photograph. There were several Chinese businesses on Concho Avenue in early San Angelo. Nothing is known about the role Saru played in early San Angelo, but he had his picture taken here and that alone confirms an Asian thread in the San Angelo tapestry. (WTC.)

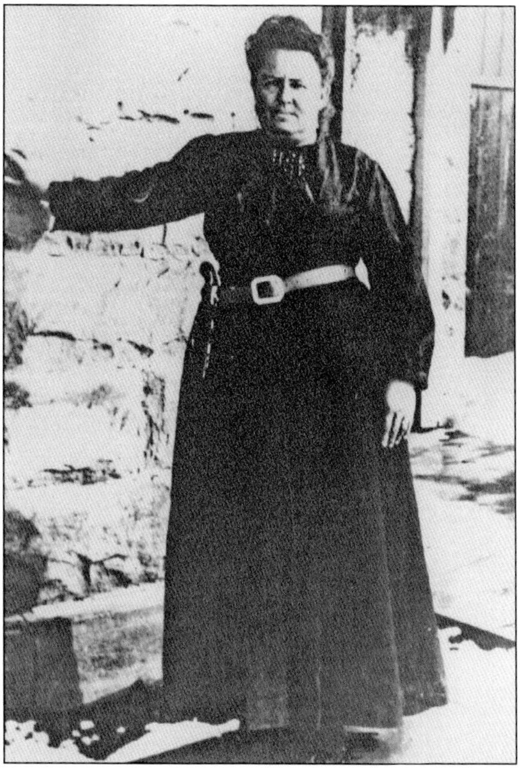

The women of the Concho Valley were as varied as the men, establishing their own traditions and leaving a definite mark on the area. This lady with a pistol on her hip was the wife of a local sheriff. Mrs. Pat Conway looks as if she is ready to take on all comers as she helps tame the West. (WTC.)

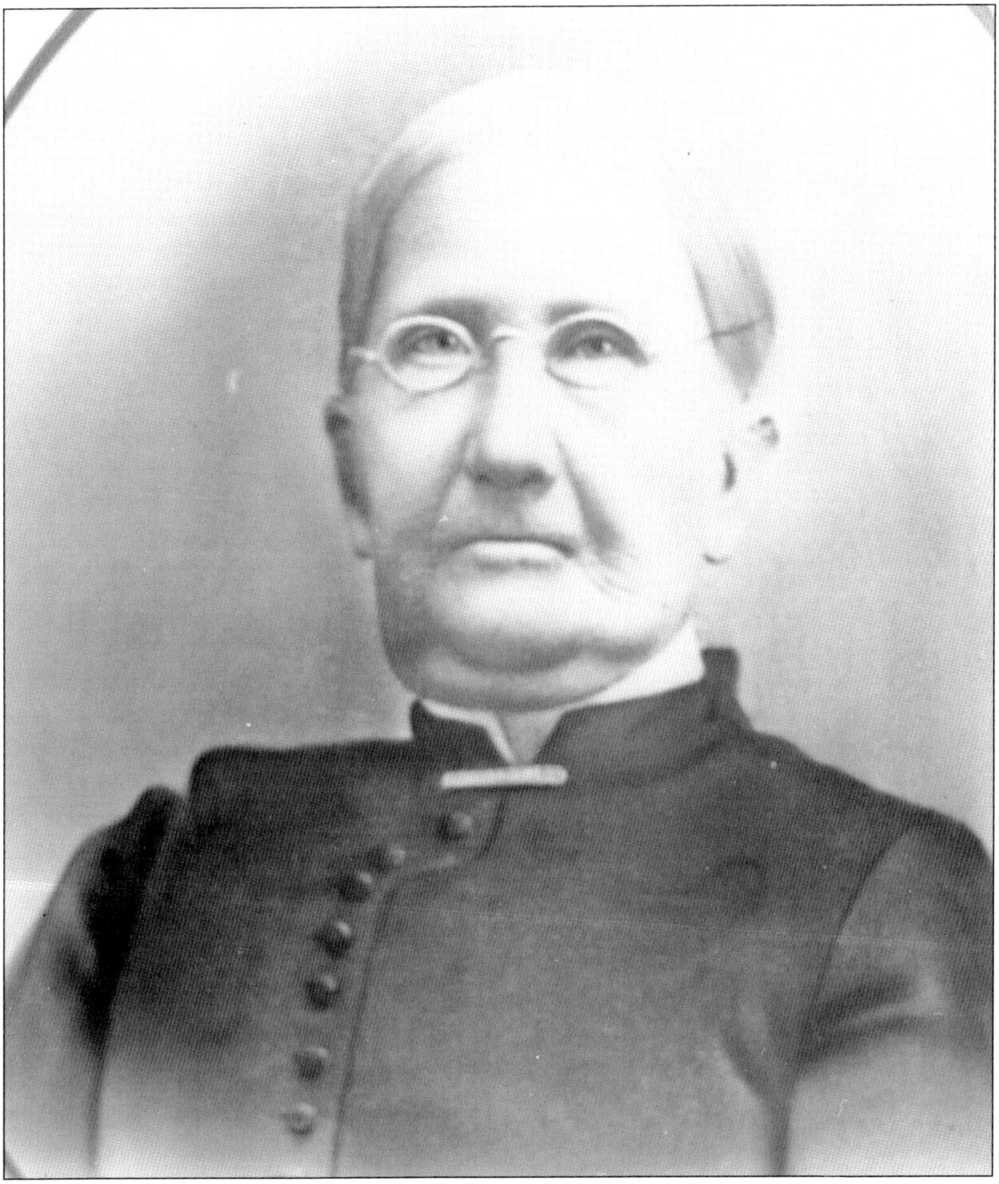

Annie Tankersley was a fabulous character. She was a wealthy Southern girl who married R.F. Tankersley and became one of the first settlers in the Concho Valley. As a ranch wife, she befriended local Indians and raised six children with a rifle close at hand to take care of anyone with hostile intent. After 30 years of marriage, she left R.F. and moved to San Angelo. Later, she would run the Concho House Hotel. Annie successfully faced down angry soldiers who wanted to shoot up her property during the McCarthy episode, took the almost unheard of step of filing for divorce from her husband, and faced down her ex-husband on the streets of San Angelo and demanded the $10,000 he owed her. She was also a devoted churchgoer and philanthropist known for her compassion and nursing ability. (FC.)

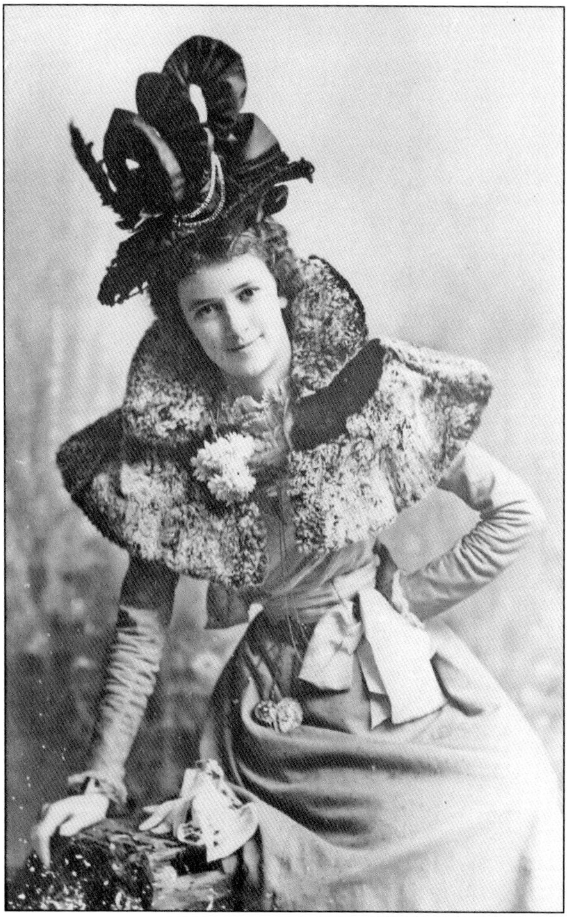

Addie Runyon worked in a local dry goods store. She was obviously fashion conscious. One of the demands made of late-19th-century women was the wasp waist, and Runyon surely had one of the smallest midsections anywhere. (WTC.)

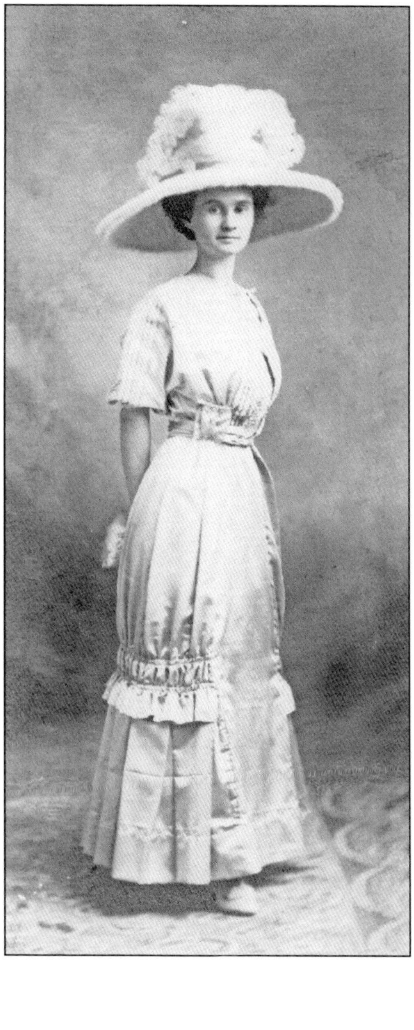

This unidentified lady was somewhat more restrained in her choice of how one should dress for a portrait. She wore this demure hobble skirt and plumed hat when she was photographed in 1910. (FC.)

Some girls were beauty queens. In this photograph is Helen Ragsdale, the photographer's daughter, when she was crowned queen of San Angelo. The Ragsdale family was very active in the life of San Angelo. Local archives have many pictures of their Christmas celebrations, their trips, and many other activities. M.C. Ragsdale left behind an interesting record of family life at the turn of the century. (FC.)

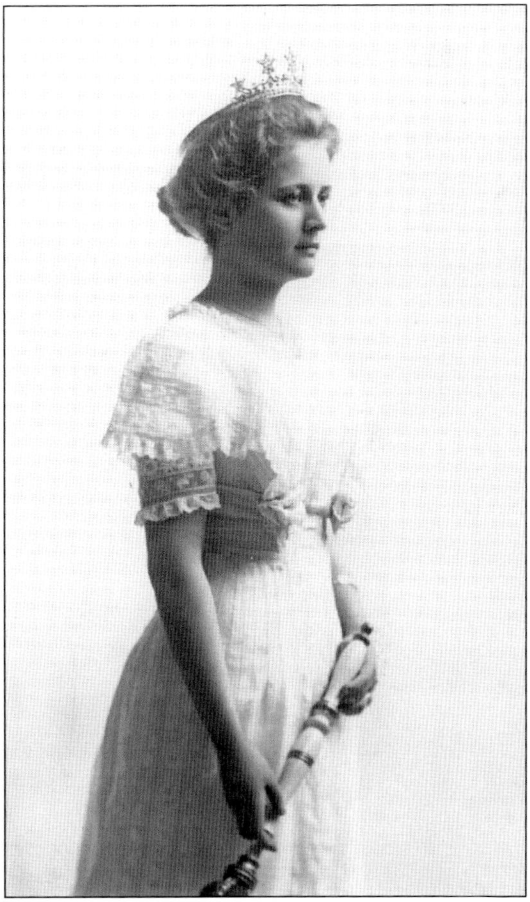

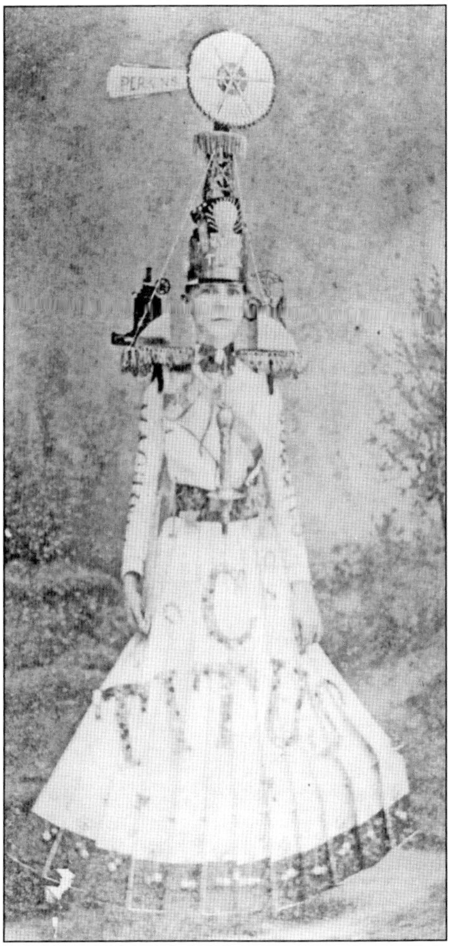

There were working girls of all types in San Angelo. While many of the women employed in town were prostitutes, their pictures have not survived. But women were also teachers, nurses, business owners, nannies, cooks, shop clerks, ranchers, and laundresses. This is a picture of Corinne Baker Wingfield advertising Titus Windmills. (FC.)

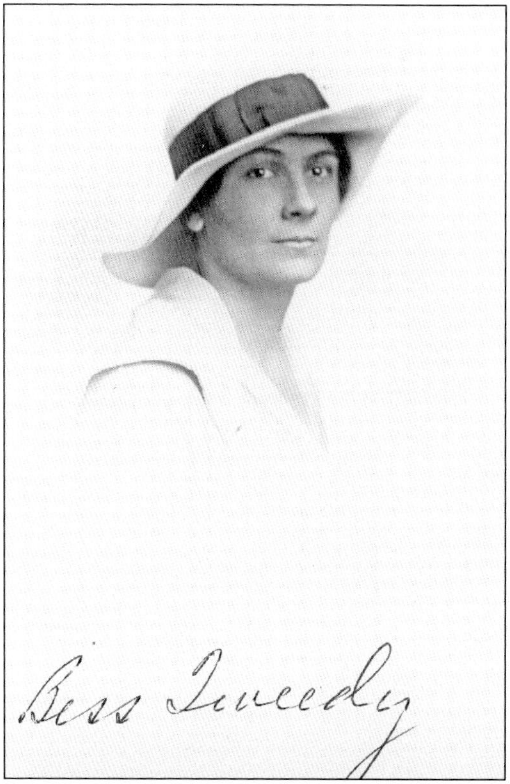

Bess Tweedy was the only daughter of Joseph Lord Tweedy, who settled in Knickerbocker. As she grew up, Bess learned about horses and cattle and sheep, but she did not make a living with her knowledge. Instead, she married Morgan Flowers and moved to California. He was a polo player and taught movie stars who needed to know how to ride or play the game of polo. (FC.)

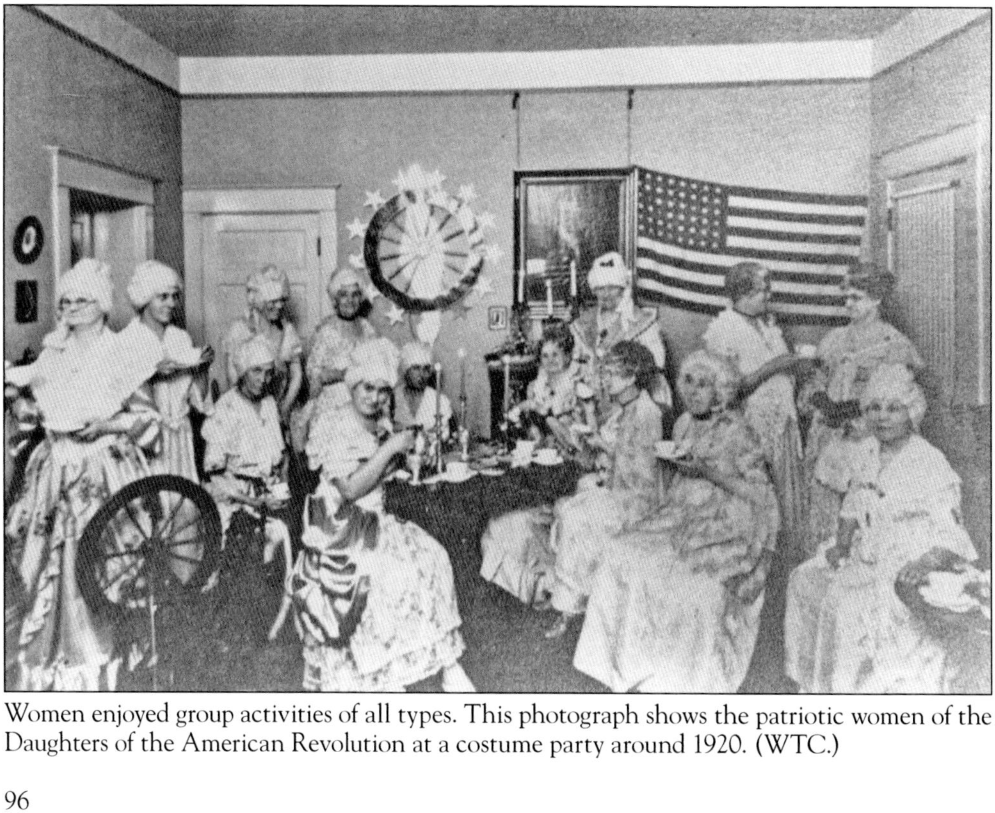

Women enjoyed group activities of all types. This photograph shows the patriotic women of the Daughters of the American Revolution at a costume party around 1920. (WTC.)

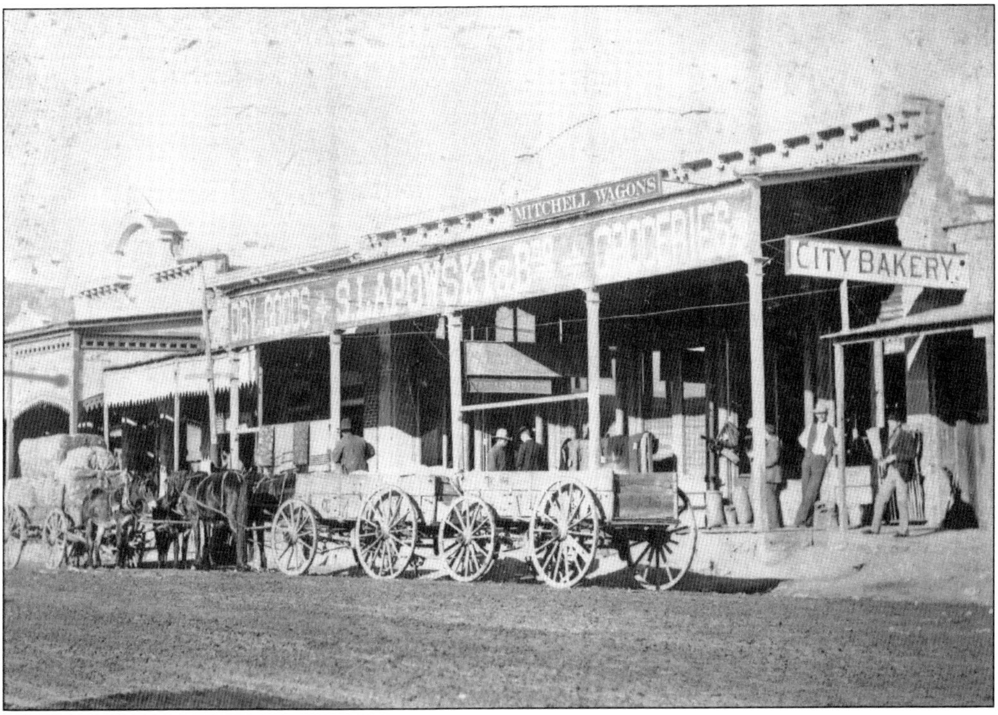

Jewish merchants were prominent in San Angelo as well as in surrounding communities such as Ballinger. The Lapowski Dry Goods store was a profitable business that enabled members of the family to become part of the educated elite in America after they left San Angelo and adopted the surname *Dillon*. (Both, WTC.)

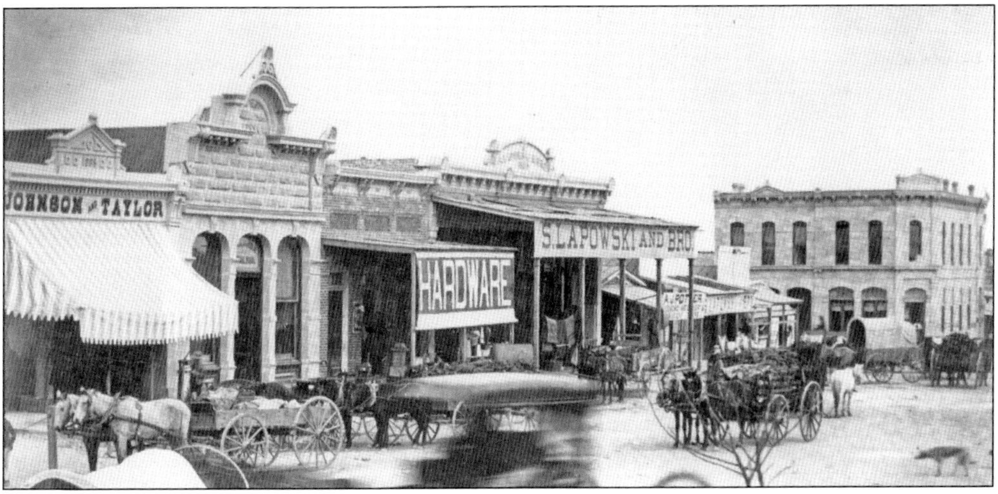

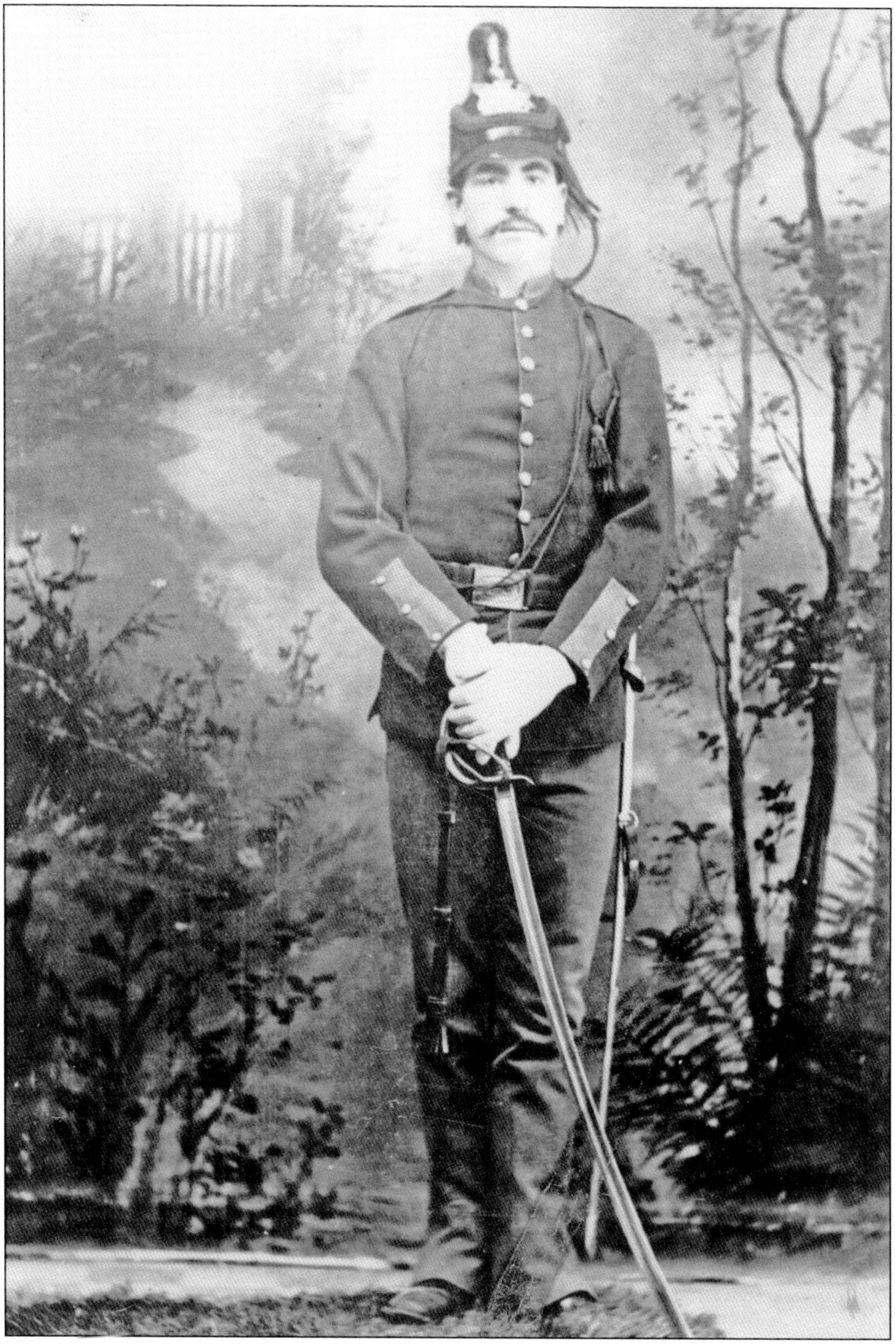

The African American population in San Angelo was always smaller than the Hispanic population, but it was a significant part of the tapestry. Sancho Mazique was a former slave who joined the army after the Civil War. He served five years in the 10th Cavalry at Fort Concho. When he was honorably discharged in 1880, Mazique used his carpentry skills to make a living in the Concho Valley. He also cooked at the Sugg Ranch. When he died on April 20, 1951, at the age of 101, the newspaper reported that he had been an amazing source of information about the history of the last century. (FC.)

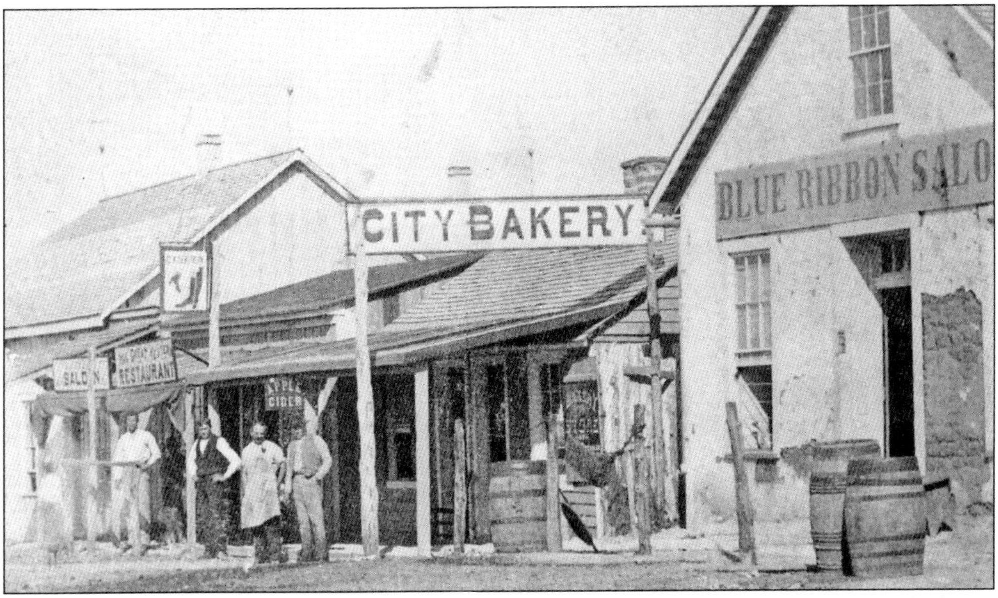

Perhaps the most extraordinary African American in early San Angelo was George B. Jackson, proprietor of the Blue Ribbon Saloon seen in this picture. He also owned a ranch and raised cattle and sheep. Prominent in the political life of the town, he was elected as a delegate to the Republican National Convention in 1900. Some argue about whether the western frontier created lasting opportunities for people of color and women. The evidence in early San Angelo suggests that a resounding "yes" is the appropriate answer. (WTC.)

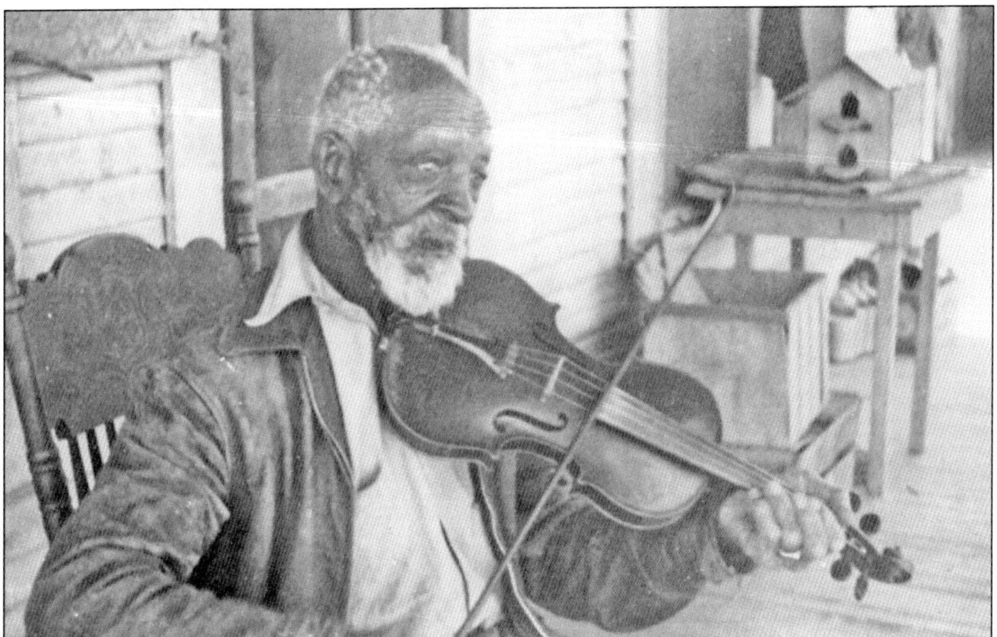

Elijah Cox was another Buffalo Soldier who stayed in San Angelo after his military service was over. Pictured here on his back porch, "Old Cox," as he was often called, was famous for playing his violin at dances at Fort Concho and in San Angelo. In an interview, he claimed to be able to play 300 waltzes from memory. (Private collection.)

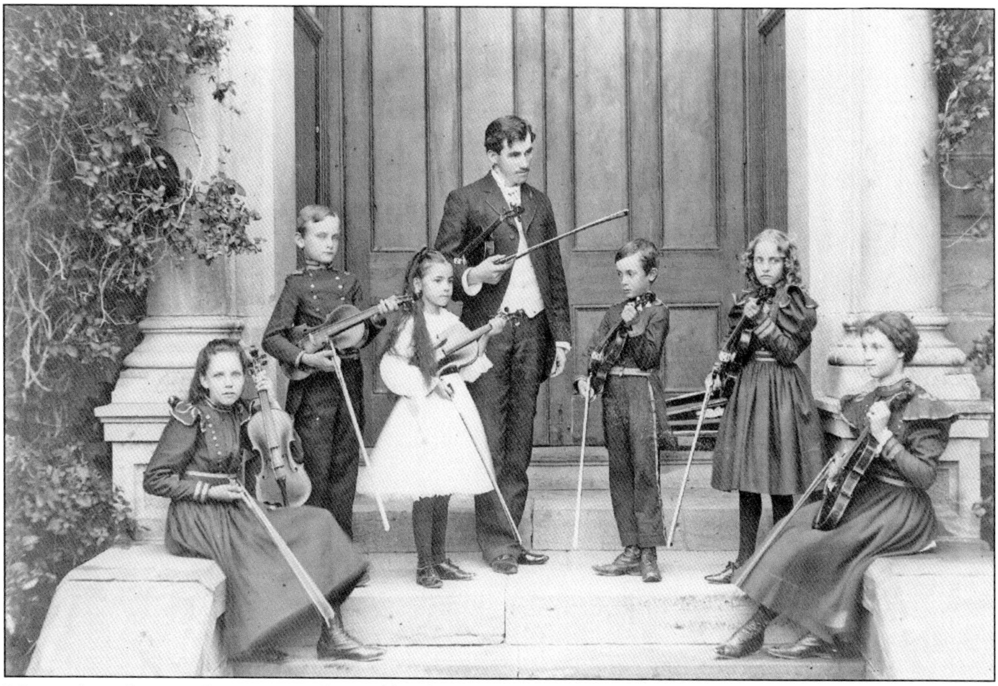

Musical traditions from a number of backgrounds are another thread of the tapestry. This is a photograph of a classical violin class posing on the steps of the San Angelo Courthouse. The pained looks on the students' faces seems to question their enthusiasm for the task. (FC.)

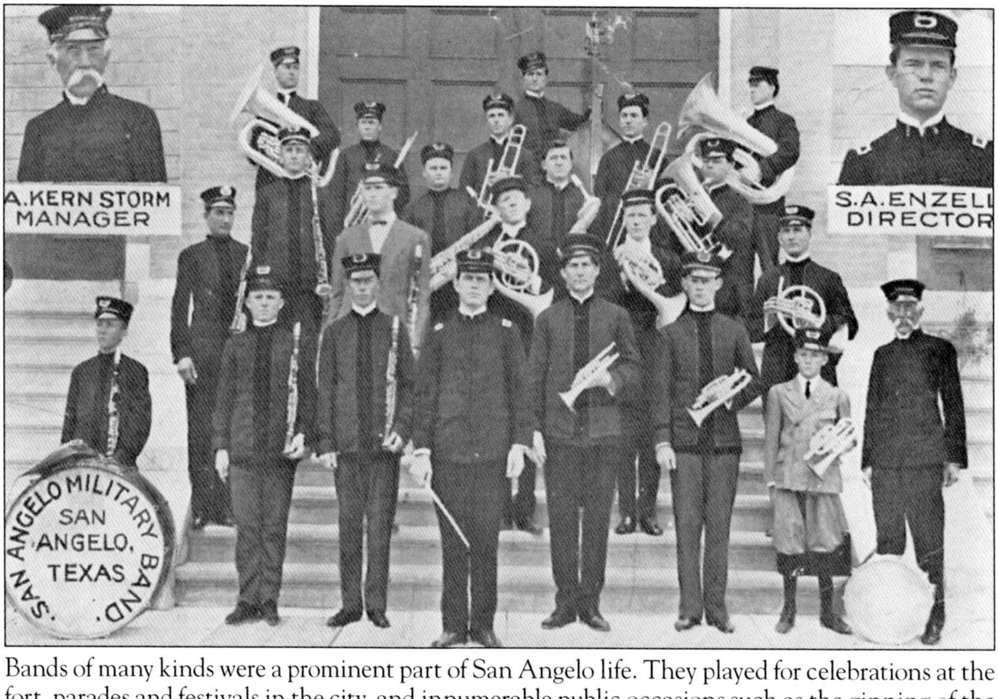

Bands of many kinds were a prominent part of San Angelo life. They played for celebrations at the fort, parades and festivals in the city, and innumerable public occasions such as the ginning of the first bale of cotton in Tom Green County. This group of young and old musicians calls themselves the San Angelo Military Band. Any connection with Fort Concho seems tenuous. (WTC.)

Individuals played guitars, pianos, mariachi instruments, and an untold number of other instruments. This is a charming portrait taken by M.C. Ragsdale of an unidentified young woman entertaining an audience. (FC.)

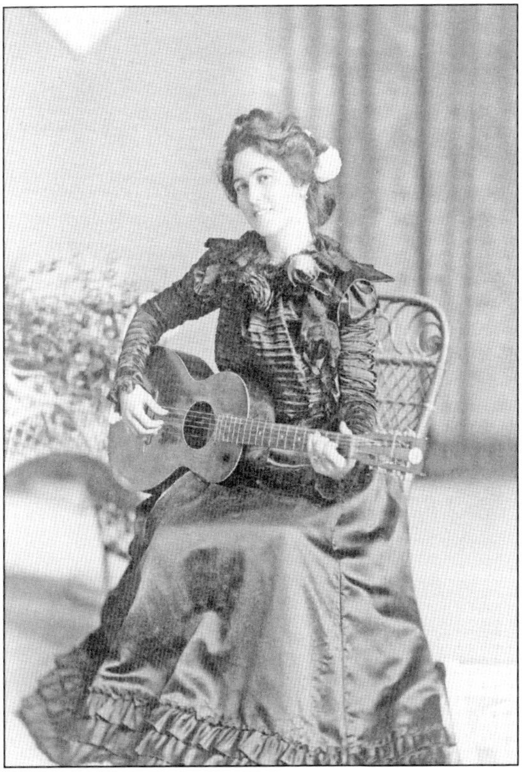

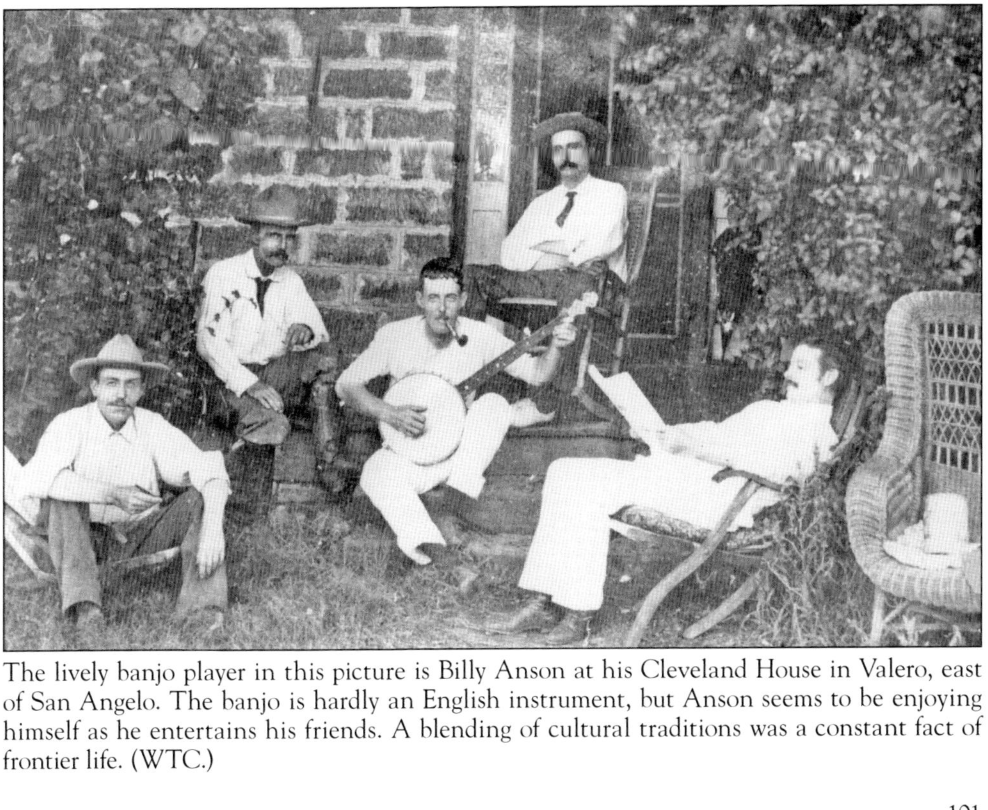

The lively banjo player in this picture is Billy Anson at his Cleveland House in Valero, east of San Angelo. The banjo is hardly an English instrument, but Anson seems to be enjoying himself as he entertains his friends. A blending of cultural traditions was a constant fact of frontier life. (WTC.)

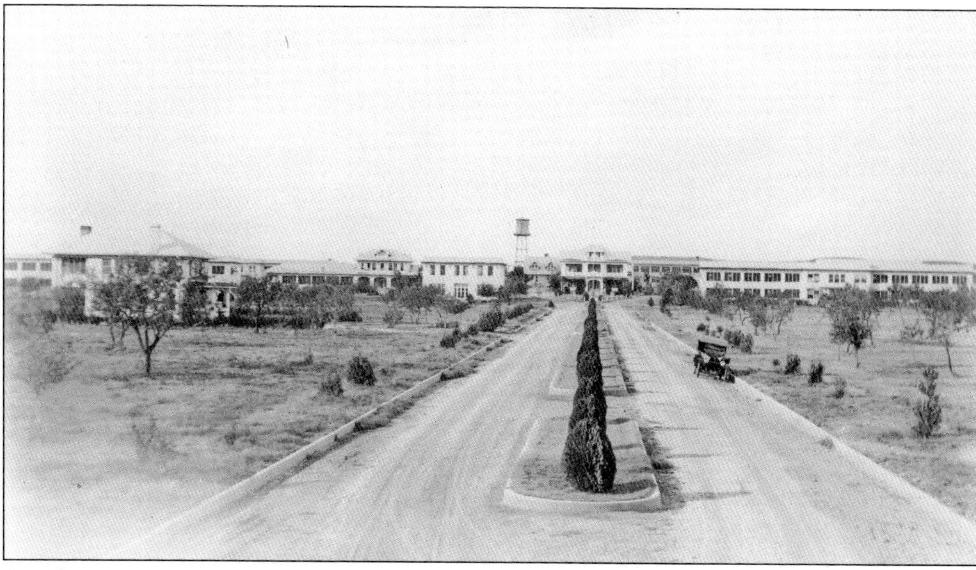

Another interesting group of people who settled in San Angelo were those with serious respiratory problems such as tuberculosis. Inelegantly called "lungers," these people came for medical treatment in a warm and dry climate. Oscar Ruffini is a perfect example of someone who came, restored his health, and decided to live in the hospitable environment of the Concho Valley. This picture shows a state sanatorium built at Carlsbad, 16 miles northwest of San Angelo. The local newspaper said it was one of five sanatoriums in the city in the early 1920s. People as varied as John Loomis, Annie Tankersley, and saloon keeper Tom McCloskey nursed people with lung problems in the early days. (FC.)

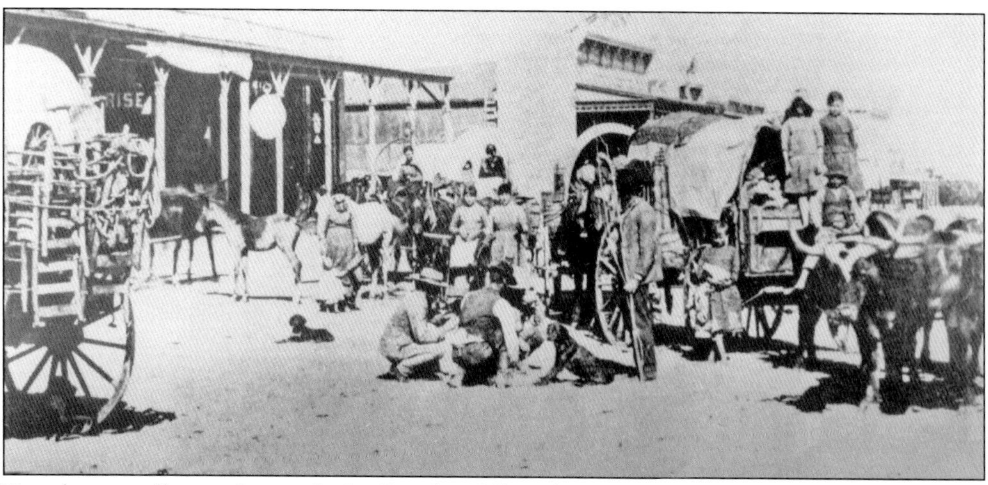

Travelers as well as settlers made the Concho Valley what it was. This photograph shows covered wagons full of immigrant families stopping in town. San Angelo was a city surrounded by a wide rural area, and in some ways it was isolated from the outside world. But it was not cut off from the many rich cultural traditions that came with those who traveled through town. (WTC.)

Five

Amusements

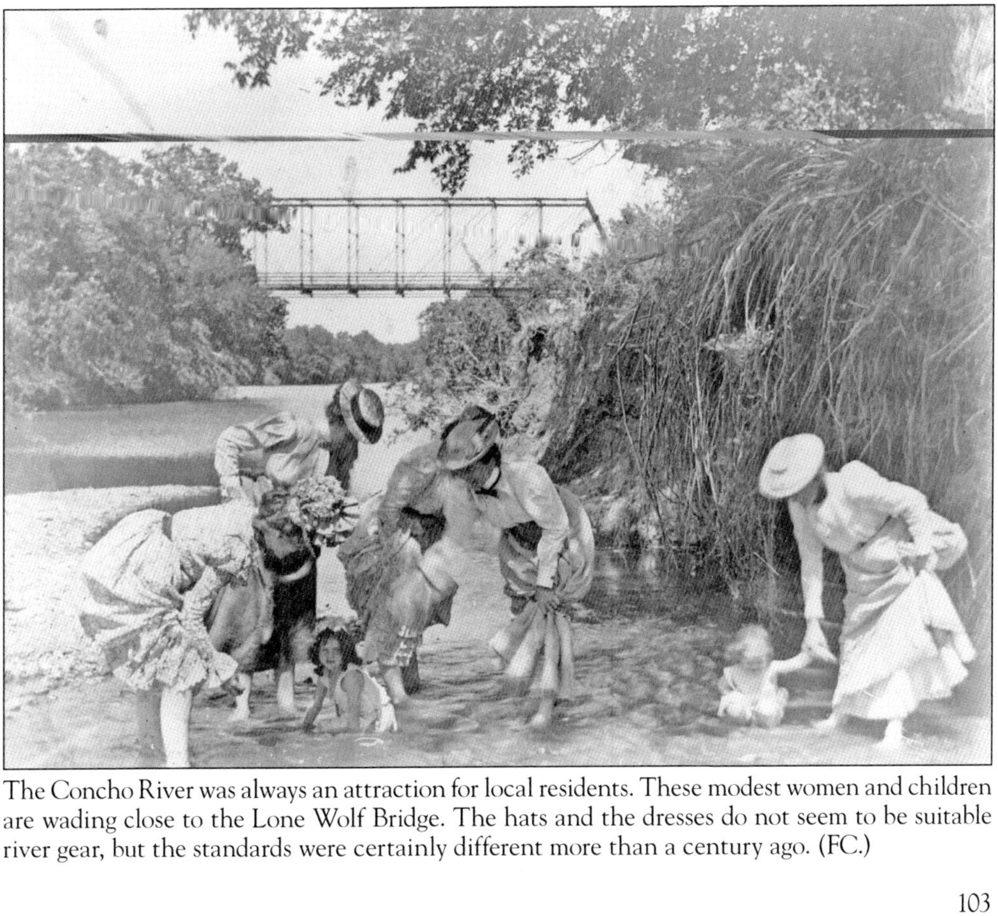

The Concho River was always an attraction for local residents. These modest women and children are wading close to the Lone Wolf Bridge. The hats and the dresses do not seem to be suitable river gear, but the standards were certainly different more than a century ago. (FC.)

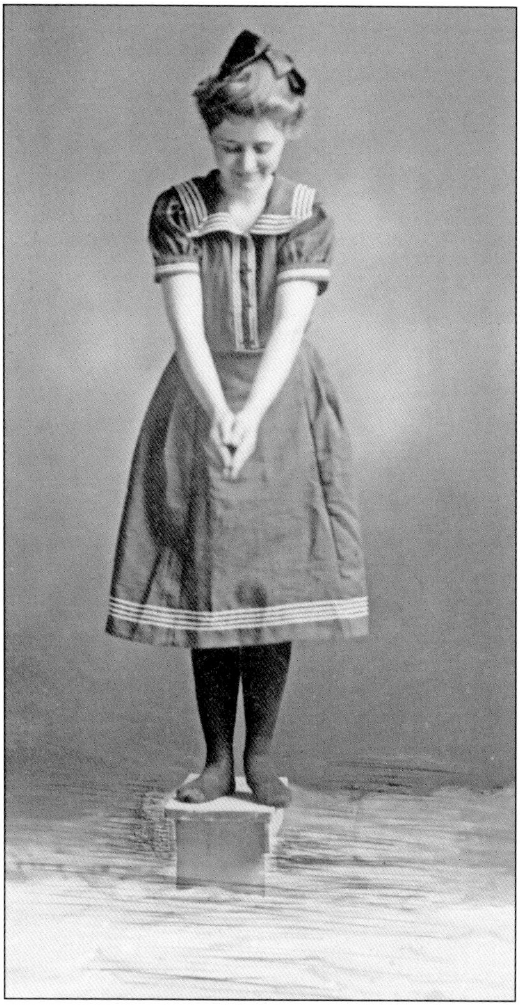

By the 1920s, it was appropriate for women to appear in public wearing swimming suits. The river was a good place to swim as well as wade. The girl in the photograph is the charming Helen Ragsdale, daughter of photographer M.C. Ragsdale. (FC.)

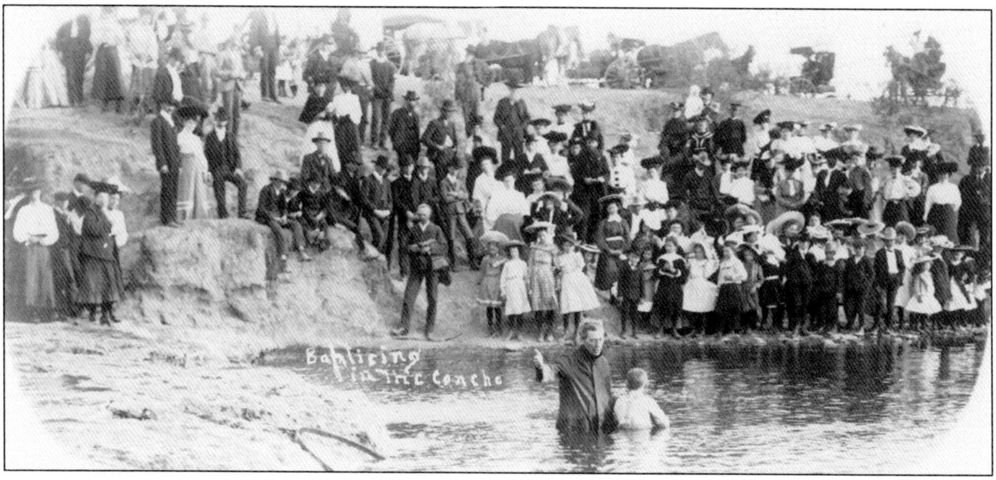

The bank of the river was a convenient place to hold a sacred event as well. Here, a baptism in the Concho River takes place as a congregation dressed in their Sunday best looks on. (FC.)

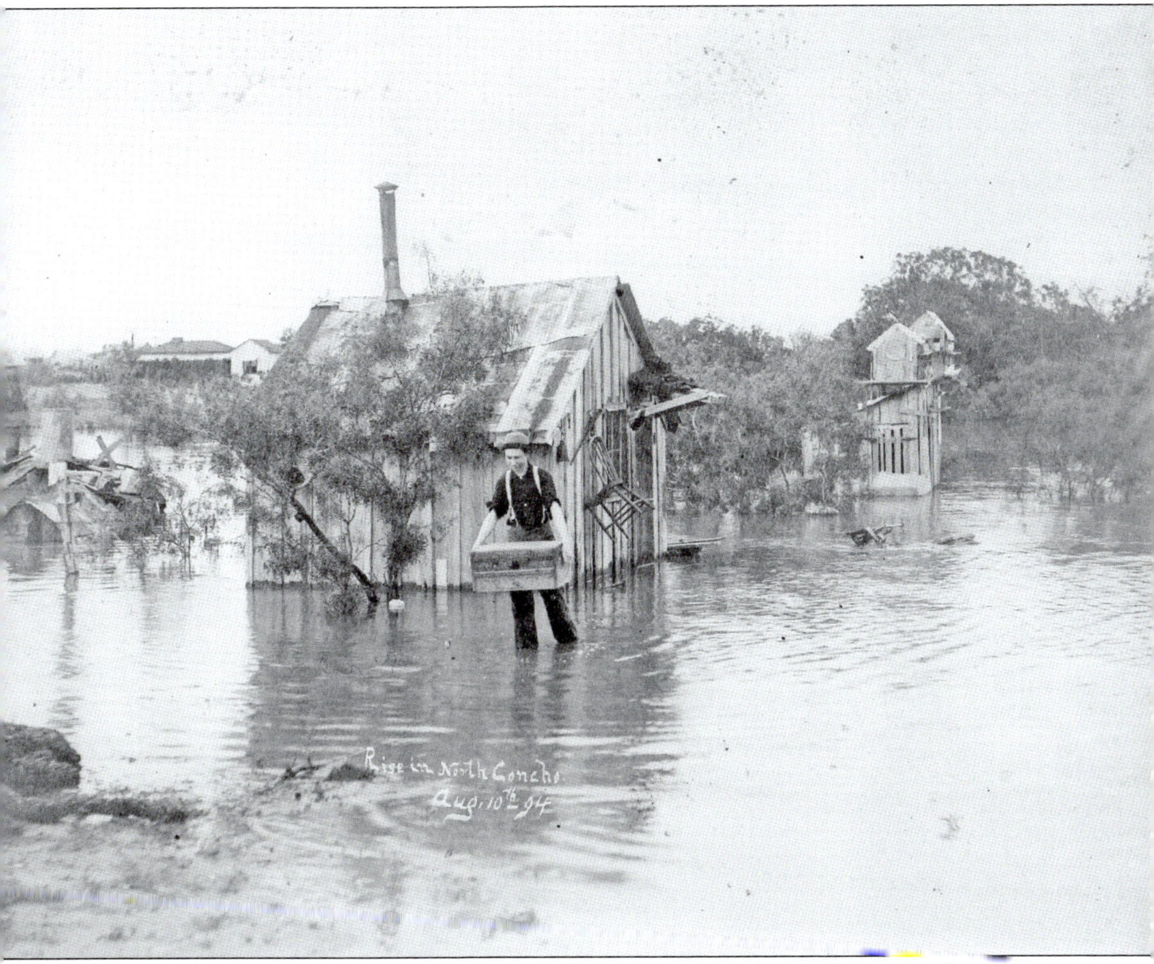

Sometimes, however, the river was dangerous or even fatal. Rainfall would come to the region and seemingly never let up, and the river would swell and destroy everything in its path. The Ben Ficklin flood of 1882 was such a devastating event in part because settlers did not recognize the destructive power of the Concho River. Concho Valley residents learned to be wary when excessive rains fell in the area. This is a photograph showing a rise on the North Concho River in 1894. (FC.)

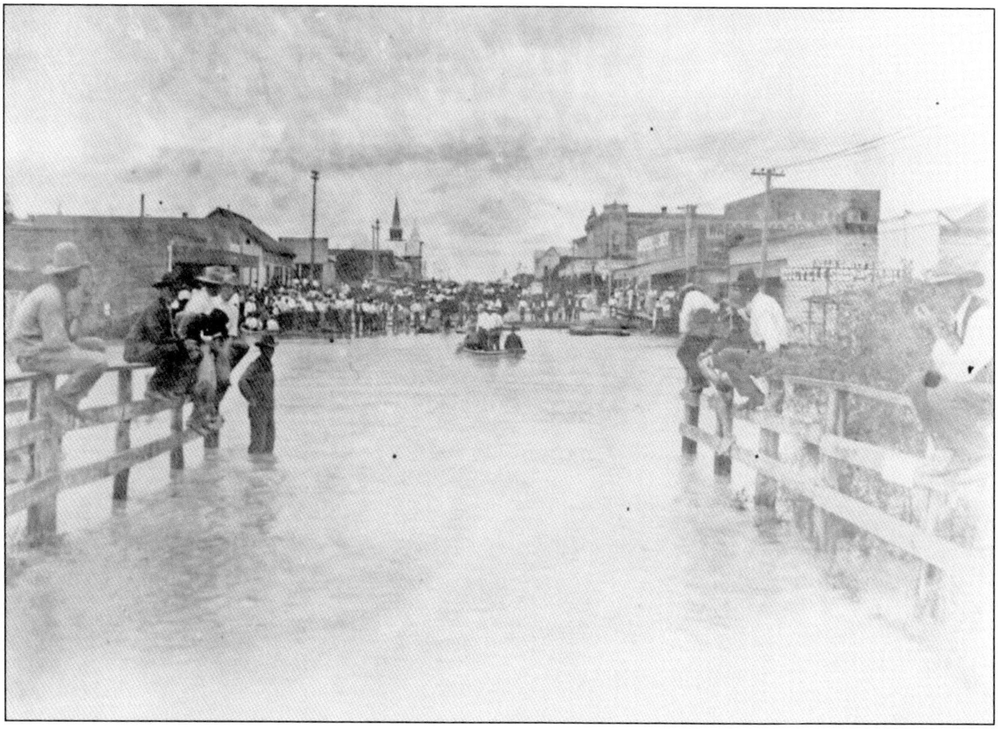

The 1894 flood affected downtown San Angelo as well. In dry periods, people prayed for rain and were thrilled to get it, even if a flood resulted. Most residents found the high water fascinating. Watching moderate floodwaters was one of the favorite amusements in the Concho Valley. (WTC.)

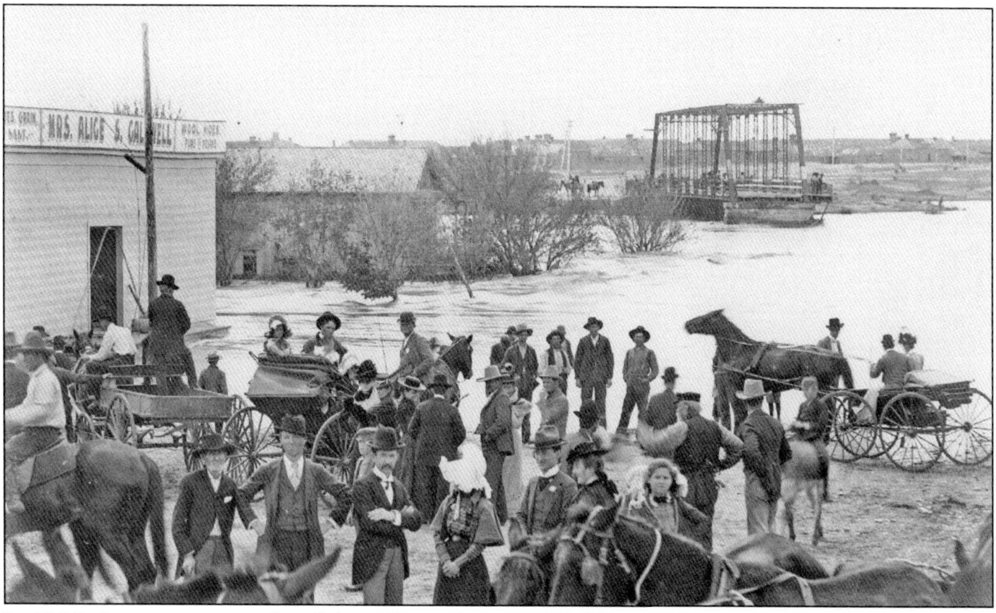

In 1906, there was yet another deluge. Here, the Long Wolf Bridge is cut off from the town by high water. Even though this was a serious problem for the city, people were attracted to and mesmerized by the dangerous waters. It looked as if onlookers even dressed for the event. On the left is Alice Caldwell's business establishment—a wagon yard, wool house, and general store. (FC.)

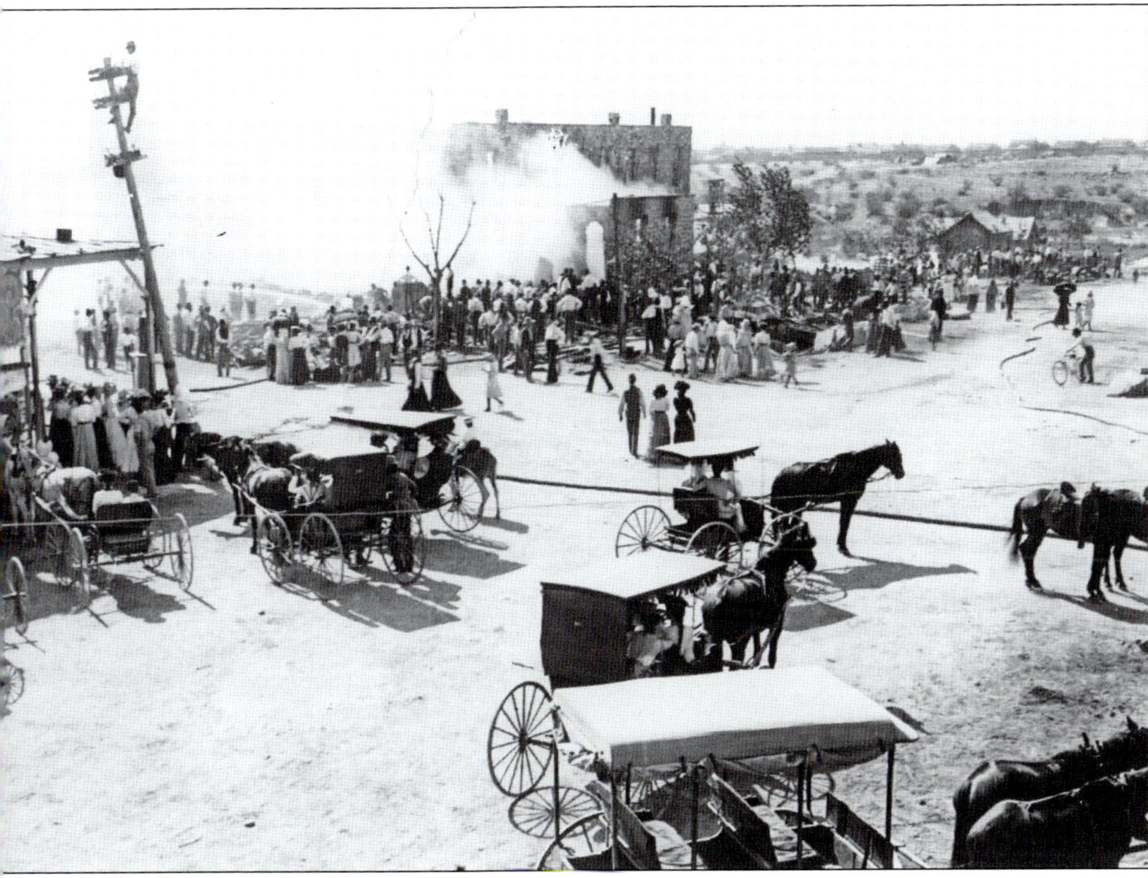

Fire was another fascinating disaster. This photograph shows the 1902 fire that destroyed the first Lundon Hotel. This spectacle was so interesting to one gentleman he had to climb the telephone pole to get an adequate view. Many people were dangerously close to this fire in which eight lives were lost. (FC.)

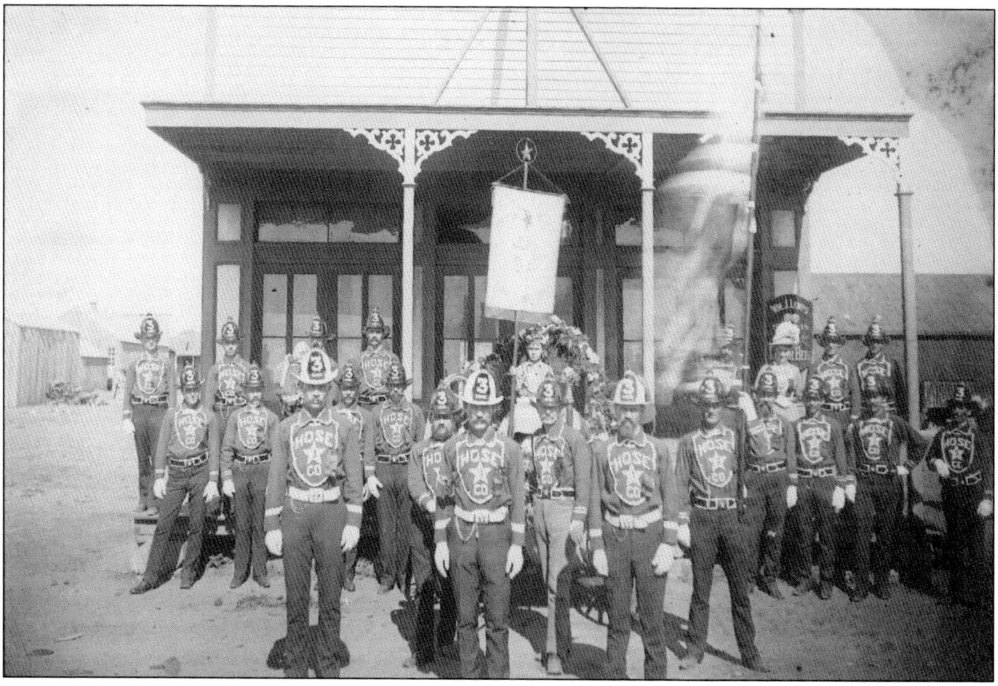

Firefighting was the work of volunteers in San Angelo. These proud gentlemen took their jobs very seriously. Here, the hose company members pose in their uniforms and white gloves. These men seem quite proud of both their pretty young mascot and the important work they do. (WTC.)

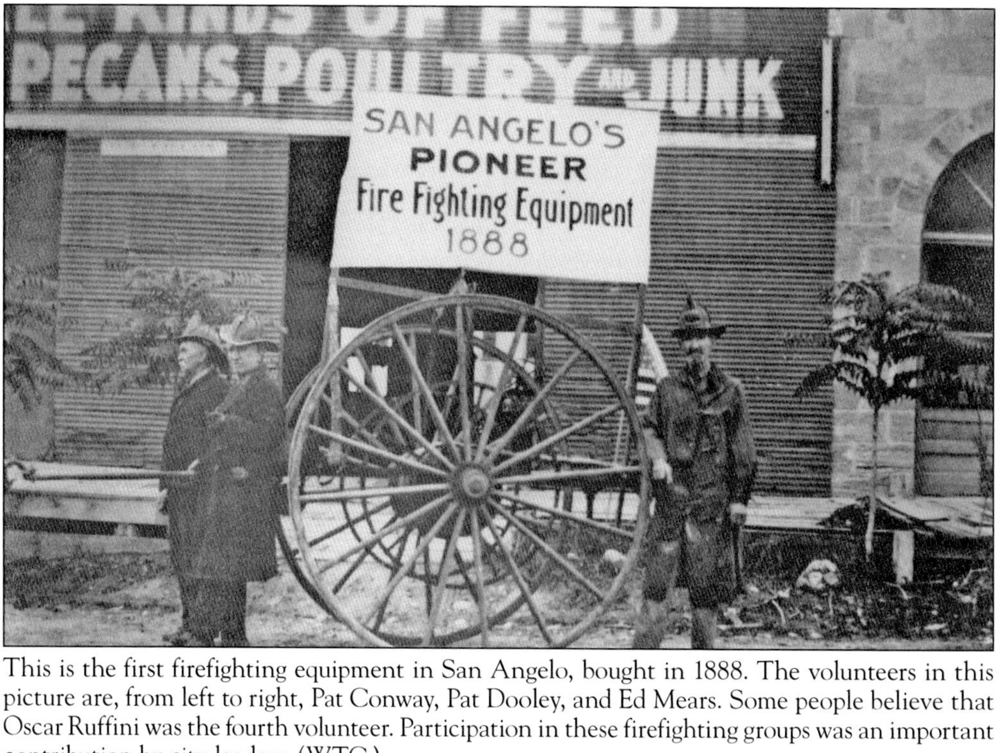

This is the first firefighting equipment in San Angelo, bought in 1888. The volunteers in this picture are, from left to right, Pat Conway, Pat Dooley, and Ed Mears. Some people believe that Oscar Ruffini was the fourth volunteer. Participation in these firefighting groups was an important contribution by city leaders. (WTC.)

Hunting and fishing were major preoccupations in early San Angelo. Col. Benjamin Grierson once complained that everyone at Fort Concho had "fishing on the brain." Civilians seemed to enjoy the pastime as much as the soldiers and their wives. Worthy citizens Jim Landon (left), Tom Grimes (center), and Clint Johnson (right) display their catch. (WTC.)

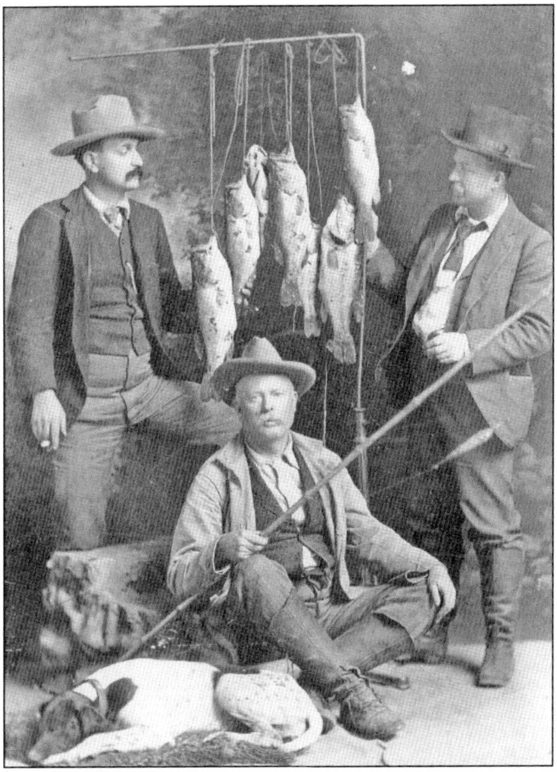

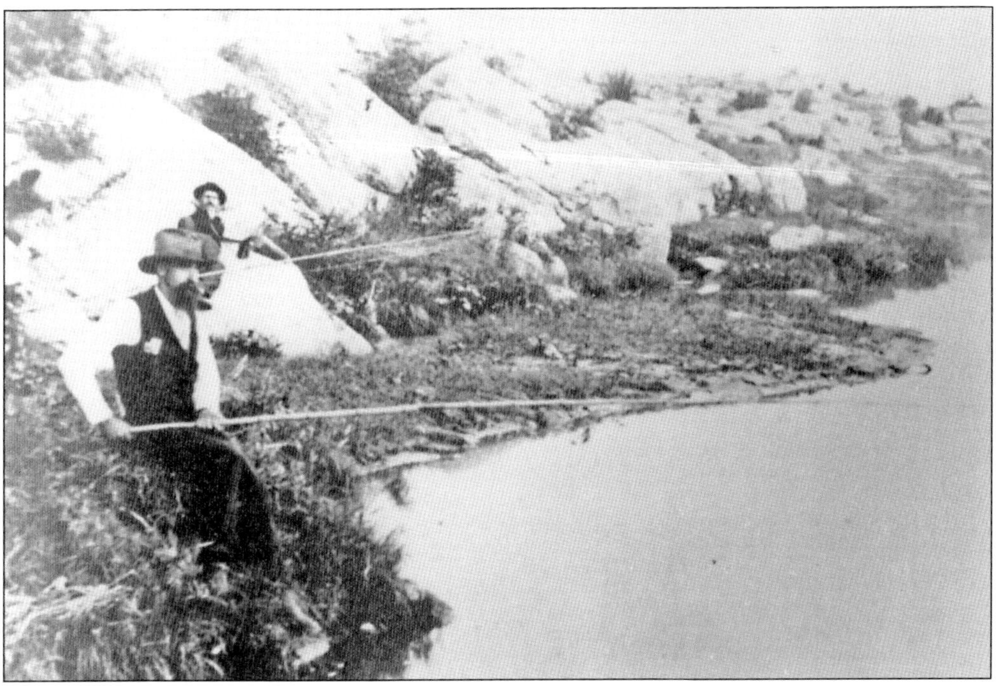

Often, fishing was not part of an organized excursion. Anyone could put a pole in the river at any time. These people were fishing under the Oakes Street Bridge. There was a community of less affluent citizens who lived close by. Sometimes one could catch dinner and supper. (FC.)

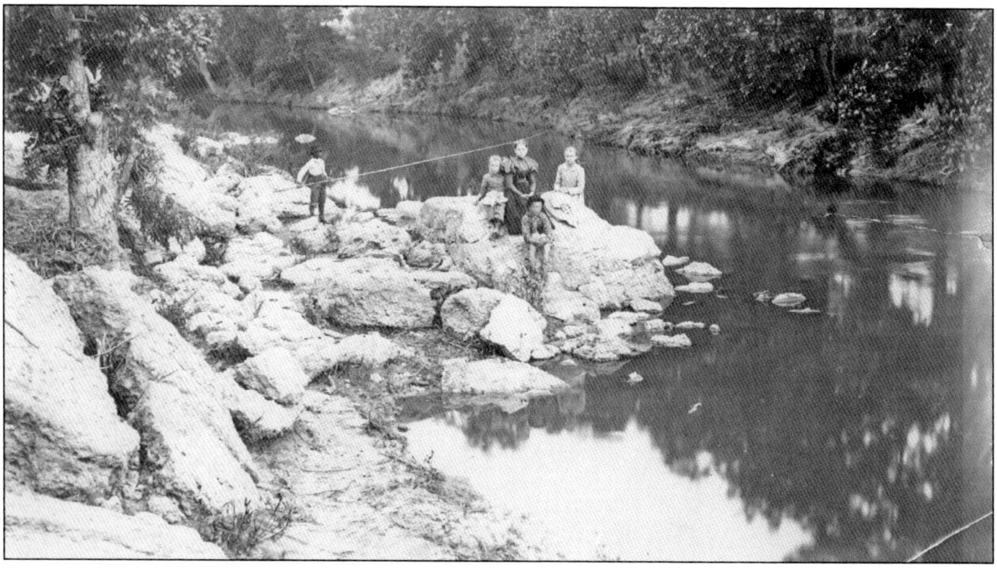

Women and children enjoyed fishing every bit as much as the grown men did. In this photograph, the Allen, Probandt, Willeke, and Wolters kids are enjoying a pleasurable time by the river. (WTC.)

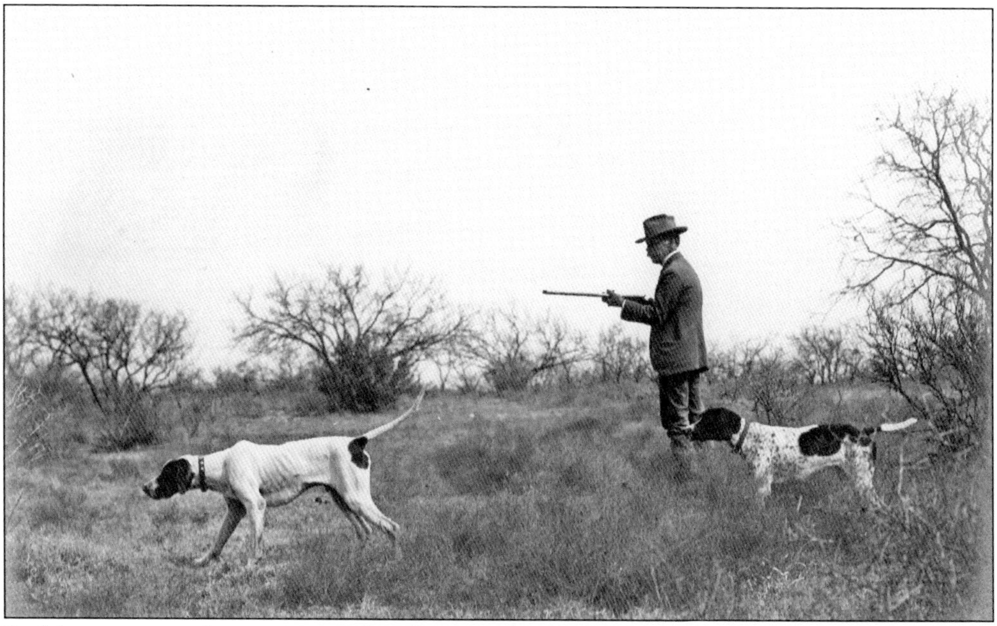

Bird hunting was always a treat. This photograph may show M. C. Ragsdale with his shotgun. The hunter in this picture is not identified, but it appeared in a private journal, which belonged to Ragsdale. The journal included many views of him and his dogs working to accumulate a dove or quail feast. (FC.)

Deer were abundant in the Concho Valley. Here, Duwain E. Hughes (left) and W.W. Carson (right) display their "Deer Kill," as it was labeled on the back of the photograph. (FC.)

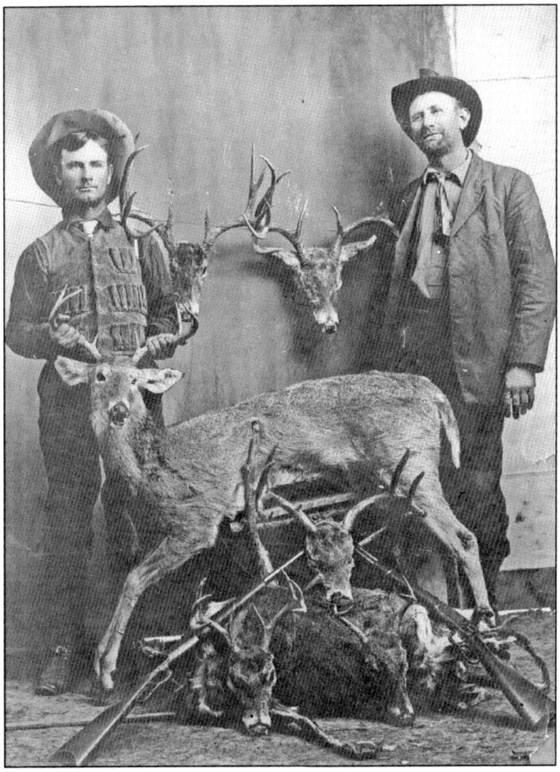

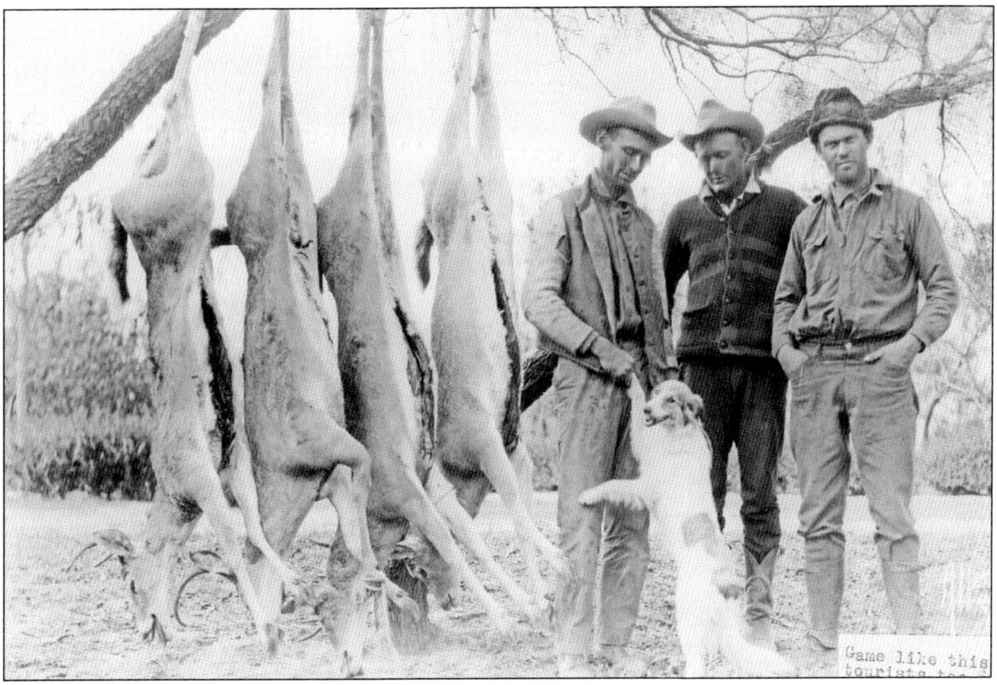

This photograph appeared in the local newspaper, the *San Angelo Standard Times*, in the early 1920s. The hunters are not identified, but the text refers to these gentlemen as tourists. Commercial bird and deer hunting became an important source of income for Concho Valley landowners.

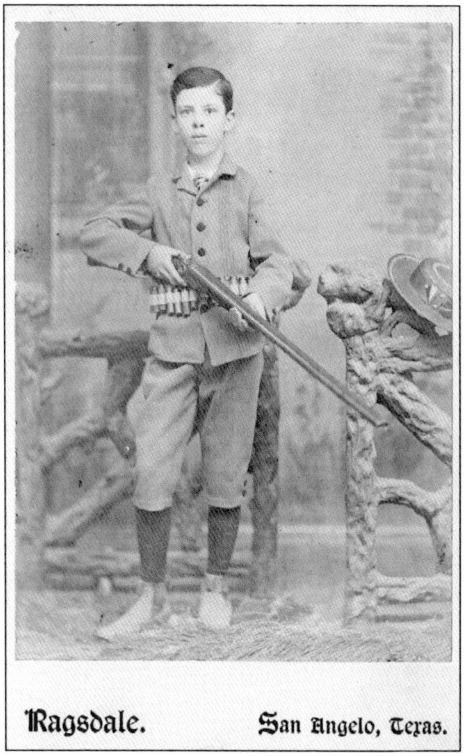

Children enjoyed this sport as well. This studio portrait shows Felix Harris ready for the hunt with his shotgun, his special belt for cartridges, and his knickers. The Ragsdale studio seemingly had a prop for any occasion. (WTC.)

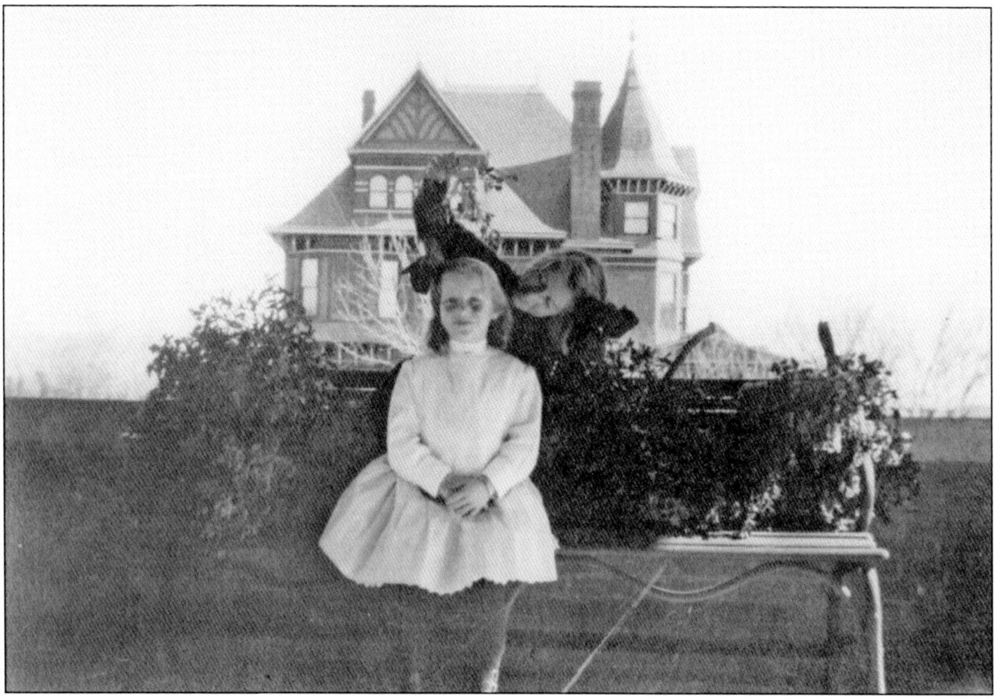

The children of the Concho Valley were able, with imagination, to make their fun wherever they might be. This picture shows two young girls, Mary Hobbs and Jeanette Millspaugh, having a grand time clowning for the photographer. (WTC.)

The children in this picture are, from left to right, young Lawrence, Mellick, and Jose Tweedy. The three look very serious as they pose for the photographer; they probably enjoyed pulling and riding in the wagon much more when the camera was not around and their clothes not so confining. (WTC.)

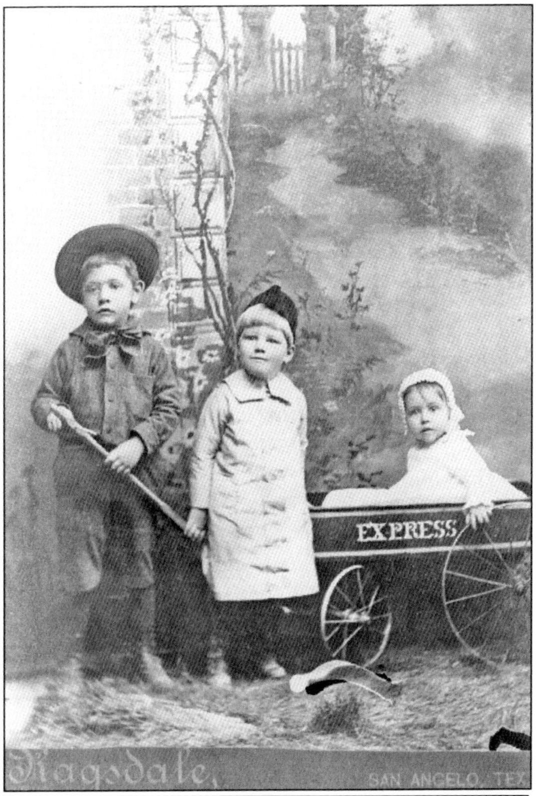

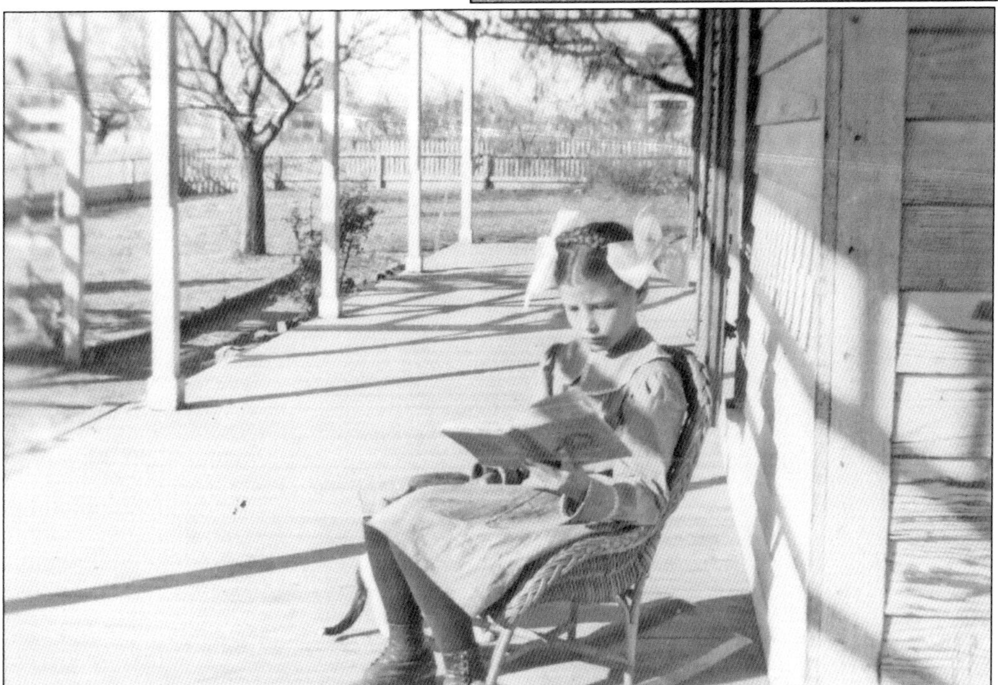

If other outdoor activities ran out, reading a book in a quiet corner was always a possibility. (WTC.)

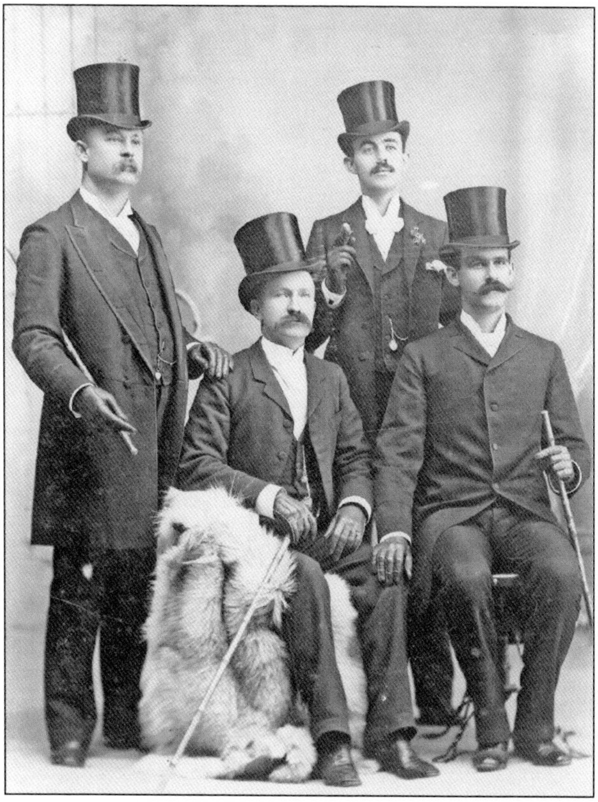

Gentlemen in the Concho Valley had special entertainments of their own. New Year's Day calling was a strong tradition. Men dressed to the nines and went, in some cases with their hangovers, to visit local hostesses and to drink some more. Birdy Cooper mentioned New Year's Day visiting at Fort Concho as well. Here, four San Angeloans pose while dressed for their New Years calls. From left to right are (seated) William Prestridge and Tom Duggan; (standing) Clint Johnson and B.C. Alexander. (FC.)

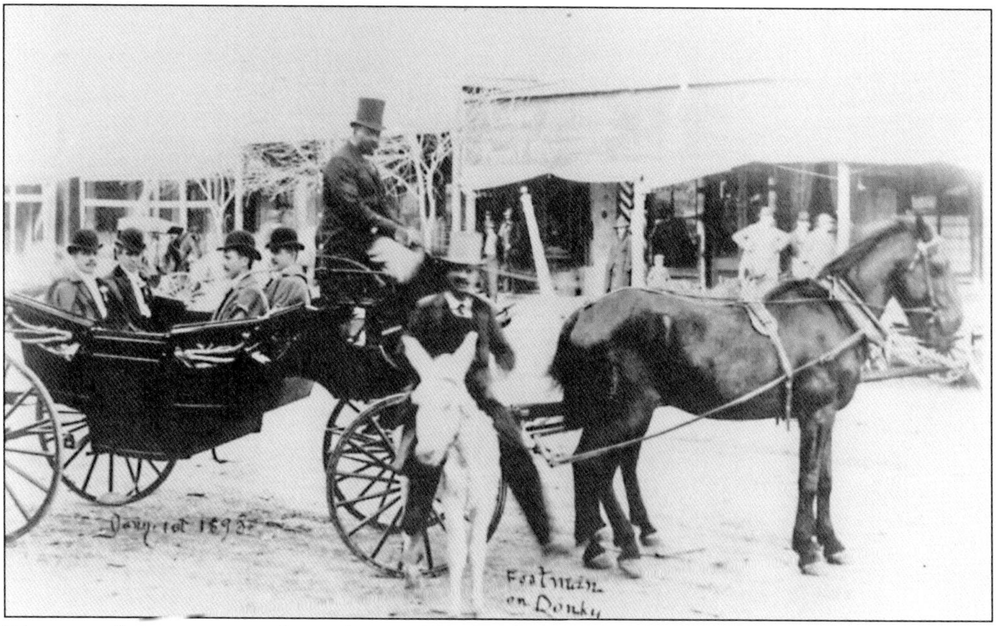

These gentlemen are actually in the process of making their New Year's Day calls in 1895. Riding in style in a fancy carriage, with a driver and even a footman, they are probably getting ready to make a call at the Legal Tender Saloon in the background. The gentlemen in the carriage are Eugene Moon, Ralph Harris, Gilmore Gwin, and a Mr. Moody. (Private collection.)

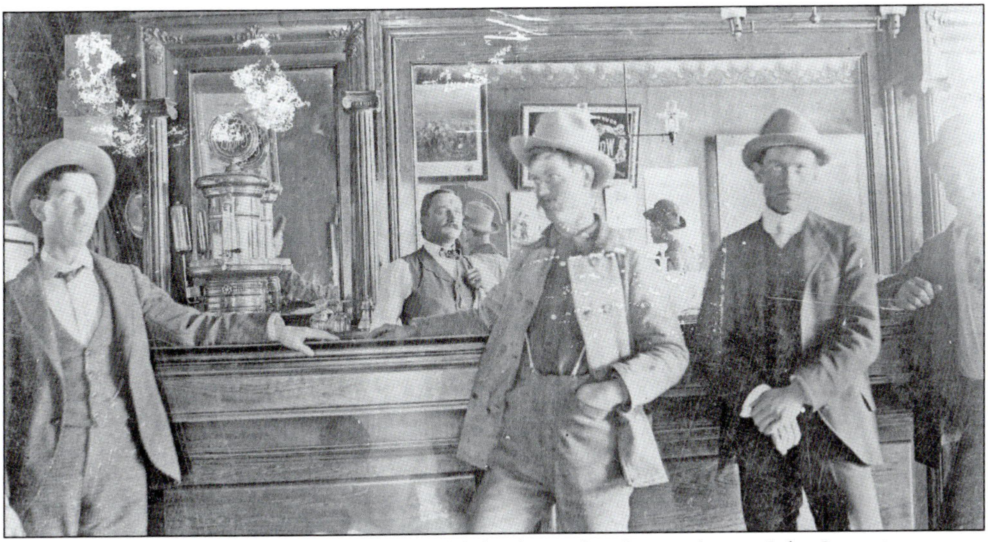

The interior of the Arc Light Saloon, a "model drinking place" according to John Loomis, appears in this picture. Tom McCloskey bought it in 1888. He was highly respected for being a good businessman and a charitable individual who gave money to those in need and nursed strangers who had tuberculosis. San Angelo had lost its Wild West image by 1888, but the saloon remained a prominent part of San Angelo life where gentlemen could stop for a meal, a drink, or a cigar. This photograph dates from the early 1900s. (FC.)

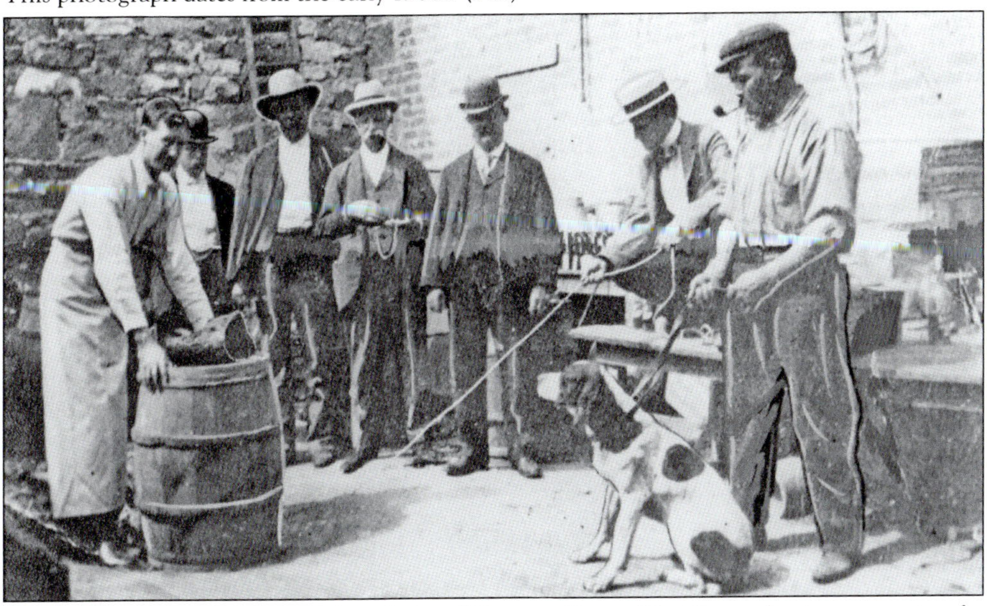

This interesting photograph is identified as "Choctaw George" holding a dog in preparation for a badger fight. John Loomis describes the practical joke that is being set up here as "pulling the badger." A new man would show up in a local saloon. A fight between the dog and the "badger" in the barrel would be arranged. Crowds gathered and much betting would take place as to which animal would win the confrontation. The greenhorn would be given the honor of pulling the rope to let the badger out, and out would fall a chamber pot. After the laughter subsided, the new man was supposed to buy a round of drinks for the crowd. Practical jokes such as this became a part of West Texas tradition. (WTC.)

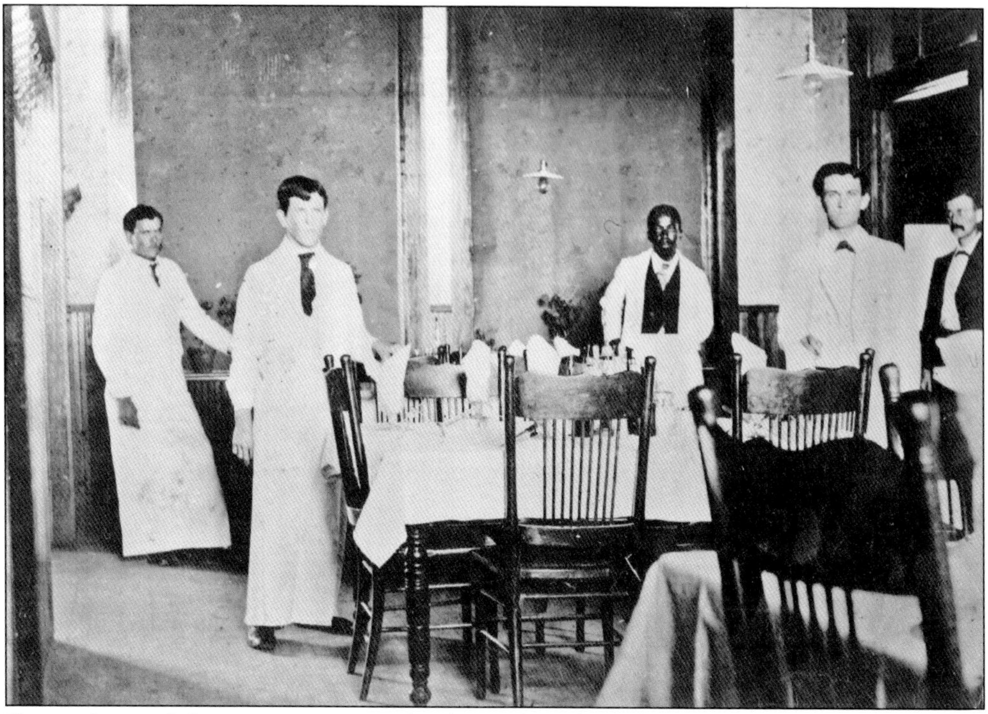

If a gentleman did not want to eat at the Arc Light Saloon, he could get an elegant dinner at the first Landon Hotel just across the street. It is interesting that there are no pictures of women in the hotels and saloons. Many of the patrons of these establishments were men from local ranches doing their business in town and enjoying a night out before returning to the isolation of country life. (WTC.)

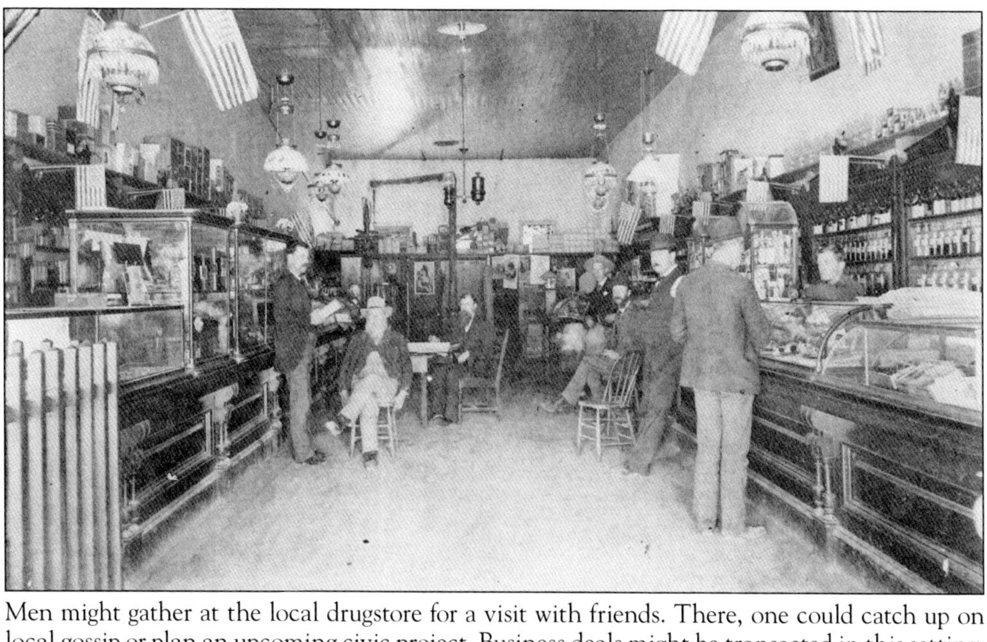

Men might gather at the local drugstore for a visit with friends. There, one could catch up on local gossip or plan an upcoming civic project. Business deals might be transacted in this setting, and medical advice could be obtained from the pharmacist. (WTC.)

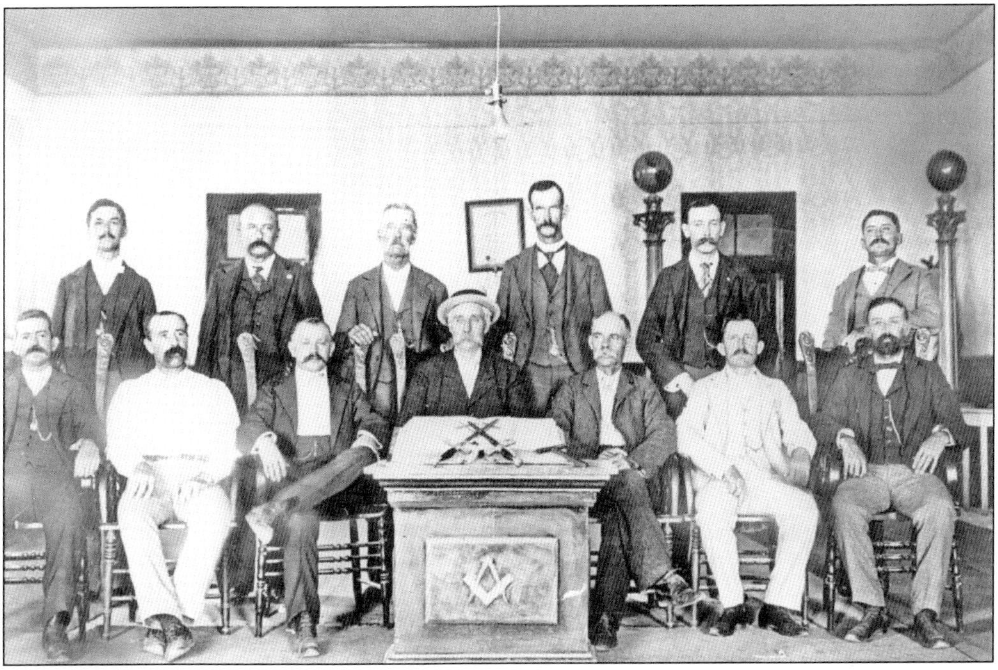

There were serious men's groups as well. This photograph shows members of the Masonic Order on June 19, 1899. Familiar names appear in the picture. From left to right are (seated) Powell, Litt, Snyder, Dr. A. B. Chambers, Knapp, Kennedy, and Norman; (standing) Houston, Findlater, Funk, Couch, March, and Mertz. (FC.)

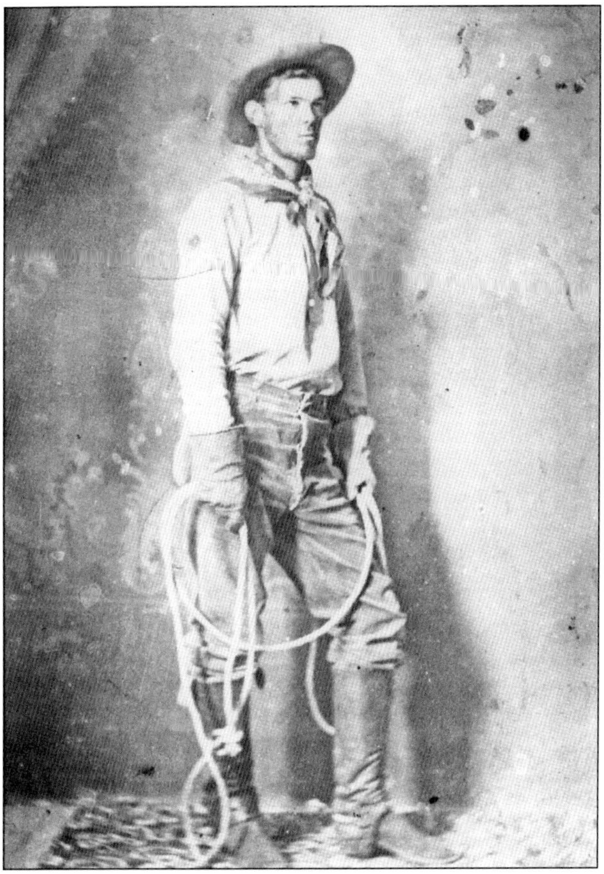

Many forms of entertainment in San Angelo related to the ranching and frontier heritage of the city. Known as "Booger Red," Samuel Thomas Privett was an expert local cowboy, rider, roper, and horse-breaker. He had suffered terrible scarring from an acid explosion. His red hair and terrible scars gave him his nickname. (FC.)

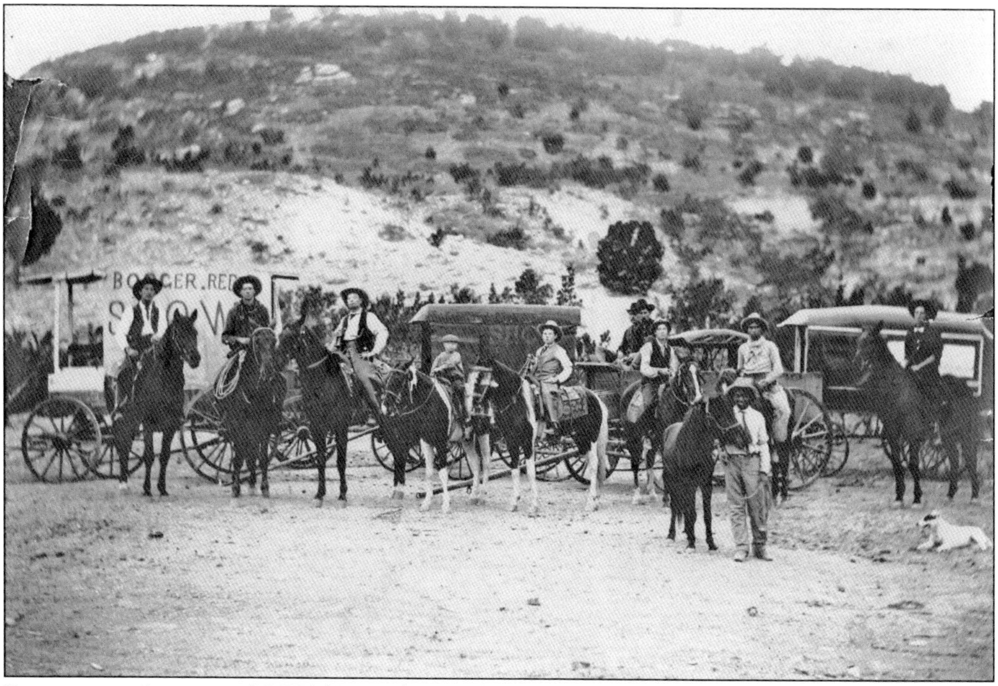

Privett started a successful Wild West show, called the Booger Red Show, which is pictured here. The company was a touring group of expert riders and ropers who traveled the state of Texas in wagons. Pawnee Bill of Oklahoma and Buffalo Bill Cody of Wyoming organized similar shows for national and international audiences. Booger Red performed in San Angelo, of course, to large crowds. (WTC.)

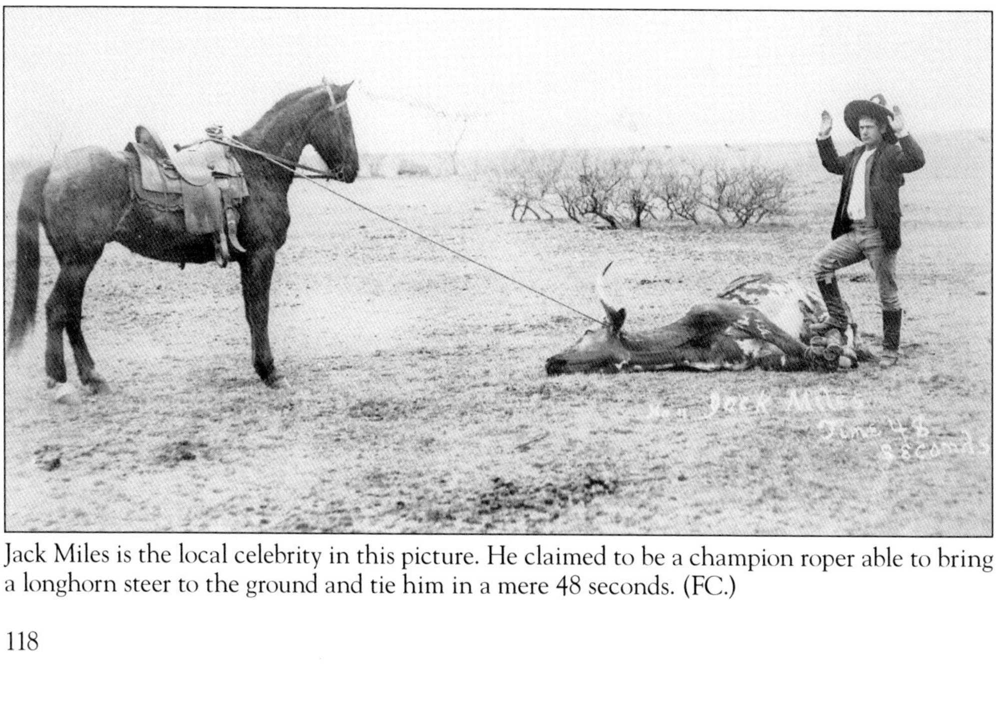

Jack Miles is the local celebrity in this picture. He claimed to be a champion roper able to bring a longhorn steer to the ground and tie him in a mere 48 seconds. (FC.)

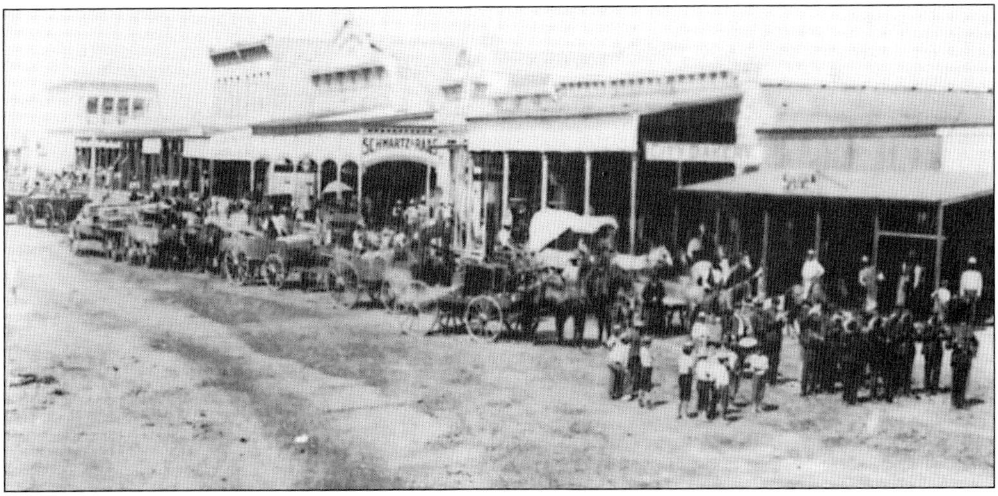

This interesting picture shows the formation of a Pioneer Parade in 1880. To put this date into some perspective, San Angelo was still a small town in the shadow of Ben Ficklin, the community that would be destroyed by a flood two years later. There is something wondrous about celebrating a town's pioneer heritage so early, just as there is something interesting about enjoying western shows and roping contests when many people around the area performed these feats when they went to work each day. Perhaps the citizens of San Angelo felt they were a significant part of history while they were living it. (WTC.)

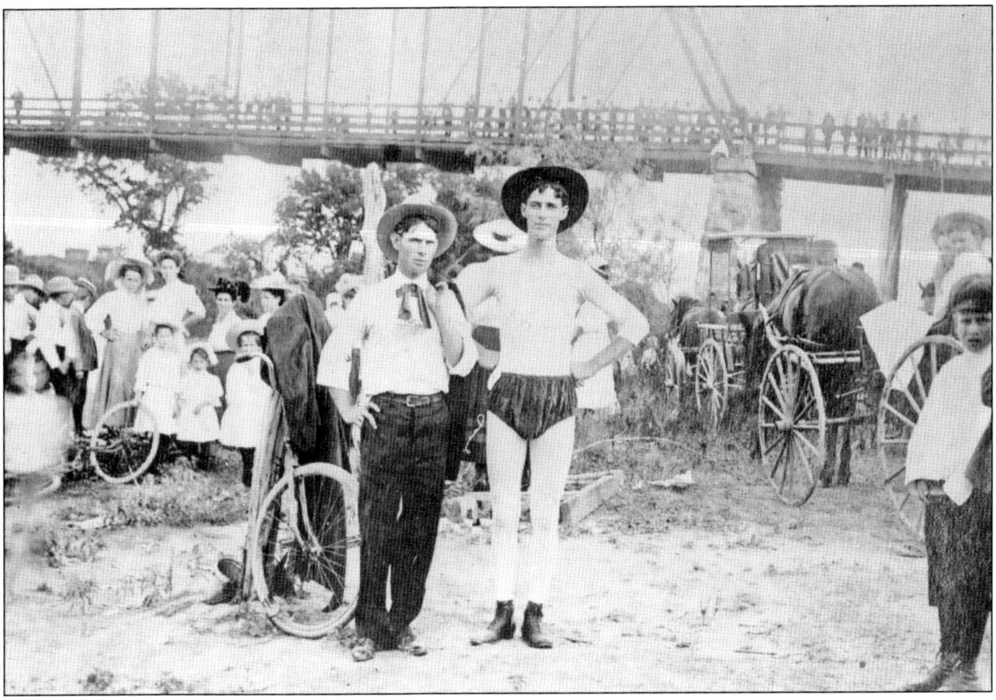

One option for residents to pass the time on a lazy Sunday afternoon was to go see John Hull in his bathing suit climb to the top of the Lone Wolf Bridge and jump off. This picture shows Hull preparing to perform in front of a sizable audience. Since he did the climb and jump every Sunday, there was quite a crowd waiting to see the performance when this photograph was taken. (WTC.)

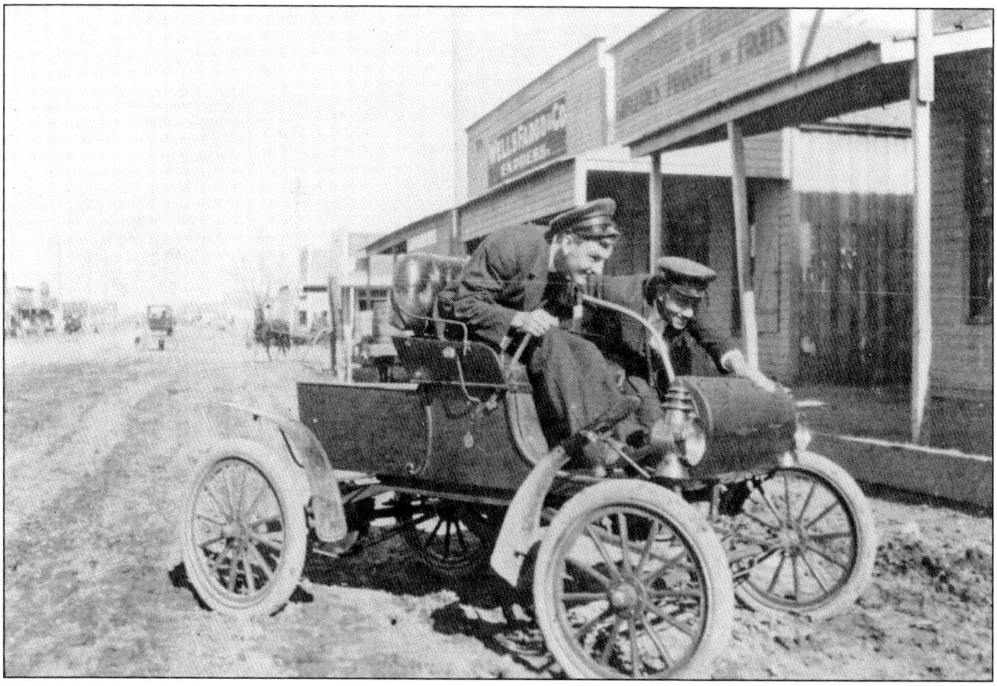

Playing around with a new automobile was obviously great entertainment. Perhaps there was irony involved in taking this picture in front of the Wells Fargo office. Transportation in America was getting ready to change dramatically as the automobile became widespread. (WTC.)

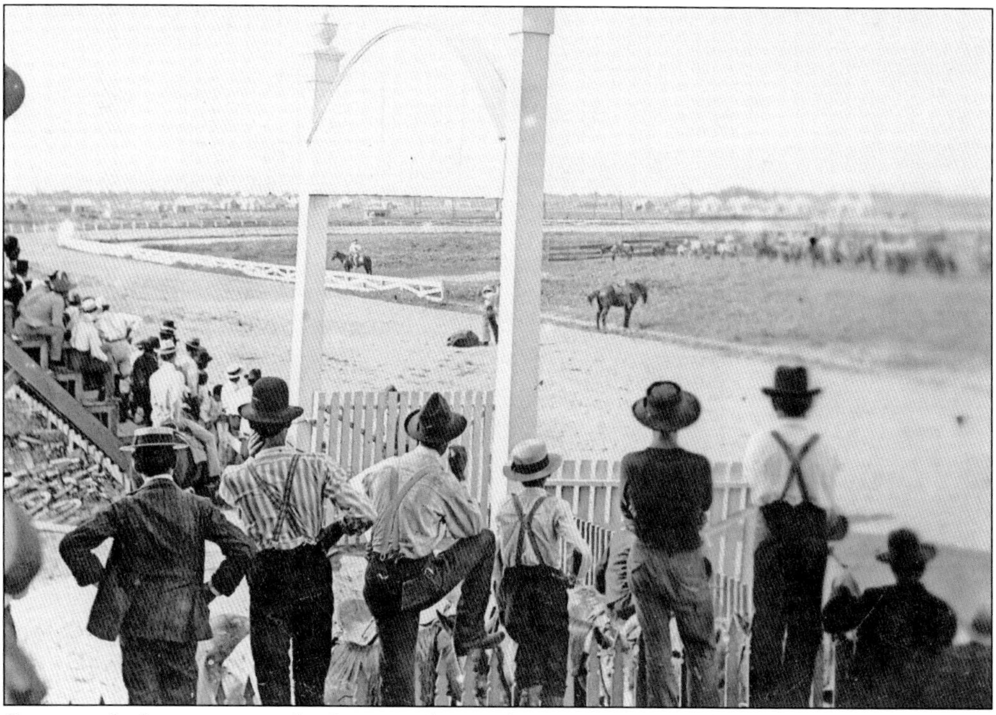

Going to the horse races at the fairgrounds was also an option. Excellent horses were raised and trained in the Concho Valley. Such races provided fun and excitement for many. (WTC.)

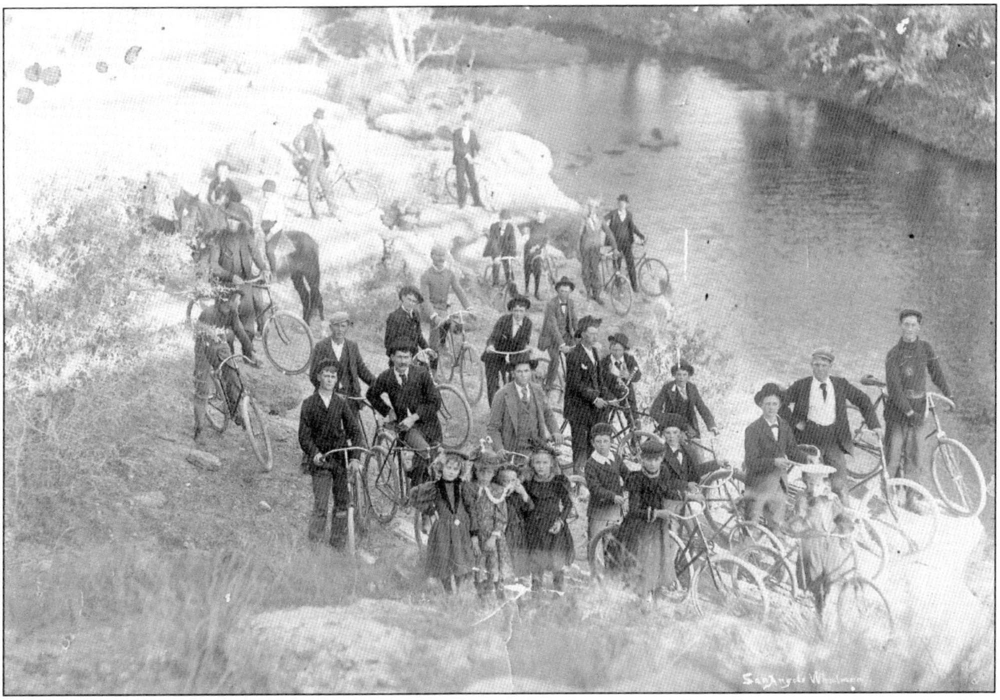

Perhaps the best choice was a bike ride on a leisurely afternoon. This photograph shows the San Angelo Wheelmen and their children on an outing. Biking was very popular in early San Angelo; there was even a bicycle sales and repair shop in town owned by Choctaw George. One could keep up with the group on horseback if his bike were in the shop for repair. Why these riders posed by the river with coats, ties, and hats is unknown. (WTC.)

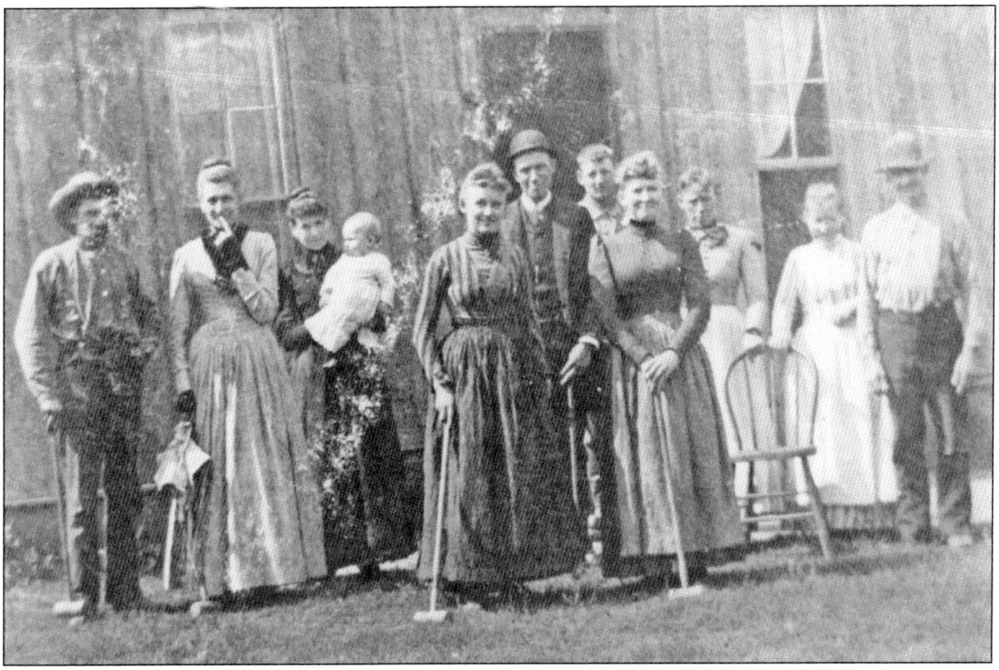

The men and women left back at the house might organize a game of croquet. (WTC.)

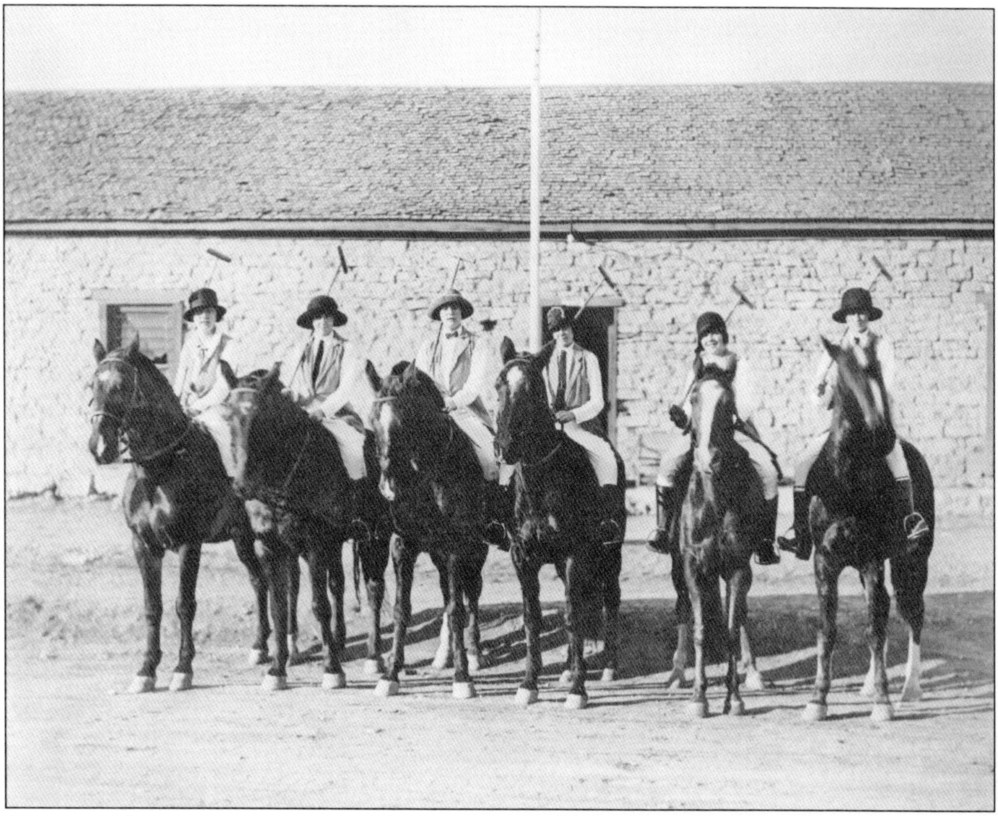

The more adventuresome women might even practice their polo skills on the Fort Concho parade ground. This photograph is of a women's polo team in the early 1920s. (FC.)

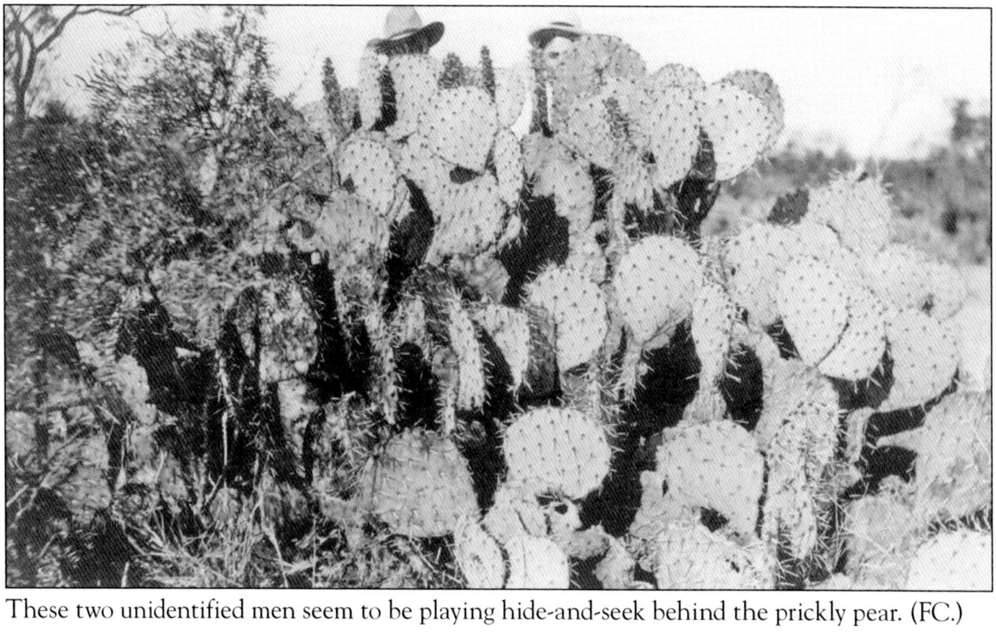

These two unidentified men seem to be playing hide-and-seek behind the prickly pear. (FC.)

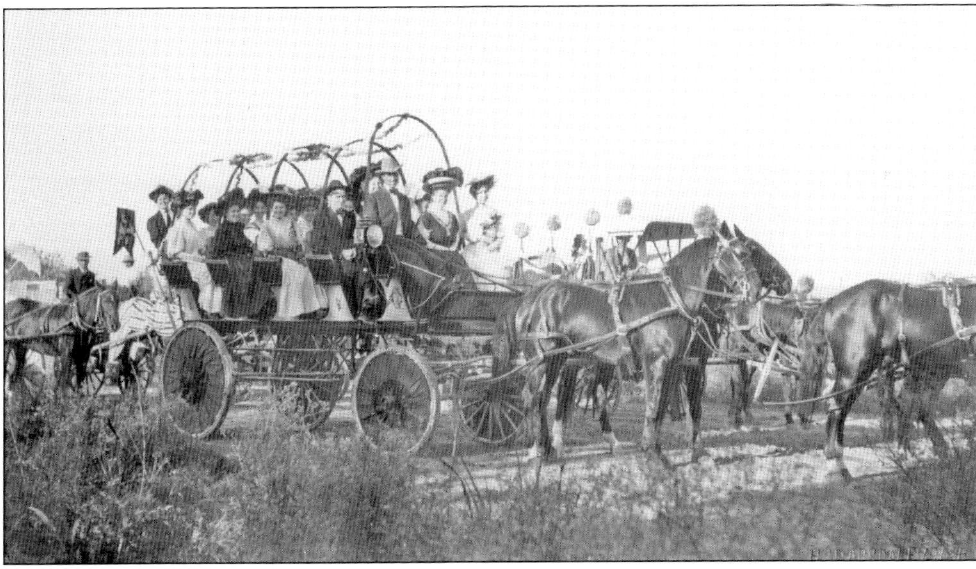

Taking excursions was a popular amusement in San Angelo. This wagon is the Tally-ho, and the riders are going for a picnic. Mary Bland Millspaugh is one of those on board, along with Sara Cunningham, who would later marry Millspaugh's brother. Picnic attire was certainly cumbersome in the early days. (Private collection.)

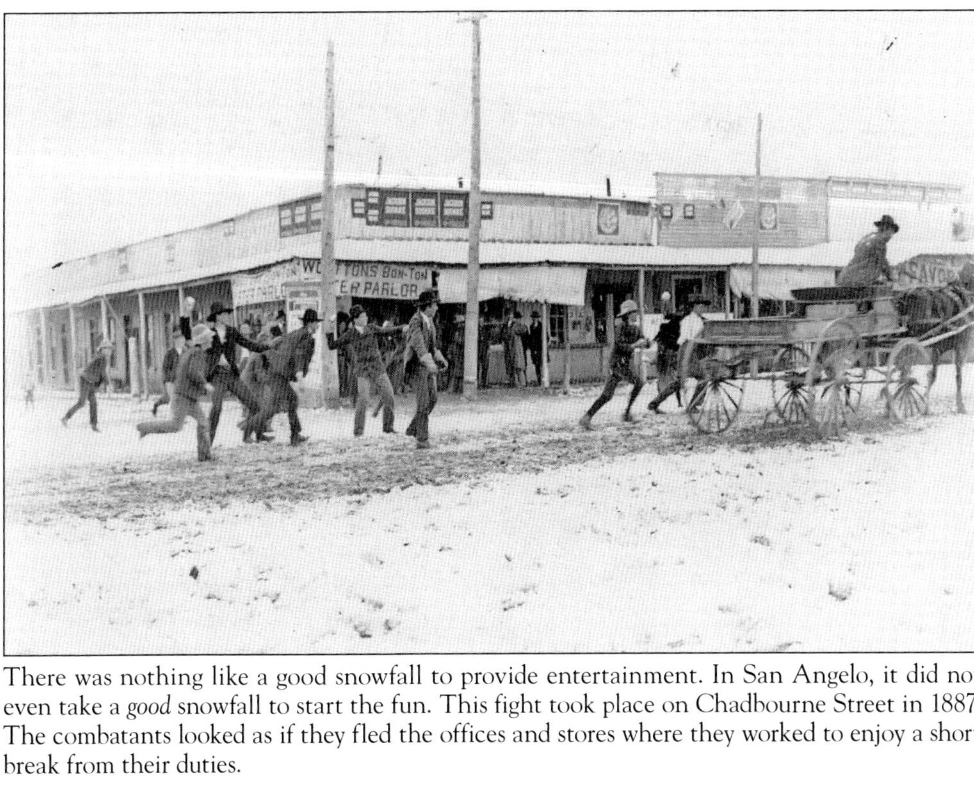

There was nothing like a good snowfall to provide entertainment. In San Angelo, it did not even take a *good* snowfall to start the fun. This fight took place on Chadbourne Street in 1887. The combatants looked as if they fled the offices and stores where they worked to enjoy a short break from their duties.

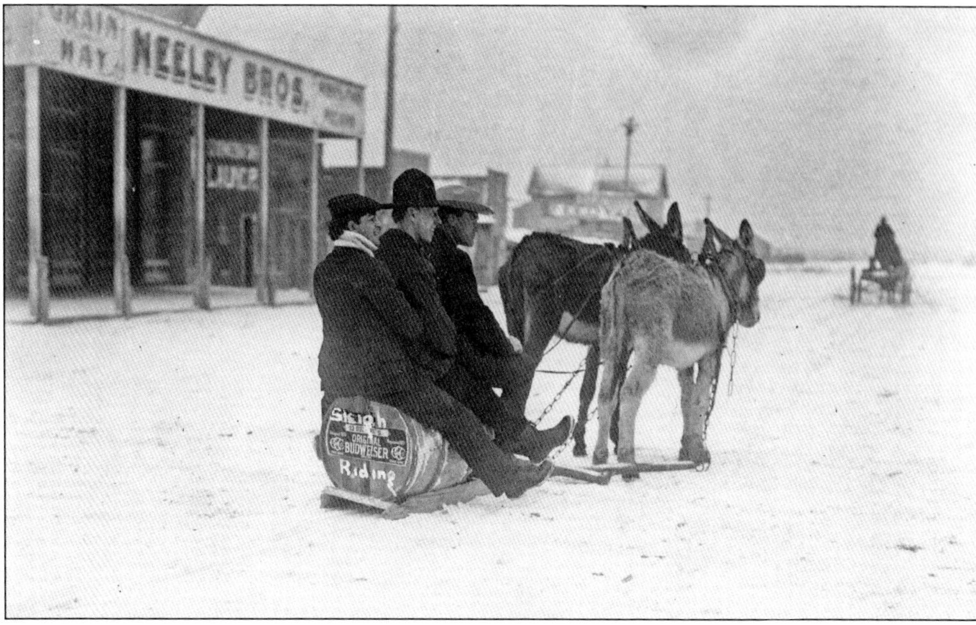

Infrequent snows meant no one had sleds or sleighs or other traditional snow equipment. Enter ingenuity, and the result is a great use for a beer keg. If these riders first helped empty the keg, they at least felt they were insulated from the cold. (FC.)

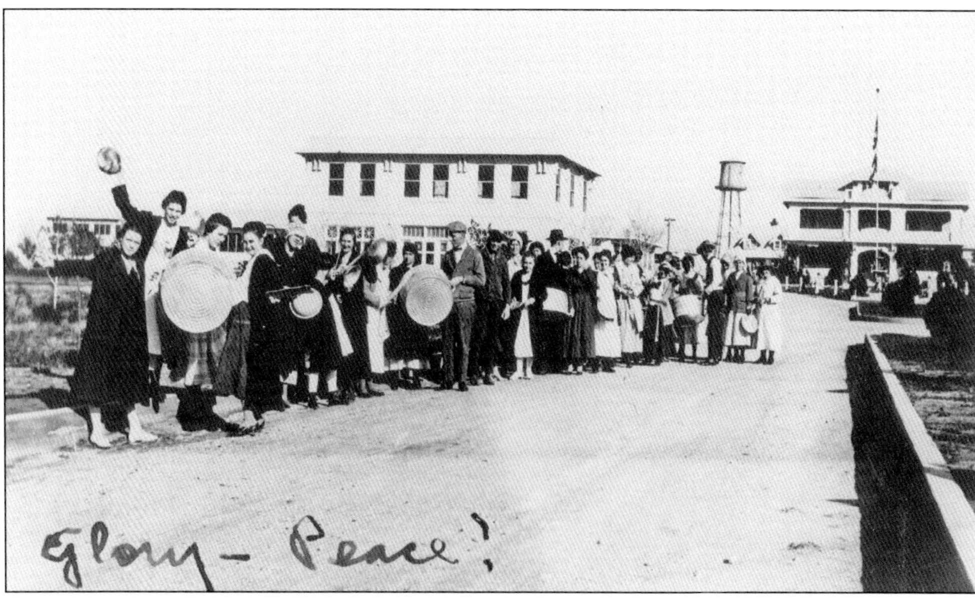

Concho Valley residents loved to celebrate. This photograph depicts the jubilation felt at the close of World War I. The location is the State Sanatorium in Carlsbad. There was no band nearby, so washtubs were quickly appropriated to make a joyful noise. (FC.)

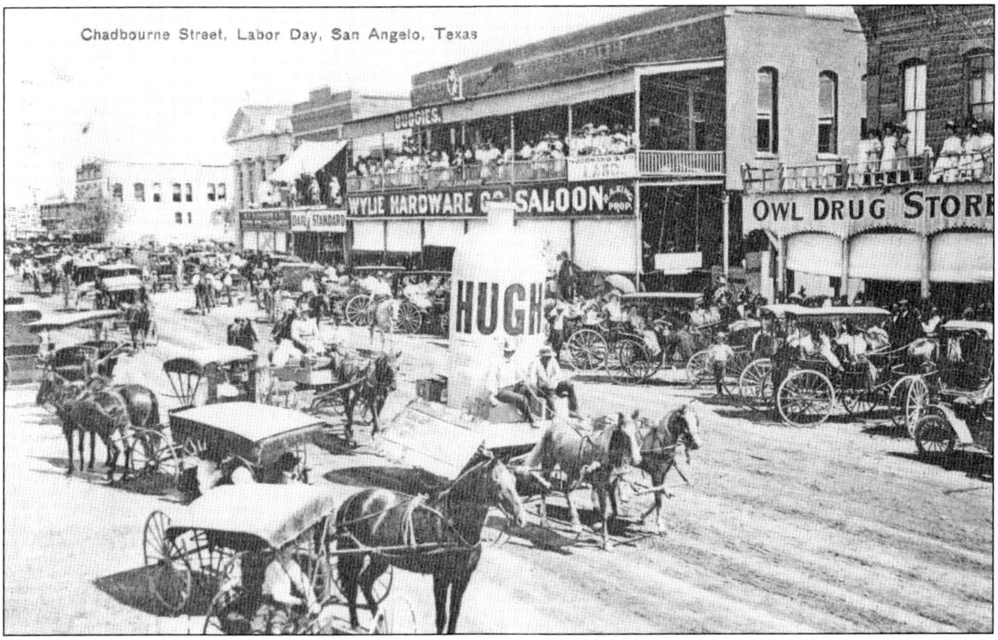

Parades were often part of any celebration. This picture shows citizens honoring Labor Day with a parade down Chadbourne Street. It would be interesting to know what the large bottle is. (WTC.)

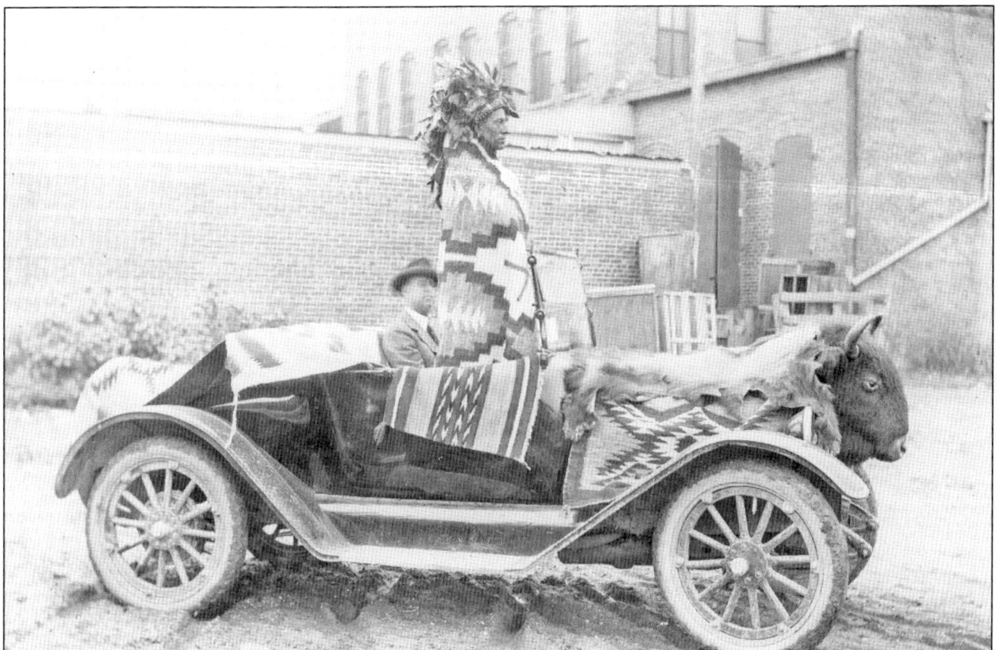

Parade floats could be very creative. This image shows grocer Silas Keeton driving a car in the 1902 Western Parade. Wade Hampton West is playing the role of an "Indian Chief" wrapped in an Indian blanket. The buffalo head on the front of the car looks very appropriate. (WTC.).

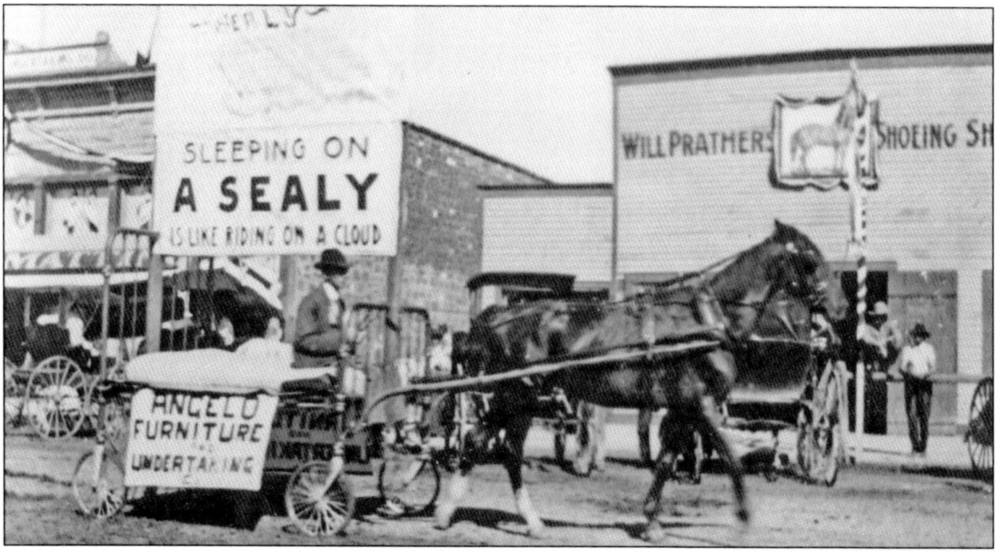

Many parade floats were advertisements. In this case, spectators learn what Angelo Furniture and Undertaking has to offer. Inquiring minds want to know: Did the deceased get a Sealy mattress in a coffin purchased from this establishment? (WTC.)

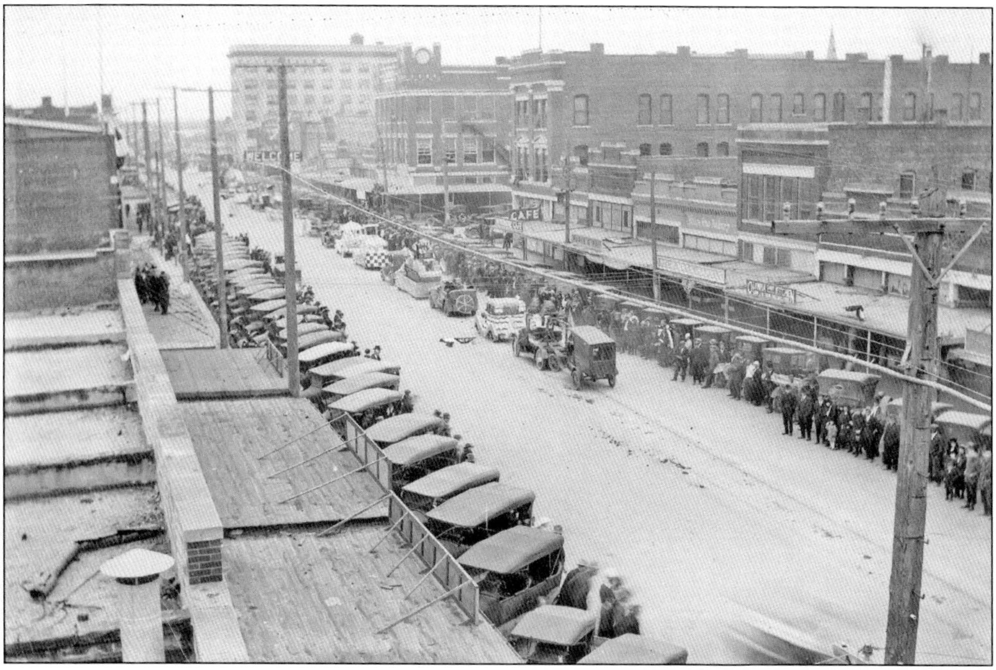

Old Settlers' Parades were an enduring part of the San Angelo tradition. This photograph was taken around 1920. It shows a mature city with cars, rather than the buggies and wagons of an earlier time, lining Chadbourne Street. Clearly, San Angelo citizens were proud of what they and their ancestors had achieved. Whether their city was called the Metropolis of the West, the End of the Rainbow, or simply San Angelo, what started as a group of rough buildings around a frontier fort in 1870 was a large and prosperous city by 1920. Soon, there would be an oil boom and plenty of change. The old settlers had created a wonderful base for future growth and development. It was appropriate that the town celebrated their work. (WTC.)

BIBLIOGRAPHY

Campbell, Suzanne. "George B. Jackson, West Texas Rancher and Entrepreneur." West Texas Collection. Peter Henderson Library, Angelo State University.

Carlson, Paul H. *Texas Woollybacks: The Range Sheep and Goat Industry*. College Station, TX: Texas A&M University Press, 1982.

Clemens, Gus Jr. *The Concho Country*. San Antonio, TX: Mulberry Avenue Books, 1980.

Dalton, C.F. "Wagon Yards." In *Historical Montage of Tom Green County, Texas*, compiled by the Tom Green County Historical Society. San Angelo, TX: Tom Green County Historical Society, 1986.

DeLeon, Arnoldo. *San Angelenos: Mexican Americans in San Angelo, Texas*. San Angelo, TX: Fort Concho Museum Press, 1985.

Green, Bill. *The Dancing was Lively: Fort Concho, Texas: A Social History, 1867 to 1882*. San Angelo, TX: Fort Concho Museum Press, 1985.

Handbook of Texas Online, a project of the Texas State Historical Association.

Hooker, Forrestine C. *Child of the Fighting Tenth: On the Frontier with the Buffalo Soldiers*. Edited by Steve Wilson. New York: Oxford University Press, 2002.

Hutton, Paul, ed. *Soldiers West: Biographies from the Military Frontier*. Lincoln, NE: University of Nebraska Press, 1987.

Kelton, Elmer. "Buffalo Hunters." In *Historical Montage of Tom Green County, Texas*, compiled by the Tom Green County Historical Society. San Angelo, TX: Tom Green County Historical Society, 1986.

Loomis, John A. *Texas Ranchman: The Memoirs of John A. Loomis*. Edited by Herman J. Viola and Sarah Loomis. Chadron, NE: Fur Press, 1982.

Matthews, James T. *Fort Concho: A History and a Guide*. Austin, TX: Texas State Historical Association, 2005.

Notson, William M. *Fort Concho Medical History, 1869 to 1872*. San Angelo, TX: Fort Concho Preservation and Museum, 1974.

Prestiano, Robert. "Oscar Ruffini: The Early Years." *Fort Concho Report*, 16 (Summer 1984): 3–23.

Wood, David. "General History of Railroading in the San Angelo Area," Railway Museum of San Angelo, http://railwaymuseumssanangelo.homestead.com.